★ THE ★ EXPERIENCE ECONOMY

★ THE ★ EXPERIENCE ECONOMY

— UPDATED EDITION —

B. JOSEPH PINE II

JAMES H. GILMORE

HARVARD BUSINESS REVIEW PRESS

Boston, Massachusetts

Printed in the United States of America

20 19 18 17 16 15 14 13 12 11

Library of Congress Cataloging-in-Publication Data

Pine, B. Joseph.
The experience economy / B. Joseph Pine II, James H. Gilmore.
p. cm.
Rev. ed. of: The experience economy : work is theatre & every business a stage. 1999.
Includes bibliographical references and index.
ISBN 978-1-4221-6197-5 (alk. paper)
1. Product management. 2. Marketing. 3. Diversification in industry. 4. Customer services. I. Gilmore, James H., 1959- II. Title.
HF5415.15.P56 2011
658.5'6—dc22

2010054391

To the Author and Perfecter of our faith.

Contents

Preview to the Updated Edition: Beyond Goods and Services

Goods and services are no longer enough. That sentence was the reading line (following the book's subtitle) that accompanied the original hardbound edition of *The Experience Economy* in 1999. Perhaps not enough people read the line, let alone took it to heart. Although the book has since been published in fifteen languages and purchased by more than three hundred thousand people worldwide, the book's thesis has not sufficiently penetrated the minds of enough business leaders (and policy makers) to give full bloom to a truly new—and desperately needed—economic order. Relying on the manufacturing of goods and the delivery of services remains the mindset of too many executives (and politicians), prohibiting the shift to more vibrant enterprises offering experiences (and thus more robust national economies). So let us here be most clear: *goods and services are no longer enough* to foster economic growth, create new jobs, and maintain economic prosperity. To realize revenue growth and increased employment, the staging of experiences must be pursued as a distinct form of economic output. Indeed, in a world saturated with largely undifferentiated goods and services the greatest opportunity for value creation resides in staging experiences.

The actions of individual entrepreneurs prove the point. Contrast the success of leading experience innovators over the past twelve years with the failure of rival companies (and whole industries, for that matter) that either missed or ignored our economic message. Take retail. Countless chains have met their demise in this time frame as they insisted on merely merchandising finished goods. Walmart and online sellers ate their lunch. Yet experiences such as Build-A-Bear Workshop flourished. In 1999, founder Maxine Clark had just opened her first bear-making venue. Told by conventional retail experts that launching such an enterprise was foolhardy, Clark drew inspiration from our July/August 1998 *Harvard Business Review* article, "Welcome to the Experience Economy." Today, Build-A-Bear profitably operates more than three hundred experience outlets in the United States alone, and almost five hundred worldwide—all venues where consumers mass customize their own plush toy animals within an engaging retail factory experience.

Similarly, Pleasant Rowland had just opened her first American Girl Place in Chicago in late 1998. From the outset she conceived her American Girl dolls—each themed to a specific period of American history—as only a prop for broader book-reading and character-building experiences. With yet additional American Girl Places in place today, American Girl thrives inside Mattel, which otherwise struggles to revive Barbie and other toys (seen as mere goods by most American girls and boys today). And what store is now the envy of every mall owner and developer? Apple. Why? Customers clearly flock there for not only the goods but also the store experience, with sales per square foot an order of magnitude greater than those of the typical retailer.

Interestingly enough, Apple studied the hospitality experiences at both Ritz-Carlton and various boutique hotels for design inspiration in creating its revolutionary new retail format. (Gateway had previously attempted selling direct via retail stores, as had Dell with kiosks, but both lacked a rich appreciation for experience design, opting instead to retain typical merchandising footprints.) Thus, experiencing the wares at an Apple Store feels uncannily like bellying up to the bar at a hotel lounge. Apple's in-store Genius Bars, iPod Studios, and classroom amphitheatres bear a remarkable resemblance to the registration areas, concierge desks, and meeting space experiences of better boutique hotels. Moreover, these "design" hotels played a role in changing the competitive landscape in their own industry. Thanks to Bill Kimpton, Ian Schrager, Chip Conley, and other boutique hoteliers, no hotel chain can today afford to merely provide basic service activities and ignore its guests' experiences. From furnishing sociable lobby spaces to providing beds that promise better sleep experiences (credit Schrager for kick-starting innovation in the former, and credit Westin's "Heavenly Bed" for the latter), the hospitality industry now clearly creates new value on the basis of experiences.

Consider next the Geek Squad. At the time of *The Experience Economy*'s release in 1999, founder Robert Stephens employed fewer than a dozen Special Agents in his 24-hour computer support task torce. Today, thanks to the Geek Squad's acquisition and rollout by Best Buy, more than twenty-four thousand Geek Squad geeks—Special Agents, Double Agents, and (inside Best Buy stores) Counter Intelligence Agents—stage compelling installation and repair experiences worldwide. Perhaps no other company matches the Geek Squad in exemplifying the experience-staging principles we outline in this book, especially the proposition that work is theatre. The thematic costuming integral to the Geek Squad being the Geek Squad (and readily and naively dismissed by other service providers) demonstrates the tangible value—to customers, to employees, and to shareholders—that you can create by boldly treating services as the stage and goods as the props for staging engaging experiences. Think of the number of fragmented service industries—car washes, home decorators, landscapers, laundromats, and educational tutors, to name a few—that would benefit from an enterprise emulating the Geek Squad's experience mindset.

The economic doldrums in which much of the advanced world found itself after the 2008 financial crisis resulted from a failure to experientially innovate like each of these companies. The Industrial Economy has had its day. The invention and production of new goods once fueled the world's advanced economies. It is today very difficult to invent—and therefore rare to encounter—a truly new good; most differentiation of goods now involves the enhancement or modification of items within existing product categories and not the creation of wholly new categories. (Consumer electronics and medical technology represent two notable exceptions; but consider that when buying these items, customers most value not the goods themselves but the experiences and transformations they enable.) Even when someone invents a truly new good, manufacturers instinctively seek to automate the work required to make it and scale up as soon as possible. Although revenue growth may follow, these manufacturers add few new jobs to the world.

The Service Economy, too, justifiably has faltered. Any growth we saw in true services—government statistics still embed experiences (and transformations) within the service sector—largely came from financial services, and most of that from artificially propping up a world of goods—beginning with automobiles and housing and extending to mall development and other commercial ventures—with increasingly desperate attempts to devise financial instruments that more highly leverage old wealth (in the form of protected classes of assets). All this incessant financing created precious little tangible value. And so, as with the dot-com craze and crash that came before, eventually the bubble burst. What does the world need instead? New wealth generated from the formation of new experience-based enterprises.

Since the original publication of *The Experience Economy*, we recognize that the experience thinking we promoted has taken root in three areas. First, experiential marketing applies experience staging to the marketing of goods and services, seeking to be less dependent on traditional media as the means of building demand. Second, the application of experience-staging prowess to operations—in what many call Customer Experience Management (or CEM)—aims to make interactions with customers friendlier, easier, and more convenient. Finally, digital experiences increasingly flourish, using the World Wide Web and other electronic platforms to create new virtual and gaming experiences.

Each of these experience-focused pursuits has its merits. More goods and services get sold because of experiential marketing; some "customer experiences" are less of a hassle because of CEM; and many bits-based experiences certainly offer capabilities unimaginable in the world of atoms. But true economic progress requires experiences in the form of new economic output, and not only new experiential promotions, customer-experience processes, or the experience-rich potential of new media. The Progression of Economic Value requires new for-fee offerings in which operations are an experience and the experience is the marketing—in either the physical or the virtual realm.

Opportunities Within the Experience Economy

Toward this end, four value-creating opportunities stand out. First, concerning goods, *more offerings should be mass customized*: what is needed is not more production of physical goods but more innovative methods for making those goods. Most manufacturers have ignored the pleas by us (and others) to shift from Mass Production to Mass Customization methods, to replace supply chains with demand chains, to convert raw materials into goods not as speculative inventory but only in response to actual demand. Mass customizing—efficiently serving customers uniquely—means producing only and exactly what individual customers want. Mass customizing any good turns that good automatically into a service; and mass customizing any service turns that service automatically into an experience. In *The Experience Economy* we devote more than two chapters to framing how best to pursue customized capabilities and offerings. Yet to this day, one cannot, for example, name a single U.S.-made model of automobile available to consumers via mass customization. It's shameful. It's why scores of dealerships have closed, with consumers awaiting new build-a-car experiences.

In encouraging more mass customization as a means of creating new value, let us call attention to perhaps the most ignored—and yet arguably the most powerful—concept in the entire book, namely the notion of reducing or eliminating *customer sacrifice*. Customer sacrifice is the gap between what individual customers settle for (in buying mass produced goods and services) and what each wants exactly. Every business would benefit from asking itself, What one dimension of sacrifice, if eliminated, would create the greatest value for customers? Once you have identified that sacrifice, you should pursue solutions to help customers experience less sacrifice.

Second, concerning services, *more companies should direct their employees to act*. Organizations that have a service mindset focus solely on *what* tasks employees do; those with an experience mindset also consider *how* those tasks are performed and thereby embrace theatre as a model for performance. By and large, despite decades of management literature proffering customer service advice, consumers still endure many miserable encounters. Consider a typical "day in the life" of consumer service interactions—talking to call centers, waiting at convenience store counters, trying to be heard in drive-through lanes, waiting in line at bank teller windows, getting rental cars, riding shuttle buses, enduring air travel, checking out groceries, visiting the mall, paying for gasoline, and so forth. Twelve years ago we characterized the scene as poor service, no service, or self-service. Unfortunately, little has changed. As a result, customers understandably hesitate to pay any premium. Profitability therefore suffers, wages stagnate, and workers disengage—creating a downward spiral to yet more miserable service.

A huge first step in staging more engaging experiences needs to be taken. As again the Geek Squad exemplifies, companies must recognize that their employees are onstage and therefore need to act in a way that engages their customers. So managers need to give employees roles to play, help them characterize those roles, and especially invest time in rehearsing before placing them on the business stage. When a business is treated as a mere service, hourly workers spend almost no offstage time preparing onstage behaviors. Actors prepare. Better human performances—focusing on the *how*, and not only the *what*—turn mundane interactions into engaging encounters. So ask yourself, What acts of theatre would turn our workers' functional activities into memorable events? Here, we devote three chapters to the principle that work is theatre. Wise business leaders champion this new paradigm in their organizations; custodians of the old order fail to see the upside in investing in better workplace acting and seek only to cut head count at every turn.

Third, concerning experiences, *more offerings should find ways to explicitly charge for time.* Time is the currency of experiences. Today, some experiential marketing events require an admission fee; some experiential operations contribute to charging a premium for the supported goods and services; and some experiences are accessible only on a subscription basis. Some. It is vital that more experiences in the future be available only by admission, for such holds the key to a full-fledged Experience Economy. What truly makes an experience a distinct economic offering, providing new sources of revenue growth, is requiring customers to explicitly pay for the time they spend in places or events. Many businesses languish today because they still have not asked themselves the fundamental question we posed twelve years ago: what would we do differently if we charged admission? Addressing this question remains most critical; identifying answers, most imperative.

To assist in finding answers, in this edition of *The Experience Economy* we add a new framework outlining six ways of charging for time: entry fees, per-event fees, per-period fees, initiation fees, access fees, and membership fees. Descriptions of these alternative ways of charging admission should help businesses conceive of new ways of creating and capturing the experiential value they create. Consider one particular pricing model ripe for such admission-fee innovation: time sharing. Think Netflix. It's no movie rental service, charging for each lent film. Rather, the company charges a monthly fee and subsumes the rental service in a movie-viewing subscription. The same sort of access-based experiences have emerged with corporate jets, recreational vehicles, snow removal equipment, and even designer women's handbags. Automobile ride-sharing programs have also met with some success, but real progress will come only when consumers can access a greater portfolio of vehicles for an assortment of driving needs. Almost any industry would benefit from seeking to differentiate based on for-fee experiences.

Finally, *more experiences should yield transformations*. Moreover, these transformations—the fifth and final economic offering in the Progression of Economic Value that begins with commodities—should themselves command a fee in the form of explicitly charging for the demonstrated outcomes that result from the underlying experiences. In other words, companies enabling transformations should charge not merely for time but for the change *resulting* from that time. They should charge for the ends and not only the means of life-changing (or company-altering) experiences.

We especially challenge enterprises in three industries: those that focus on making people healthy, wealthy, and wise.

Truly market-based approaches in the healthcare industry would free parties to charge for demonstrated outcomes and not mere attempts to gain such noteworthy ends. Endless debate over health *insurance* would shift to actual innovation in health*care*, in which people would be charged only for the ongoing ensurance of wellness. Unsuccessful treatments that fail to remedy ailments would not be compensated (just as one doesn't pay a plumber who fails to fix a leaky sink), and new financial instruments tied to actual performance—perhaps securitizing future earnings streams of successfully treated patients—would necessarily emerge. Similarly, the reward systems in financial institutions would reflect the true results of investment decisions—and then move away from an exclusive spotlight on investments to granting wise counsel on life decisions concerning how best to spend and gift wealth. And colleges and universities, which graduate barely half those who enroll (would we ever tolerate such dismal performance from any other industry?), should focus on the actual educational, personal, and societal outcomes achieved, collecting all or part of the tuition only when those outcomes become clear at graduation and beyond. To do otherwise, in each of these fields, does a disservice to all.

Do not take our admonition for greater experience innovation to mean that there has not been great progress over the past twelve years toward offering new experiences. Much has indeed emerged, whether because of companies embracing the principles we espoused in the first edition or the natural evolution of competitive advantage as their goods and services become commoditized. But much more needs to follow. This comes as no surprise to us, because we have always viewed the Experience Economy as a long-term structural shift in the very fabric of advanced economies. The forces of creative destruction take time. New forms of economic output do not come automatically. They require individual people and individual enterprises to take action, to abandon old Industrial and Service Economy paradigms in order to introduce new experiences and transformations.

Issues Surrounding the Experience Economy

We want no misconceptions to prohibit progress. So let us formally address some of the objections we have heard over the years concerning *The Experience Economy*.

Some object to the word *stage* to describe the primary work activity, or economic function, of experiences. One could substitute an alternative verb—*orchestrate* comes to mind—but only at the risk of diluting our emphasis on the importance of stagecraft in, well, staging engaging experiences. Stagecraft it is, and frankly, more businesses besides show business need to embrace theatre as a model for directing work. A related objection truly annoys us. Some readers balk at our use of theatre "as a metaphor" when we could not be clearer: it's not a metaphor but a *model* for human performance in staging experiences. We also wish others who agree that an economic shift is indeed under way would stop trying to advance alternative terms for this wave of economic history, pushing such terms as the "Knowledge Economy" or the "Attention Economy." Economic eras have always been named based on the corresponding nature of output (Service Economy for services) or dominant domain of work (Agrarian Economy for commodities, Industrial Economy for goods), so the only legitimate alternative to the Experience Economy would rightfully be the "Theatrical Economy"—which seems less practical given the aforementioned theatre misconception. Yet others simply need to be more precise with their terminology. We have no objection to referencing the "Dream Society" or "Creative Class," gladly recognizing and embracing these terms as properly identifying trends emerging alongside the Experience Economy. But it does not help to then occasionally make reference to a "Dream Economy" or a "Creative Economy." Having dreams and being creative have fueled innovation in previous economic eras (but so much so, in today's era, that they may give rise to a new social class); what is new about this new economy is that *experiences* represent the basis of *economic* activity. People rarely if ever bought birthday parties, as one example, in previous economic eras; today they do so regularly.

Beyond these language issues, other readers misread our intentions (perhaps reading in their own apprehensions as our aspirations). Some viewed experiences only as entertainment. Any careful reading of chapter 2 should dissuade readers from this mistaken notion. Indeed, we see the "four E's"—entertainment plus the educational, escapist, and esthetic realms of experience—as a means to avoid amusing ourselves to death. Showing full-length movies in the classroom, putting up PowerPoint screens in church sanctuaries, and showing non-sports-related video clips on ballpark scoreboards do not indicate thoughtful application of experience-staging excellence for teaching students, preaching to disciples, and connecting with fans, respectively. Another mistaken interpretation: assuming that all experiences must necessarily trend toward the inauthentic or the virtual. (We address these subjects in our subsequent books *Authenticity: What Consumers* Really *Want* and *Infinite Possibility: Creating Customer Value on the Digital Frontier*, respectively.) In fact, the Experience Economy allows for a vast array of alternative offerings, ranging from the more or less natural/artificial, original/imitative, genuine/disingenuous, real/fake, self-centered/other-focused—across all dimensions of time, space, and matter. Contrary to yet another objection—that we seek to turn "all of life" into "a paid-for experience"—we certainly recognize noneconomic spheres of social and personal experience. As undeniably more of life becomes commodified, we should all carefully examine our lives as citizens, donors, students, and worshippers—not to mention as parents and lovers—in terms of what we choose to buy and not buy, to sell and not sell, to experience and not experience. Yet for developed economies to remain prosperous, a shift to experiences must occur: goods and services are no longer enough to employ the masses. We would hope that concern about the possible deleterious impact of certain experiences (and, moreover, transformations) would prompt critics to enter the economic arena and offer more virtuous forms of these economic offerings.

Two particular criticisms of *The Experience Economy* provide a very useful perspective, especially as they serve to propel further study into the nature of engaging experiences. The first comes in the form of emphasizing the role of co-creation in the formation of experiences—and viewing our work as lacking sufficient appreciation for the role of guests in creating their own experiences. The view is understandable, as our concern in 1999—and even now—focuses primarily on the supply side of experiences. Our primary goal has been to encourage the creation of new experiences. Therefore, we focus much more on the stager of experiences, while recognizing that to a degree all experiences are co-created, as they happen inside the individual person in reaction to what is staged outside that person. That said, we agree that a supply of new experiences indeed prompts many guests to want a more participatory role. Moreover, this desire spills over to the relationships between clients and providers of services, and between users and manufacturers of goods as well (something that Joe recognized in his first book, *Mass Customization: The New Frontier in Business Competition*). Alvin Toffler nailed it when he anticipated the rise of "prosumers." No one approach, however, should be rigidly imposed on experience design. It would be a mistake to suppose that all consumers want openly co-created offerings in every circumstance and in every category of good, service, and experience (transformations in free societies are by their very nature co-created, with the company only guiding what customers, in the end, must themselves undergo; to treat transformation otherwise is tyranny). What should be considered is the degree of control afforded in any given situation. Even at Disneyland or Walt Disney World—places with a high degree of staging—guests themselves exert a great deal of control over where and when they roam between rides. And one of us (OK, it's Jim) takes particular delight in being just a little too enthusiastic in shows like Country Bear Jamboree, with his over-the-top hooting and hollering effectively co-ruining the experience for others. At issue is the intentionality of the stager and the adaptability for the guest in terms of the co-creation. We would welcome greater excellence in both dimensions.

The second valid concern contends we place too much emphasis on experiences as memorable events. Let us share our twofold perspective. First, in envisioning engaging experiences, you can and should consider a multiplicity of dimensions. These include, but are not limited to, the multisensory nature of experiences, their level of personal meaningfulness, the way the experience is shared with others (if at all), the intensity and duration of various experiential elements, complexity (or simplicity), and untold other characteristics of how people spend time. Cultural considerations and national and local sensitivities, as well as the prior life experiences of guests, all impact how people perceive experiences. Our belief is that no matter how it's viewed, any dimension of enjoyment usually translates into the experience being more memorable—even if few or no details can be recollected. This takes us to a second aspect of the matter: recognizing the distinction between the memory of an experience and the enjoyment of the experience in the moment (apart from how memorable it later proves). Even here, people at least remember that they enjoyed the experience, even if they cannot recall or explain why. Of critical importance is how the experience concludes. Here, one new model added to this edition of

The Experience Economy, the mid-nineteenth-century model of Gustav Freytag found in chapter 6, explains the structure of compelling dramas and offers considerable insight. In a nutshell, failure to adequately establish proper context, interweave building action, or allow for falling action and a dénouement adversely diminishes the audience's memory of even the most climactic highs of an enjoyable experience (and even more adversely magnifies the memory of an unpleasant one). Bottom line: no, a strong memory is not required for every experience, but the greater the (positive) memory created and the longer it lasts, the more value is created.

With that, we now leave you to this, the updated edition of *The Experience Economy*. It updates many of the examples used to illustrate the plethora of models and tools we put forward to help executives see the world differently. In addition to reaching a new readership, we do hope those who read the original book read it anew, refreshing their memory of lessons learned. And we hope they will introduce the tome to many new readers. For in shifting to an Experience Economy, we can use fellow laborers. We wish all well and sincerely hope *The Experience Economy* speeds up the day when the Experience Economy reaches its full potential.

—James H. Gilmore
Shaker Heights, Ohio

—B. Joseph Pine II
Dellwood, Minnesota

February 2011

Strategic Horizons LLP
P.O. Box 548
Aurora, Ohio 44202-0548 USA
+1 (330) 995-4680
PineGilmore@strategichorizons.com

★ PREVIEW ★

Step Right Up

OVERSTOCKED! Undersold. Ten, 20, 30, 40 percent discounts. Half off everything! Buy one, get one free. Free financing for a year. Guaranteed lowest prices! Going out of business sale. . . . In a word: commoditized.

This book offers an escape from the all-too-easy practice of competing on the basis of price. While customers love a sale, businesses perish from relying on low prices as a means of hawking their offerings. That approach worked for years, indeed decades, as economies of scale associated with mass producing goods and services resulted in a corresponding cost savings with every successive price reduction. But in industry after industry, that system of competition no longer sustains growth and profitability. You know it; we all know it. But what do we do about it?

We wrote this book for those searching for new ways to add value to their enterprises—fully aware that executives and managers have been bombarded with business books with the same aim. We've all been continuously improved, reengineered, and downsized. We've embraced time-based competition and the one-to-one future. We're now demassified, informationalized, digitized, and, yes, even mass customized—perhaps self-organizing and thriving on chaos to boot. Every business competing for the future is customer-centric, customer-driven, customer-focused, customer-yadda-yadda-yadda. So what's new?

This is new: experiences represent an existing but previously unarticulated *genre of economic output*. Decoupling experiences from services in accounting for what businesses create opens up possibilities for extraordinary economic expansion—just as recognizing services as a distinct and legitimate offering led to a vibrant economic foundation in the face of a declining industrial base. And a new base is emerging. Ignore the familiar hype: information is not the foundation of the "New Economy," for information is not an economic offering. As our friend John Perry Barlow likes to say, information wants to be free. Only when companies constitute it in the form of information *services*—or informational *goods* and informing *experiences*—do they create economic value. Economic offerings, not forms of intelligence, comprise the substance of buying and selling.

Recognizing experiences as a distinct economic offering provides the key to future economic growth, as shown in chapter 1. Economic pessimist Jeremy Rifkin is right to suggest that businesses will need fewer workers to deliver services in the future, just as in the past due to innovations and higher productivity they needed fewer factory workers to produce goods, and before that fewer farm workers to harvest agricultural commodities. But those who decry the loss of agricultural and manufacturing jobs are wrong in asserting that the total number of jobs available will soon go down. Future waves of economic activity based on new economic offerings will provide ample opportunities to generate more wealth and create new jobs—if only businesses remain free to compete, unencumbered by government's view of what constitutes appropriate economic offerings to promote or protect.

Those businesses that recognize this dramatic shift and respond to it effectively—both are required—will forestall the forces of commoditization and create new economic value. (That is not to say that all companies must stage experiences to be profitable.

Commodity companies can make money, at least on the up cycles. But watch out for those downturns!) Chapters 2 and 3 show how to stage engaging and compelling experiences using two frameworks we've gleaned from studying companies that have already successfully shifted to the Experience Economy. For those not yet ready to do so directly, a second route is provided by understanding that mass customizing automatically turns goods into services and services into experiences. Embracing the principles of Mass Customization articulated in chapters 4 and 5—and thereby helping customers experience less sacrifice in their interactions with you and your offerings—may first be required for many goods manufacturers and service providers to enter the Experience Economy. (And don't neglect to read the short Intermission for an extension of this route.)

This new economy also demands new models for work. At every level in any company, workers need to understand that in the Experience Economy every business is a stage, and therefore work is theatre. That may sound strange, but it is true: chapter 6 makes the case that whenever a customer happens across your bare stage of business, the workers are acting. It then introduces techniques for performing accordingly. Chapter 7 goes through four forms of theatre and in what situations each should be applied, while chapter 8 sets down basic guidelines for those taking on each of the various roles required for any enterprise to stage experiences. All workers—from boardroom executives to frontline staffers—should be able to see themselves anew in this chapter, and those in human resource and organizational development departments should read it particularly closely to gain insight into changes required in the new economy.

Of course, not everyone will agree that we are shifting to an Experience Economy or that such a development is a good thing. Consider Las Vegas, the experience capital of America (although

Orlando, Los Angeles, Manhattan, and even Branson, Missouri, would win their share of votes in any poll). Virtually *everything* about Vegas is a designed experience, from the slot machines at the airport to the gambling casinos that line the Strip; from the themed hotels and restaurants to the singing, circus, and magic shows; and from the Forum Shops mall that recreates ancient Rome to the amusement parks, thrill rides, video arcades, and carnival-style games that attract the twentysomethings and give older parents a reason to bring their kids in tow.

Of course, there is another side to the Vegas experience: the readily available alcohol, drugs, nudity-filled nightclubs, and prostitution. Unfortunately, these are every bit as much a part of the Experience Economy as any other entertainment or escapist fare. True, as we shift to this new economy, some people (perhaps more people) will make unwise and immoral choices due to the ready availability and slicker staging of prurient experiences. And most of the experiences mentioned above, while engaging and memorable, are certainly not virtuous. Further, many people object, with reason, to the artificiality of Disney World, the simulated nature of various motion-based attractions, and the technocentric remoteness of the Internet (although these "artificial" experiences are counterbalanced to some degree by the concatenate rise of such "real" experiences as camping at Yellowstone National Park, donkey-riding down the Grand Canyon, kayaking on the Colorado River, and, more recently, a host of such "extreme sports" as rollerblading, snowboarding, skysurfing, and the like).

Despite the great improvements in working conditions, health, life expectancy, and the standard of living associated with every previous economic shift, those shifts were not without their dislocations and negative effects; we should not expect otherwise in the shift from the Service to the Experience Economy. All the issues mentioned above are legitimate and worthy of debate. But it is clear that we cannot retreat from the impending reality of the Experience Economy already surrounding us. Commendable or deleterious, virtuous or immoral, natural or artificial—these are all choices we make as together we create this new economy.

Those who decried previous economic shifts—two centuries ago to the Industrial Economy and in the past twenty years to the Service Economy—failed to stop the Progression of Economic Value to higher-echelon offerings. It happened despite their protestations. Therefore, we believe that the moral emphasis should not lie on whether commerce should shift to experiential offerings. If societies are to seek continued economic prosperity, they must stage experiences to add sufficient value to their economies to employ the masses (goods and services are no longer enough). The moral emphasis must be placed instead on *what kinds of experiences will be staged.* The business executive, like everyone else, must in the end concern himself with the ultimate aims of man. That will be our focus in chapters 9 and 10, as we explore the business world when experiences become commoditized, and the fifth, and final, economic offering—transformations—comes to the fore. You won't want to miss these last two chapters, nor the encore, for the implications for your business, whatever it is today, may be profound. And we won't back away from stating what we believe when it is the right thing to do.

We hope all readers discover a clear and compelling articulation of the new competitive landscape for the strategic options facing their enterprises. But even more, we hope you personally find the tools to begin staging compelling experiences and guiding vital transformations for your customers, present and future.

—Joe Pine
Dellwood, Minnesota

—Jim Gilmore
Shaker Heights, Ohio

December 1998

CHAPTER 1

Welcome to the Experience Economy

COMMODITIZED. No company wants that word applied to its goods or services. Merely mentioning *commoditization* sends shivers down the spines of executives and entrepreneurs alike. Differentiation disappears, margins fall through the floor, and customers buy solely on the basis of price, price, price.

Consider, however, a true commodity: the coffee bean. Companies that harvest coffee or trade it on the futures market receive—at the time of this writing—a little more than 75 cents per pound, which translates into 1 or 2 cents a cup. When a manufacturer roasts, grinds, packages, and sells those same beans in a grocery store, turning them into a good, the price to a consumer jumps to between 5 and 25 cents a cup (depending on brand and package size). Brew the ground beans in a run-of-the-mill diner, quick-serve restaurant, or bodega, and that coffee-making service now sells for 50 cents to a dollar or so per cup.

So depending on what a business does with it, coffee can be any of three economic offerings—commodity, good, or service—with three distinct ranges of value customers attach to the offering.

FIGURE 1-1

Price of coffee offerings

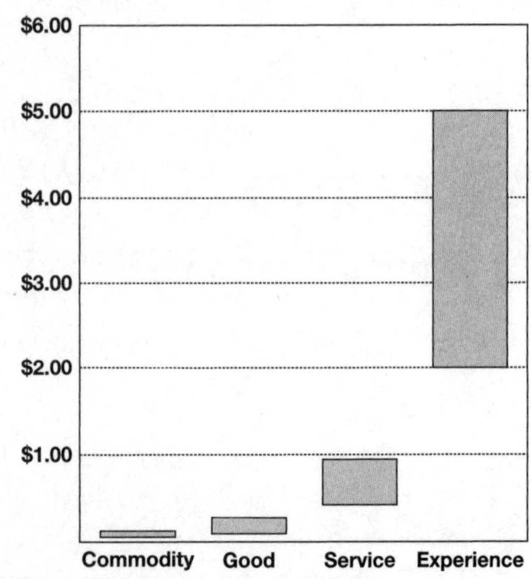

But wait: serve that same coffee in a five-star restaurant or a cafe such as Starbucks—where the ordering, creation, and consumption of the cup embody a heightened ambience or sense of theatre—and consumers gladly pay $2 to $5 a cup. Businesses that ascend to this fourth level of value (see figure 1-1) establish a distinctive experience that envelops the purchase of coffee, increasing its value (and therefore its price) by two orders of magnitude over the original commodity.

Or more. Immediately upon arriving in Venice, a friend of ours asked a hotel concierge where he and his wife could go to enjoy the city's best. Without hesitation he directed them to the Caffè Florian in St. Mark's Square. The two of them were soon at the cafe in the crisp morning air, sipping cups of steaming coffee, fully immersed in the sights and sounds of the most remarkable of Old

World cities. More than an hour later, our friend received the bill and discovered the experience had cost more than $15 a cup. "Was the coffee worth it?" we asked. "*Assolutamente*!"

A New Source of Value

Experiences are a fourth economic offering, as distinct from services as services are from goods, but one that has until now gone largely unrecognized. Experiences have always been around, but consumers, businesses, and economists lumped them into the service sector along with such uneventful activities as dry cleaning, auto repair, wholesale distribution, and telephone access. When a person buys a service, he purchases a set of intangible activities carried out on his behalf. But when he buys an experience, he pays to spend time enjoying a series of memorable events that a company stages—as in a theatrical play—to engage him in an inherently personal way.

Experiences have always been at the heart of entertainment offerings, from plays and concerts to movies and TV shows. Over the past few decades, however, the number of entertainment options has exploded to encompass many, many new experiences. We trace the beginnings of this experience expansion to one man and the company he founded: Walt Disney. After making his name by continually layering new levels of experiential effects on to cartoons (he innovated synchronized sound, color animation, three-dimensional backgrounds, stereophonic sound, audio-animatronics, and so forth), Disney capped his career in 1955 by opening Disneyland—a living, immersive cartoon world—in California. Before his death in 1966, Disney had also envisioned Walt Disney World, which opened in Florida in 1971. Rather than create another amusement park, Disney created the world's first *theme* parks, which immerse guests (never "customers" or "clients") in rides that not only entertain but also involve them in an unfolding story. For every guest, cast members (never "employees") stage a complete production of sights, sounds, tastes, aromas, and textures to create a unique experience.[1] Today, The Walt Disney Company carries on its founder's heritage by continually "imagineering" new offerings to apply its experiential expertise, from TV shows on the Disney Channel to "character worlds" at Disney.com, from Broadway shows to the Disney Cruise Line, complete with its own Caribbean island.

Whereas Disney used to be the only theme park proprietor, it now faces scores of competitors in every line of business, both traditional and experimental. New technologies encourage whole new genres of experience, such as video games, online games, motion-based attractions, 3-D movies, virtual worlds, and augmented reality. Desire for ever greater processing power to render ever more immersive experiences drives demand for the goods and services of the computer industry. Former Intel chairman (now senior adviser) Andrew Grove anticipated the explosion of technology-enabled offerings in a mid-1990s speech at the COMDEX computer show (itself an experience), when he declared, "We need to look at our business as more than simply the building and selling of personal computers [that is, goods]. Our business is the delivery of information [that is, services] and lifelike interactive experiences." Exactly.

Many traditional service industries, now competing for the same dollar with these new experiences, are themselves becoming more experiential. At theme restaurants such as Benihana, the Hard Rock Cafe, Ed Debevic's, Joe's Crab Shack, and the Bubba Gump Shrimp Co., the food functions as a prop for what's known in the industry as an "eatertainment" experience. And stores such as Build-A-Bear Workshop, Jordan's Furniture, and Niketown draw consumers through fun activities and promotional events (sometimes called "entertailing," or what The Mills Corp. trademarked as "shoppertainment").

But this doesn't mean that experiences rely exclusively on entertainment; as we explain fully in chapter 2, entertainment is only one aspect of an experience. Rather, companies stage an experience whenever they *engage* customers, connecting with them in a personal, memorable way. Many dining experiences have less to do with the entertainment motif than with the merging of dining with comedy, art, history, or nature, as happens at such restaurants as Teatro ZinZanni, Café Ti Tu Tango, Medieval Times, and the Rainforest Cafe, respectively.[2] In each place, the food service provides a stage for layering on a larger feast of sensations that resonate with consumers. Retailers such as Jungle Jim's International Market, The Home Depot, and the Viking Cooking School offer tours, workshops, and classes that combine shopping and education in ways that we can rightly describe as "edutailing" or "shopperscapism."

The "commodity mindset," according to former British Airways chairman Sir Colin Marshall, means mistakenly thinking "that a business is merely performing a function—in our case, transporting people from point A to point B on time and at the lowest possible price." What British Airways does, he continued, "is to go beyond the function and compete on the basis of providing an experience."[3] The company uses its base service (the travel itself) as a stage for a distinctive en route experience, one that gives the traveler a respite from the inevitable stress and strain of a long trip.

Even the most mundane transactions can be turned into memorable experiences. Standard Parking of Chicago plays a signature song on each level of its parking garage at O'Hare Airport and decorates walls with icons of a local sports franchise—the Bulls on one floor, the Blackhawks on another, and so forth. As one Chicago resident told us, "You never forget where you parked!" Trips to the grocery store, often a burden for families, become exciting events at places such as Bristol Farms Gourmet Specialty Foods Markets in Southern California. This upscale chain "operates its stores as if they were theatres," according to *Stores* magazine, featuring "music, live entertainment, exotic scenery, free refreshments, a video-equipped amphitheater, famous-name guest stars and full audience participation."[4] Russell Vernon, owner of West Point Market in Akron, Ohio—where fresh flowers decorate the aisles, restrooms feature original artwork, and classical music wafts down the aisles—describes his store as "a stage for the products we sell. Our ceiling heights, lighting and color create a theatrical shopping environment."[5] Grocers such as The Fresh Market and Whole Foods Markets replicate these local food experiences and scale them on a regional and national basis, respectively.

Consumers aren't the only ones to appreciate such experiences. Businesses are made up of people, and business-to-business settings also present stages for experiences. A Minneapolis-based computer installation and repair firm first dubbed itself the Geek Squad in 1994 and began focusing on home-office and small business customers. With its special agents costumed in white shirts with thin black ties, carrying badges, and driving black-and-white Beetles, called Geekmobiles, painted like squad cars, the company turns mundane services into truly memorable encounters. Today the "24-Hour Computer Support Task Force" employs more than twenty-four thousand agents as part of Best Buy. Costumed entrepreneurs in other industries followed suit, such as a garbage collector calling itself the Junk Squad ("Satisfaction Guaranteed or Double Your Junk Back"). Many companies hire theatre troupes to turn otherwise ordinary meetings into improvisational events. Minneapolis-based LiveSpark (formerly Interactive Personalities, Inc.), for example, stages rehearsed plays and "spontaneous scenes" for corporate customers, engaging audience members in a variety of ways, including computer-generated characters that interact in real time.[6]

Business-to-business marketers increasingly orchestrate events at elaborate venues to pitch prospects. Scores of B2B companies turn mundane conference rooms into experiential "executive briefing centers"—and some go beyond that, such as Johnson Controls' Showcase in Milwaukee, where the company plunges business guests into a power outage to show off its products in action. Steelcase recently launched a venue called WorkSpring, the first one in Chicago, offering unique office space so that corporate guests experience furniture in actual meetings before making purchasing decisions. TST, Inc., an engineering firm in Fort Collins, Colorado, gutted its office to create the TST Engineerium, a place for staff to host "visioneering experiences" for its land development customers. Autodesk, Inc., developers of engineering and design software, curates the Autodesk Gallery at One Market in San Francisco as a place to showcase clients' use of its technology in innovative design projects (and opens the B2B interactive art exhibition to the general public every Wednesday afternoon). One B2B experience takes place outdoors: the Case Tomahawk Customer Experience Center in the Northwoods of Wisconsin. Prospective buyers play in a giant sandbox with large construction equipment—bulldozers, backhoes, cherry pickers, and the like—as part of the selling process.

Valuable Distinctions

The foregoing examples—from consumer to business customer, theme restaurant to computer support task force—only hint at the newfound prominence of such experiences within the U.S.

economy and, increasingly, those of other developed nations as well. They herald the still emerging Experience Economy.

Why now? Part of the answer lies with technology, which powers many experiences, and part with increasing competitive intensity, which drives the ongoing search for differentiation. But the most encompassing answer resides in the nature of economic value and its natural progression—like that of the coffee bean—from commodity to good to service and then to experience. An additional reason for the rise of the Experience Economy is, of course, rising affluence over time. Economist Tibor Scitovsky notes that "man's main response to increasing affluence seems to be an increase in the frequency of festive meals; he adds to the number of special occasions and holidays considered worthy of them and, ultimately, he makes them routine—in the form, say, of Sunday dinners."[7] The same is true of experiences we pay for. We are going out to eat more frequently at increasingly experiential venues, and even drinking "festive" types of coffee. As summarized in table 1-1, each economic offering differs from the others in fundamental ways, including just what, exactly, it is. These distinctions demonstrate how each successive offering creates greater economic value. Often a manager claims a company is "in a commodity business" when in fact the offering sold is not a true commodity. The perception results in part from a self-fulfilling commoditization that occurs whenever an organization fails to fully recognize the distinctions between higher-value offerings and pure commodities. (And if an analyst or pundit says your company sells a commodity when you don't, you have been insulted, as well as challenged to shift up to a higher level in economic value.) If you fear that your offerings are being commoditized, read the simple descriptions given next. And if you think your offerings could never be commoditized—think again. A haughty spirit goes before a great fall (in prices).

TABLE 1-1

Economic distinctions

Economic offering	Commodities	Goods	Services	Experiences
Economy	Agrarian	Industrial	Service	Experience
Economic function	Extract	Make	Deliver	Stage
Nature of offering	Fungible	Tangible	Intangible	Memorable
Key attribute	Natural	Standardized	Customized	Personal
Method of supply	Stored in bulk	Inventoried after production	Delivered on demand	Revealed over a duration
Seller	Trader	Manufacturer	Provider	Stager
Buyer	Market	User	Client	Guest
Factors of demand	Characteristics	Features	Benefits	Sensations

Commodities

True commodities are materials extracted from the natural world: animal, mineral, vegetable. People raise them on the ground, dig for them under the ground, or grow them in the ground. After slaughtering, mining, or harvesting the commodity, companies generally process or refine it to yield certain characteristics and then store it in bulk before transporting it to market. By definition, commodities are fungible—they are what they are and therefore interchangeable. Because commodities cannot be differentiated, commodity traders sell them largely into nameless markets where a company purchases them for a price determined by supply and demand. (Companies do of course supply gradations in categories of commodities, such as different varieties of coffee beans or different grades of oil, but within each grade the commodity is purely fungible.) Every commodity trader commands the same price as everyone else selling the same stuff, and when demand greatly exceeds supply, handsome profits ensue. When supply outstrips demand, however, profits prove hard to come by. Over the short term, the cost of extracting the commodity bears no relationship to its price, and over the long term the invisible hand of the market determines the price as it encourages companies to move in or out of commodity businesses.

Agricultural commodities formed the basis of the Agrarian Economy, which for millennia provided subsistence for families and small communities. When the United States was founded in 1776, more than 90 percent of the employed population worked on farms. In 2009, that number had dropped to 1.3 percent.[8]

What happened? The tremendous technological and productivity improvements that became known as the Industrial Revolution drastically altered this way of life, beginning on the farm but quickly extending into the factory (such as the pin-making factory made famous by Adam Smith in *The Wealth of Nations*, published, coincidentally, in 1776). Building on the success of companies in England from the 1750s onward, flourishing U.S. factories developed their own production innovations that in the 1850s collectively became known as the American System of Manufactures.[9] As manufacturers the world over learned and copied these techniques, automating millions of craft jobs in the process, the foundation for all advanced economies irrevocably shifted to goods as farm employment plummeted.

Goods

Using commodities as their raw materials, companies make and then inventory goods—tangible items sold to largely anonymous customers who buy them off the shelf, from the lot, out of the catalog, or on the Web. Because manufacturing processes actually convert the raw materials in making a variety of goods, leeway exists to set prices based on the costs of production as well as product differentiation. Significant differences exist in the features of various makes of automobiles, computers, soft drinks, and, to some degree, even lowly pins. And because they can be put to immediate use—to get places, write reports, quench thirsts, fasten things together—their users value them more highly than the commodities from whence they came.

Although people have turned commodities into useful goods throughout history, the time-intensive means of extracting commodities and the high-cost methods of craft-producing goods long prevented manufacturing from dominating the economy.[10] This changed when companies learned to standardize goods and gain economies of scale. People left the farm in droves to work in factories, and by the 1880s the United States had overtaken England as the world's leading manufacturer.[11] With the advent of Mass Production, brought about in the first assembly line at Henry Ford's Highland Park, Michigan, plant on April 1, 1913, the United States solidified its position as the number one economic power in the world.[12]

As continued process innovations gradually reduced the number of workers required to produce a given output, the need for manufacturing workers leveled off and eventually began to decline. Simultaneously, the vast wealth generated by the manufacturing sector, as well as the sheer number of physical goods accumulated, drove a greatly increased demand for services and, as a result, service workers. It was in the 1950s, when services first employed more than 50 percent of the U.S. population, that the Service Economy overtook the Industrial (although this was not recognized until long after the fact). In 2009, manufacturing jobs—people actually making things with their hands—employed a mere 10 percent of the working population.[13] With farming employing 1.3 percent, what economists today categorize as services makes up almost 90 percent of U.S. workers. Globally, service jobs recently eclipsed agricultural ones for the first time in human history: some 42 percent of worldwide workers find employment in the service sector, 36 percent in agriculture, and only 22 percent in manufacturing.[14] (Of course, these statistics, from the United Nations International Labour Organization, fail to distinguish those working in experience-staging employment; so the service sector figure includes experience-staging jobs as well.)

Services

Services are intangible activities customized to the individual request of known clients. Service providers use goods to perform operations on a particular client (such as haircuts or eye exams) or on his property or possessions (such as lawn care or computer repair). Clients generally value the benefits of services more highly than the goods required to provide them. Services accomplish specific tasks clients want done but do not want to do themselves; goods merely supply the means.

Just as gray areas lie between commodities and goods (extensive processing or refining may merge into making), the line between goods and services can be blurry. Even though restaurants deliver tangible food, for example, economists place them in the service sector because they do not inventory their offerings but deliver them on demand in response to an individual patron's order. Although fast-food restaurants that make the food in advance share fewer of these attributes and so lie closer to the realm of goods than others, economists rightly count those employed at McDonald's, for instance, in the service sector.

While employment continues to shift to services, output in the commodity and goods sectors has not abated. Today, fewer farmers harvest far more than their ancestors ever conceived possible, and the sheer quantity of goods rolling off assembly lines would shock even Adam Smith. Thanks to continued technological and operational innovations, extracting commodities from the ground and making goods in factories simply require a diminishing number of people. Still, the percentage of gross domestic product (GDP) devoted to the service sector today dwarfs the other offerings. After fearing for many years the hollowing of the U.S. industrial base, most pundits now recognize it as a positive development that the United States, along with most advanced countries, has shifted full-bore to a Service Economy.

With this shift comes another little-realized or -discussed dynamic: In a Service Economy, *individuals desire service*. Whether consumers or businesses, they scrimp and save on goods (buying at Walmart, squeezing suppliers) in order to purchase services (eating out, managing the company cafeteria) they value more highly. That's precisely why many manufacturers today find their goods commoditized. In a Service Economy, the lack of differentiation in customers' minds causes goods to face the constant price pressure indelibly associated with commodities. As a result, customers more and more purchase goods solely on price and availability.

To escape this commoditization trap, manufacturers often deliver services wrapped around their core goods. This provides fuller, more complete economic offerings that better meet customer desires.[15] So automakers, for example, increase the coverage and length of their warranties while financing and leasing cars, consumer goods manufacturers manage inventory for grocery stores, and so forth. Initially, manufacturers tend to give away these services to better sell their goods. Many later realize that customers value the services so highly that the companies can charge separately for them. Eventually, astute manufacturers shift away from a goods mentality to become predominantly service providers.

Look at IBM. In its heyday in the 1960s and 1970s the hardware manufacturer's well-earned slogan was "IBM Means Service," as it lavished services—at no cost—on any company that would buy its hardware goods. It planned facilities, programmed code, integrated other companies' equipment, and repaired its own machines so prodigiously as to overwhelm nearly all competitors. But as time went on and the industry matured, customer demand for service (not to mention the Justice Department suit that forced IBM to unbundle its hardware and software) surpassed the company's ability to give it away, and it began to charge explicitly for its services. Company executives eventually discovered that the services it once provided for free were, in fact, its most valued offerings. Today, with its mainframe computers long since commoditized, IBM's Global Services unit grows at double-digit rates. The company no longer gives away its services to sell its goods. Indeed, the deal is reversed: IBM buys its clients' hardware when they contract with Global Services to manage their information systems. IBM still manufactures computers, but it's now in the *business* of providing services.

Buying goods to sell services—or at least giving them away below cost or for nothing, as mobile phone operators do—signifies that the Service Economy has reached a level once thought unimaginable and, by many, undesirable. Not very long ago academics and pundits still decried the takeover by services as the engine of economic growth, asserting that no economic power could afford to lose its industrial base and that an economy based overwhelmingly on services would become transient, destined to lose its prowess and its place among nations. That concern is now obviously unfounded. In fact, only the shift to services allowed for continued prosperity in the face of the ever-increasing automation of commoditized goods.

The dynamic continues. The commoditization trap that forced manufacturers to add services to the mix now attacks services with a similar vengeance. Telephone companies sell long-distance service solely on price, price, price. Airplanes resemble cattle cars, with a significant number of passengers flying on free awards; in a last-ditch effort, airlines consolidate, and nickel-and-dime customers for ancillary services, to maintain profitability. Fast-food restaurants all stress "value" pricing; few have managed to avoid offering a "dollar menu." (Interestingly, the *Economist* created the Big Mac Index to compare the price levels in different countries based on the price of a local Big Mac.[16] Perhaps a new metric should measure the number of items now available for a mere buck.) And price wars abound in the financial services industry as first discount and then Internet-based brokers constantly drive down commissions, charging as little as $3 for what a full-service broker would charge more than $100. J. Joseph Ricketts, founder of Ameritrade, even told *BusinessWeek,* "I can see a time when, for a customer with a certain size margin account, we won't charge commissions. We might even pay a customer, on a per trade basis, to bring the account to us."[17] An absurdity? Only if one fails to recognize that any shift up to a new, higher-value offering entails giving away the old, lower-value offering.

Indeed, the Internet is the greatest known force of commoditization for goods as well as services. It eliminates much of the human element in traditional buying and selling. Its capability for friction-free transactions enables instant price comparisons across myriad sources. And its ability to quickly execute these transactions allows customers to benefit from time as well as cost savings. With time-starved consumers and speed-obsessed businesses, the Internet increasingly turns transactions for goods and services into a virtual commodity pit.[18] Web-based enterprises busy commoditizing both consumer and business-to-business industries include specialty commoditizers—such as CarsDirect.com (automobiles), compare.net (consumer electronics), getsmart.com (financial services), insweb.com (insurance), and priceline.com (airline travel)—and general commoditizers that help buyers find lower prices for virtually all goods and services, such as bizrate.com, netmarket.com, NexTag.com, pricegrabber.com, and mySimon.com, to name a few. Consider, too, the ease with which consumers can perform such commoditizing tasks as finding used books via Amazon.com or searching for items via Google. And of course newspaper classified ads, the once dominant means for price-conscious consumers to find low-cost secondhand items, now have unprecedented competition from the commoditizing presence of eBay and CraigsList.

The other great force of commoditization? Walmart. That is the $400 billion behemoth's entire modus operandi, accomplished by squeezing its suppliers, increasing its package sizes, enhancing its logistics—whatever it takes to lower the costs of the goods it sells. Note, too, that Walmart increasingly sells services, beginning with food and photographic services but now encompassing optometric, financial, and healthcare services and becoming a force for commoditization in that sector as well.

Service providers also face another adverse trend unknown to goods manufacturers: *disintermediation.* Companies such as Dell, USAA, and Southwest Airlines generally sidestep retailers, distributors, and agents to connect directly with their end buyers. Decreased employment in these intermediaries, as well as bankruptcies and consolidations, invariably results. And a third trend further curtails service sector employment: that old boogeyman *automation,* which today hits many service jobs (telephone operators, bank clerks, and the like) with the same force and intensity that technological progress hit employment in the goods sector during the twentieth century.

Even professional service providers increasingly discover that their offerings have been "productized"—embedded into software, such as tax preparation programs.[19] Or they have been offshored to India, as with manufacturing moving to China, in what amounts to a fourth force of commoditization.

All this points to an inevitable conclusion: the Service Economy has peaked. A new economy has arisen to increase revenues and create new jobs, one based on a distinct kind of economic output. Goods and services are no longer enough.

Experiences

Experiences have necessarily emerged to create new value. Such experience offerings occur whenever a company intentionally uses services as the stage and goods as props to engage an individual. Whereas commodities are fungible, goods tangible, and services intangible, experiences are *memorable*. Buyers of experiences—we'll follow Disney's lead and call them *guests*—value being engaged by what the company reveals over a duration of time. Just as people have cut back on goods to spend more money on services, now they also scrutinize the time and money they spend on services to make way for more memorable—and more highly valued—experiences.

The company—we'll call it an *experience stager*—no longer offers goods or services alone but the resulting experience, rich with sensations, created within each customer. All prior economic offerings remain at arm's length, outside the buyer, but experiences are inherently personal. They actually occur within any individual who has been engaged on an emotional, physical, intellectual, or even spiritual level. The result? No two people can have the same experience—period. Each experience derives from the interaction between the staged event and the individual's prior state of mind and being.

Even so, some observers might argue that experiences are only a subclass of services, merely the latest twist to get people to buy certain services. Interestingly, the esteemed Adam Smith made the same argument about the relationship between goods and services more than two hundred years ago in *The Wealth of Nations*. He regarded services almost as a necessary evil—what he called "unproductive labour"—and not as an economic offering in itself, precisely because services cannot be physically inventoried and therefore create no tangible testament that work has been done. Smith did not limit his view of unproductive activity to such workers as household servants. He included the "sovereign" and other "servants of the public," the "protection, security, and defence of the commonwealth," and a number of professionals ("churchmen, lawyers, physicians, men of letters of all kinds") whose efforts the current market has determined to be of far more value than that of most laborers. Smith then singled out the experience stagers of his day ("players, buffoons, musicians, opera-singers, opera-dancers, &c.") and concluded, "The labour of the meanest of these has a certain value, regulated by the very same principles which regulate that of every other sort of labour; and that of the noblest and most useful, produces nothing which could afterwards purchase or procure an equal quantity of labour. Like the declamation of the actor, the harangue of the orator, or the tune of the musician, the work of all of them perishes in the very instant of its production."[20] However, even though the *work* of the experience stager perishes with its performance (precisely the right word), the *value* of the experience lingers in the memory of any individual who was engaged by the event.[21] Most parents do not take their kids to Walt Disney World only for the venue itself but rather to make the shared experience part of everyday family conversations for months, or years, afterward.

Although experiences themselves lack tangibility, people greatly desire them because the value of experiences lies within them, where it remains long afterward. That's why the studies performed by Cornell psychology professors Travis Carter and Thomas Gilovich determined that buying experiences makes people happier, with a greater sense of well-being, than purchasing goods.[22] Similarly, the *Economist* summarized recent economic research into happiness as "'experiences' over commodities, pastimes over knick-knacks, doing over having."[23]

Companies that create such happiness-generating experiences not only earn a place in the hearts of consumers but also capture their hard-earned dollars—and harder-earned time. The notion of inflation as purely the result of companies passing along increased costs is not valid; higher prices also indicate greater value, especially in the way people spend their time. The shift in consumer (and business) demand from commodities to goods to services and now to experiences shifts the prototypical "market basket" to these higher-valued offerings—more than government statisticians take into account, we believe. In 2009, barely 60 percent of the total Consumer Price Index (CPI) was in services, which weren't even included in the Producer Price Index until 1995.[24] But if we examine the CPI statistics, as shown in figure 1-2, we see that the CPI for goods (using new vehicles, the prototypical Industrial Economy product) increases less than the CPI for services, which in turn increases less than the CPI for the one prototypical experience that can be found in the statistics: admissions to recreational events such as movies, concerts, and sports, which the government began tracking separately only in 1978.[25] Note, too, the volatility of the CPI for a typical commodity, pork, relative to the other offerings. Increased price volatility as pure market forces take over awaits the sellers of all commoditized goods and services.[26] (Pork actually surpasses

FIGURE 1-2

Consumer Price Index (CPI) by economic offering

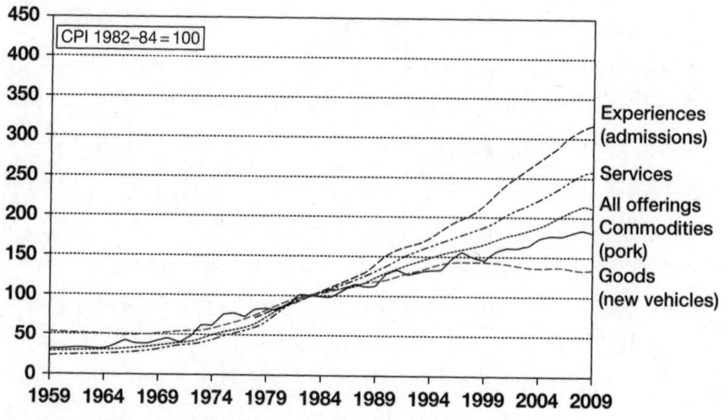

Source: U.S. Bureau of Labor Statistics; Lee S. Kaplan, Lee3Consultants.com.

new vehicles in these statistics because of not only its own volatility but also the increasing price pressure on the commoditizing automobile industry over the past decade or two while it simultaneously increased quality, which the government discounts in any price increases. We suspect these lines will once again cross.) Companies that stage experiences, on the other hand, increase the price of their offerings much faster than the rate of inflation because consumers value experiences more highly.

The employment and nominal GDP statistics show the same effect as the CPI, as figure 1-3 makes clear.[27] In the fifty-year period 1959–2009, commodity output produced in the United States increased by a compound annual growth rate (CAGR) of 5.2%, while employment in commodity industries actually *decreased*. Manufacturing output increased only slightly more than commodity output, while also losing jobs on average every year, albeit only slightly (although the *relative* number of people

FIGURE 1-3

Growth in employment and nominal gross domestic product (GDP) by economic offering

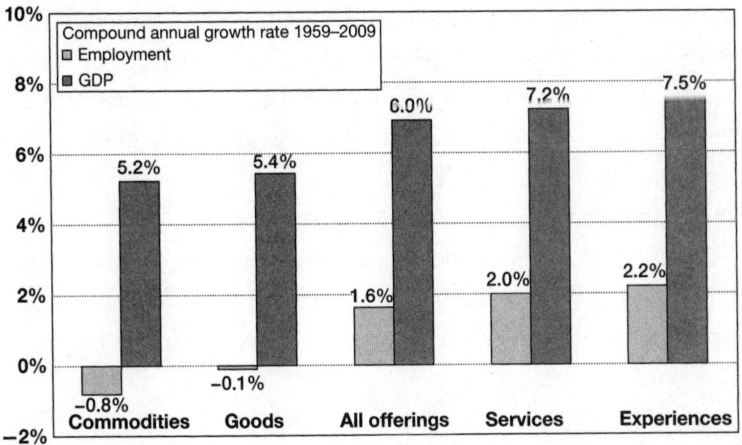

Source: U.S. Bureau of Economic Analysis; Strategic Horizons LLP; and Lee S. Kaplan, Lee3Consultants.com analysis.

employed in the manufacturing sector decreased greatly in the past fifty years). Services overpowered these sectors with a 2.0 percent CAGR in employment and more than 7 percent in GDP. But those industries (or portions) that could be pulled out of the government's service sector statistics as experiential grew even faster: 2.2 percent employment and 7.5 percent GDP.[28]

No wonder many companies today wrap experiences around their existing goods and services to differentiate their offerings. Service providers may have an edge in this regard, because they are not wedded to tangible offerings. They can enhance the environment in which clients purchase or receive the service, layer on inviting sensations encountered while in that company-controlled environment, and otherwise figure out how to better engage clients to turn the service into a memorable event.

Ing the Thing

What's a manufacturer to do? Short of leapfrogging into the experience business—quite a stretch for most diehard manufacturers—manufacturers must focus on the experience customers have while using their goods.[29] Most product designers focus primarily on the internal mechanics of the good itself: what *it* does. What if the attention centered instead on the individual's use of the good? The focus would then shift to the user: how the individual experiences the *using* of the good.

Notice, for example, the diverse set of experiences highlighted in a travel guide from Fodor's Travel Publications, an "escapist scrapbook" featuring the photography and essays of Peter Guttman. In *Adventures to Imagine,* Guttman documents twenty-eight adventures in which potential travelers can immerse themselves. Consider the range of activities—some old, some new, but all engaging: houseboating, portaging, mountain biking, cattle driving, bobsledding, tall ship sailing, tornado chasing, canyoneering, wagon training, seal viewing, iceberg tracking, puffin birding, race car driving, hot-air ballooning, rock climbing, spelunking, white-water rafting, canoeing, heli-hiking, hut-to-hut hiking, whale kissing, llama trekking, barnstorming, land yachting, historic battle reenacting, iceboating, polar bearing, and dogsledding.[30] Companies constantly introduce new *ing* experiences to the outdoor adventure world. Just to add a few to the list: cross-golfing and guerilla-golfing (golfing without a golf course, playing instead in undeveloped rural terrains or abandoned urban settings, respectively), noboarding (snowboarding on boards that lack bindings), canyoning (bodysurfing in rapid mountain streams, usually in Switzerland or New Zealand) or riverboarding (with more protective gear in larger rapids), and glacier-walking (in places like Norway).

Retailers like Bass Pro Shops Outdoor World, Recreational Equipment, Inc. (REI), and Cabela's sell goods as equipment for use in these types of experiences, and they lead the way in making their retail space an experience itself. Bass Pro Shops brings the outdoor environment indoors, REI provides a fifty-five-foot mountain in many stores so that customers can test its climbing gear, and Cabela's displays a thirty-five-foot dioramic mountain filled with taxidermist-stuffed wild animals. Manufacturers, too, must explicitly design their goods to enhance the user's experience—essentially *experientializing* the goods—even when customers pursue less-adventurous activities. Automakers do this when they focus on enhancing the *driving* experience, but they must also focus on other non-driving experiences that occur in cars. For example, many women are still waiting for a carmaker to accommodate *purse storing* in their vehicles. And certainly *in-car dining* could be enhanced for the millions who daily buy fast food via drive-through lanes.

Executives in the appliance industry already think this way. Former Maytag executive William Beer once told *Industry Week*, "The eating experience is now wherever a person is at the moment. We have people eating in the car on the way back and forth to work, in front of the TV." This leads Beer to deduce that "people may need a refrigerated compartment in an automobile or in the arm of a chair," innovations that would greatly enhance various eating occasions but would never surface within the framework of the industry's old mindset, which focused on how appliances perform rather than on what users do when eating.[31] The Maytag brand is now part of Whirlpool Corporation, which has embraced this experience perspective in its companywide innovation efforts. Its Duet washer-and-dryer system focuses on making the set *good-looking* in the laundry room (like parking a luxury sports car in a garage). For garages, Whirlpool invented Gladiator GarageWorks, a set of appliances for *garage-organizing*. And its new Personal Valet offers a "clothes *vitalizing* system"—a device that is neither dry cleaning nor drying clothes on an outside line, but somehow feels like both. Innovators conceived of all these new *inged* things by rethinking the experiences consumers had while using appliances (and rooms) in the home.

Many goods encompass more than one experiential aspect, opening up multiple areas for differentiation. Apparel manufacturers, for instance, could focus on the *wearing* experience, the *cleaning* experience, and perhaps even the *hanging* or *drawering* experience. (And, like Guttman, they should not be afraid to make up new gerunds whenever needed.) Office supply businesses might create a better *briefcasing* experience, *wastebasketing* experience, or *computer-screening* experience. If you as a manufacturer start thinking in these terms—*inging* your things—you'll soon be surrounding your goods with services that add value to the activity of using them and then surrounding those services with experiences that make using them more memorable—and therefore make more money.

Any good can be *inged*. Consider duct tape. ShurTech Brands of Avon, Ohio, employs a number of exemplary methods to turn *duct-taping* into a more memorably engaging experience via its Duck Tape brand. It does this first by *embedding the goods in an experiential brand.*[32] The brand sports a duck mascot named Trust E. Duck. More than a logo, the duck serves as an all-encompassing motif for organizing almost every customer interaction with the inged brand. This embedding even extends to (or arguably begins with) the brand's interactions with employees: ShurTech's corporate offices, dubbed "The Duck Tape Capital of the World," represent a themed office that does to office parks what Disney did to amusement parks. The company also emphasizes that it is *producing goods experience stagers need*. The website for Duck Tape provides a place for the company and its customers to share ideas for various "Ducktivities" that show how the goods can be used in staging various experiences. For example, you can find instructions on how to make a stylish Halloween bag entirely out of Duck Tape.

These kinds of experience-supporting insights are enabled by first *sensorializing the goods*. This represents perhaps the most straightforward way of making goods more experiential—by adding elements that enhance the customer's *sensory interaction* with them. Some goods richly engage the senses by their very nature: toys, cotton candy, home videos, music CDs, cigars, wine, and so forth. While the very use of these goods creates a sensory experience, companies can sensorialize any good by accentuating the sensations created from its use.[33] Doing so requires being aware of which senses most affect customers (but are perhaps most ignored in the traditional design of goods), focusing on those senses and the sensations they yield, and then redesigning the good to make it more experientially appealing. One way ShurTech does this is by *colorizing* the goods, offering Duck Tape in twenty colors and challenging customers to "Show Your True Colors."

The company then allows customers to show off their Duck Tape creations by *forming a goods club*. Members of the "Duck Tape Club" share tips and tell stories about their adventures using the goods (Duck Tape hammock-swinging, anyone?) as well as gain access to exclusive promotional offers. The company itself gets into the *inging* action by *making some goods scarce*. For example, ShurTech made the "world's largest roll of Duck Tape" and sent the one-of-a-kind product on a tour of select retail outlets for fans to get a special look (and feel) of the thing.

Finally, and perhaps most importantly, the company keeps busy *staging goods events*. Each year, the brand sponsors its "Stuck on Prom" contest, in which high school seniors win college scholarships by donning their tuxedos and gowns—made entirely out of Duck Tape—at their proms and then submitting photographs to ShurTech for judging. Similarly, a "Duck Tape Dad of the Year" contest finds many duct-taping fathers vying for accolades. And ShurTech helps host the "Avon Heritage Duct Tape Festival," held each June in the company's hometown. The goods event features, among other *inged* things, a parade of Duck Tape creations.

Many manufacturers stage their own goods events—although these experiences generally exist as a sideline—when they add museums, amusement parks, or other attractions to their factory output. Hershey's Chocolate World—where else but in Hershey, Pennsylvania?—is perhaps the most famous, but there are others, including Spamtown USA (Hormel Foods, Austin, Minnesota), Goodyear World of Rubber (Akron, Ohio), The Crayola Factory (Binney & Smith, Easton, Pennsylvania), LEGOLAND Billund (Denmark), The Guinness Storehouse (Dublin, Ireland), and the Heineken Experience (Amsterdam, The Netherlands).[34] Not every manufacturer can turn extra space into a ticket-taking museum, but any company can recast production as a miniaturized plant tour, thus turning the everyday acquisition and consumption of a candy bar, toy, drink, or any other good into a memorable event. The goal is to draw the customer into the process of designing, producing, packaging, and delivering the item. Customers often value the way in which they obtain something as much as the good itself: witness the great feeling Volkswagen engenders when customers pick up their new cars at the company's Autostadt theme park, next to its plant in Wolfsburg, Germany.

The purpose of *inging* anything is to shift the attention from the underlying goods (and supporting services) to an experience wrapped around these traditional offerings, forestalling commoditization and increasing sales of the goods. Consider the Gumball Wizard machines found outside untold numbers of retail stores around the world. Put in a coin and the gumball spirals around and around before being dispensed, clickety-clacking as it goes. The device offers the same old goods—while, arguably, providing worse service because it takes longer to deliver the gumball. But the *gumball-spiraling* experience, atop the goods and service, drives increased sales.

The First Principle of Experience Staging

Staging compelling experiences begins with embracing an experience-directed mindset, thinking not only about the design and production of things but also about the design and orchestration of experiences using these things. Achieving this mindset begins with thinking in terms of *ing* words. Consider this *ing* thinking the first principle of effective experience staging.

This principle furnishes a powerful first step in helping businesses and industries shift from goods and services to experiences. For example, thinking in *ing* words led to the formation of the Go RVing Alliance—composed of the Recreational Vehicle Industry Association, the Recreational Vehicle Dealers Association, and other industry groups—to collectively promote the pleasures of RVing in lieu of individual manufacturers being left to pitch the features and benefits of competing RVs.

Wholeheartedly embracing the "*ing* the thing" principle can even lead to the launch of new experience-based businesses. Consider Build-A-Bear Workshop. Instead of just creating new teddy bear goods, founder Maxine Clark envisioned a special place where "kids aged 3 to 103" could create their own stuffed animals. The experience consists of eight stuffed *animal-making* stations: Choose Me (with kids *choosing* from some thirty animal skins), Hear Me (for *recording* a message or *selecting* a prerecorded sound for an inserted sound chip), Stuff Me (*helping* stuff the animal and then *hugging* it to test for the right amount of stuffiness), Stitch Me (including *making-a-wish* and then *heart-inserting*), Fluff Me (where kids enjoy *hair-brushing* and *pampering* their new creations in a spa treatment), Name Me (*naming* the animal and *receiving* a birth certificate), Dress Me (*dressing* the animal to show personality), and finally Take Me Home (instead of putting the animal in a shopping bag, *housing* the custom-made animal in a "Cub Condo Carrying Case," a home-shaped box doubling as a coloring book—make that a *coloring house*). Online, the company posts ideas about *house-cationing* while enabling virtual *playing* in Build-A-Bearville.

Ing One and *Ing* Two

You can uncover two types of experiences in the process of thinking about how to *ing*. The first category consists of those *ing* words that exist in your company's everyday lexicon but are neglected as an experience in its offerings. Addressing these dormant opportunities can yield immediate experience enhancements. Consultant John DiJulius, for example, works with retailers to turn mundane store *greetings* into engaging encounters. You know the typical drill: the store associate says, "Can I help you?" only to have customers respond with "I'm just looking." To *ing* the greeting at JoAnn Fabrics, DiJulius suggested asking, "What are you working on?" Most customers enjoy talking about their craft projects enthusiastically, so the new welcoming experience creates greater opportunity for sales floor staff to make suggestions about possible supplies. Almost every retailer stands to gain from rethinking its greeting. Similarly, almost every airline could stand to *ing* the intrusive *reviewing* of in-flight safety instructions by flight attendants over the plane's loudspeakers. Southwest Airlines, of course, *ings* the thing by allowing staff to sprinkle these announcements with humor and even song. Virgin America rivals this with animated cartoon characters reviewing procedures on the entertainment system screen mounted on each seat.

Some neglected *ing* words provide fodder for significant innovation. Recognizing *milk-drinking* as an opportunity, cereal restaurateur Cereality invented a new utensil called the sloop. "The spoon that sips like a straw" has a hollow core running from the curved spoon end to the tip of the handle. Chick-fil-A saw store *openings* as a neglected experience. Whenever the Atlanta-based company opens a new location, it offers free chicken for a year to the first one hundred customers. These people always show up twenty-four hours in advance to camp out overnight on the store grounds. Chick-fil-A hosts ongoing games and other events in the parking lot throughout the gathering. CEO Dan Cathy typically joins the festivities in the evening to give a motivational speech and play his trumpet at key moments ("Revelry" as the morning wake-up call, and horse racing's "Call to Post" when the store officially opens). Many customers post pictures and videos online as well as blog about their experiences.

In Simsbury, Connecticut, kitchen and bathroom remodeler Mark Brady of Mark Brady Kitchens seized on the *selecting* of appliances, cabinetry, fixtures, paint, wallpaper, and other renovation accessories as an opportunity to create a "shopping cruise" for prospective customers. Brady books a stretch limousine and chaperones customers (usually couples) on a tour of more than a dozen supply houses, guiding them through a workbook he prepared for fostering discussion between stops. The shopping cruise not only saves time (customers no longer have to navigate their way to all these outlets in the industrial parts of towns), but it also doubles as a great date (the limo driver opens doors and offers snacks, and Brady himself proposes a Champagne toast at the end of the tour). Customers not only make all the necessary selections for their room but also get to know Mark Brady and get comfortable with him as their contractor. (Brady also offers to apply the $750 cost of the shopping cruise to the price of his proposed work.)

So ask yourself, What *ing* word is being most neglected within our enterprise? Once you identify the opportunity, make it your focus for creating an engaging experience for your customers.

But go one step further. A second category of *ing* words consists of newly created words—like *puffin birding, cross-golfing, noboarding,* and *housecationing*—coined to describe new-to-the-world experiences. (Of course, any new and therefore unfamiliar *ing* word and its corresponding experience, once popularized, become familiar and therefore "existing" in the sense used here; think of bungee-jumping, which was once a foreign concept but now is enjoyed in almost every resort city in the world.) This approach focuses on inventing new experiences suggested by made-up *ing* words. The emergence of new *ing* words arises naturally whenever a truly new good serves as a prop or a new service sets the stage for a new experience. Think about how Apple's iPod (a good) and iTunes (a service) gave rise to *podcasting*—now familiar to most of us—and *podjacking*—not yet so familiar: it refers to two people exchanging iPods to check out each other's playlists. (Of note: the spell-checker associated with the software used to write this chapter recognized the former pod-based *ing* word but not the latter.)

Although the objective—experience innovation—remains the same with either mental model, people often find it easier to imagine new experiences emerging from new words. U.K.-based TopGolf, for example, operates facilities on multiple continents that go beyond mere improvement on the driving range (generally designed only for practicing for subsequent eighteen-hole golf course experiences). Instead, TopGolf offers a self-contained golfing experience in and of itself. With microchips embedded in each golf ball and landing areas that detect which person hit what ball where, it scores buckets, with results for each round posted on computer monitors—a kind of everyman's leaderboard tracking for those *topgolfing* at any particular time. Or consider *zorbing.*

New Zealand-based Zorb places people inside three-meter-diameter transparent plastic balls—they're actually spheres within spheres—dubbed zorbs, and then rolls them down a hill!

Chicago provides the scene for two other examples of creating new experiences that no existing *ing* words suffice to describe. Call the one "cow-parading" and the other "bobble-buzzing." The Greater North Michigan Growth Association hosted "Cows on Parade" in the mid-1990s, commissioning local artists to decorate three hundred bronze cows imported from Switzerland and, once they were completed, placed the finished art pieces throughout the city to promote tourism. The event proved so popular that untold cities followed suit, using other objects ranging from guitars (Cleveland) to flying pigs (Cincinnati) to *Peanuts* characters (St. Paul, Minnesota) to huge resin ducks (Eugene, Oregon, home of University of Oregon Ducks sports teams).

The other Chicago experience was a B2B marketing experience. Well, actually, it might be better described as an A2A experience, conducted by the Association Forum of Chicagoland, a professional society for directors and managers of other associations based in the greater Chicago area. After years of struggling to recruit members from the ranks of readily identifiable nonmember associations, the group conceived a new *inged* approach. Rather than conduct yet another direct-mail campaign to thousands of prospects yielding only a handful of new members, the society sent bobblehead dolls of the association's executive director and volunteer president (customized at whoopassenterprises.com) to only the thirty most active members. Each bobblehead was packed in a "Care and Nurturing" kit that included postcards of the figures photographed at various Chicago landmarks (for mailing to friends in other associations), instructions for displaying the bobblehead for visitors to see in the members' offices, and, most pertinently, applications for membership. As a result of the bobble-buzzing experience, more than three hundred new members joined the Association Forum of Chicagoland, representing a tenfold return on mailings versus the less than 1 percent success rate associated with previous efforts.

So ask yourself, What new *ing* word could be the basis of creating a wholly new experience? Once you have articulated the word, explore the elements that would help turn the new term into a wildly successful experiential reality.

The Progression of Economic Value

As the placard Rebecca Pine once gave to her father for his birthday says, "The best things in life are not things." Consider a common event everyone experiences growing up: the birthday party. Most baby boomers can remember childhood birthday parties when Mom baked a cake from scratch. Which meant what, exactly? That she actually *touched* such commodities as butter, sugar, eggs, flour, milk, and cocoa. And how much did these ingredients cost back then? A dime or two, maybe three.

Such commodities became less relevant to the needs of consumers when companies such as General Mills, with its Betty Crocker brand, and Procter & Gamble, with Duncan Hines, packaged most of the necessary ingredients into cake mixes and canned frostings. And how much did these goods cost as they increasingly flew off the supermarket shelf in the 1960s and 1970s? Not much, perhaps a dollar or two at most, but still quite a bit more than the cost of the basic commodities. The higher cost was recompense for the increased value of the goods in terms of flavor and texture consistency, ease of mixing, and overall time savings.

In the 1980s, many parents stopped baking cakes at all. Instead, Mom or Dad called the supermarket or local bakery and ordered a cake, specifying the exact type of cake and frosting, when it would be picked up, and the desired words and designs on top. At $10 to $20, this cake-making service cost ten times the price of the goods needed to make the cake at home while still involving less than a dollar's worth of ingredients. Many parents thought this a great bargain, however, enabling them to focus their time and energy on planning and throwing the actual party.

What do families do now in the twenty-first century? They outsource the entire party to companies such as Chuck E. Cheese's, Jeepers!, Dave & Buster's, or myriad other local "family entertainment centers," or this Zone or that Plex of one kind or another. These companies stage a birthday experience for family and friends for $100 to $250 or more, as depicted in figure 1-4. For Elizabeth Pine's seventh birthday, the Pine family went to an old-time farm called the New Pond Farm in Redding, Connecticut,

FIGURE 1-4

Price of birthday offerings

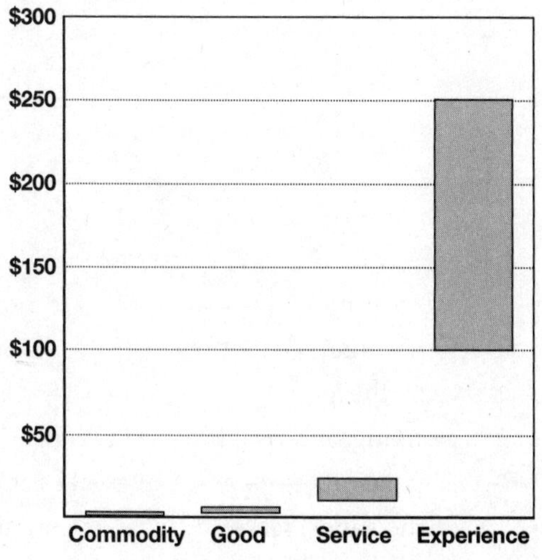

where Elizabeth and fourteen of her closest friends experienced a taste of the old Agrarian Economy by brushing cows, petting sheep, feeding chickens, making their own apple cider, and taking a hay ride over the hill and through the woods.[35] When the last present had been opened and the last guest had departed, Elizabeth's mom, Julie, got out her checkbook. When Dad asked how much the party cost, Julie replied, "A hundred and forty-six dollars—not including the cake"!

The simple saga of the birthday party illustrates the Progression of Economic Value depicted in figure 1-5.[36] Each successive offering—pure ingredients (commodities), packaged mixes (goods), finished cakes (services), and thrown parties (experiences)—greatly increases in value because the buyer finds each more relevant to what he truly wants (in this case, hosting a fun-filled and effortless birthday party). And because companies stage

FIGURE 1-5

Progression of Economic Value

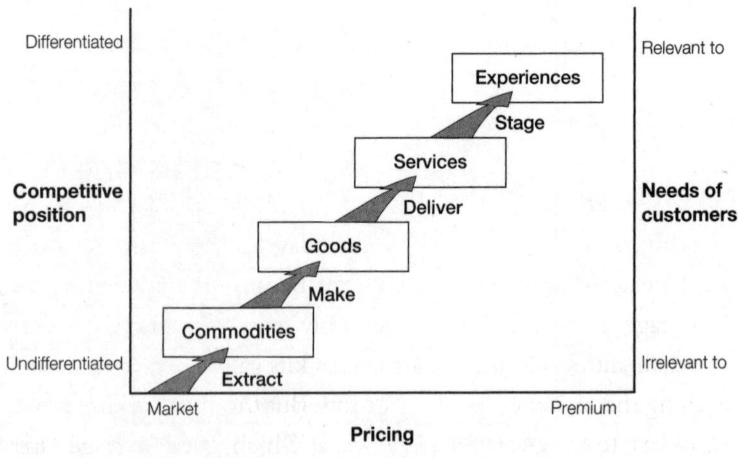

many kinds of experiences, they more easily differentiate their offerings and thereby charge a premium price based on the distinctive value provided, and not the market price of the competition. Those moms who baked from scratch paid only a few dimes' worth of ingredients. Similarly, the old-time farm accrues relatively little marginal cost to stage the birthday experience (a few dollars for labor, a little feed, and an hour or two's worth of depreciation) to turn a nice profit.[37]

One company that illustrates how to generate increased revenue and profits by shifting up the Progression of Economic Value is The Pleasant Company, now a part of Mattel. Founded in the 1980s by Pleasant Rowland, a former schoolteacher, the business manufactures a collection of American Girl dolls. Each one is cast in a period of American history and has its own set of a half-dozen fictional books placed in that time period. Girls learn U.S. history from owning the dolls and reading the books, which are marketed to their parents via catalog and the Web. In November 1998, the company opened its first American Girl Place off Michigan Avenue in Chicago, an ingeniously themed venue supported by sensation-filled sets (a doll hair salon, a photo studio, a restaurant simply called "Cafe," showcase displays for each doll, and various nooks for cuddling up with a book or doll), engaging staff performances (arriving at the concierge desk, visiting the hospital reception used for dolls in need of mending, and at nearly every turn), and a host of special events (theme parties, "Late Night" after-hours tours, and of course birthday parties). It's hard to call the American Girl Place a retail store, because it is indeed a business stage for experiences. Certainly you can purchase dolls, books, furniture, clothing, and various kits galore—even children's clothing that matches the dolls' outfits. But the merchandise proves secondary to the overall experience, at which guests average (*average!*) more than four hours per visit.

And do the math. A family may visit an American Girl Place and shell out $20 for a photography shoot—complete with preparatory makeup session—with the photo printed on a customized cover of *American Girl* magazine (subscriptions sold separately for $19.95 for six non-customized issues per year), pay another $20 in the hair salon for the doll to be restored to its original coiffed condition, and then dine at the Cafe at prix fixe prices, including gratuity, ranging from $17 to $26 for brunch, lunch, tea, and dinner. Even if they forgo a birthday celebration (at $32 per person, or $50–$65 for deluxe versions) or a late night event (for $200–$240 per girl), a family can easily spend hundreds of dollars—without buying a single physical thing! Of course, spending that much time and money on experiences then creates greater demand for traditional American Girl goods to commemorate the visit.

The company has expanded its portfolio of experiences to include American Girl Places in New York City (off Madison Avenue) and Los Angeles (at The Grove), as well as new (smaller footprint) American Girl Boutique & Bistros in Atlanta, Boston, Dallas, Denver, and the Mall of America. Sales soar, not only from the revenue generated at these retail venues but also from home via catalog shopping and at the company's website. These sales from home have undoubtedly accelerated as a result of the company's creating these away-from-home experiences to fuel the demand, for in today's Experience Economy, the experience *is* the marketing.

Let the Action Begin

Other children's experiences, such as The Little Gym and KidZania, now circle the world. Kids' camps are big business, as are various "travel teams" in their associated sports leagues, often supported with additional payments for ongoing sports lessons and personal coaching. Adults frequent cooking schools, fantasy camps, and wellness spas, among other indulgent experiences. Unique experiences constantly emerge: a place called Dig This in Steamboat Springs, Colorado, offers the B2C equivalent of the Case Tomahawk digging experience; one of its offerings, Excavate & Exfoliate, combines construction equipment play with follow-up spa treatments. Thus whole new genres of tourism arise; witness film tourism, culinary tourism, medical tourism, disaster tourism, climate change tourism, even "PhD tourism" (Context Travel of Philadelphia assigns doctorate experts to travel with tourists to various European cities). Airports, foremost among them the Amsterdam Airport Schiphol, have become experiential shopping centers. They serve as way stations to bizarre new attractions and destinations, such as Ski Dubai, Icehotel and its spinoff Icebars, and Atlantis in the Bahamas and Dubai—only to be topped by the Burning Man festival in the Black Rock Desert in Nevada. Back home, malls have become "lifestyle centers." Cafe culture abounds, from Starbucks and Caribou to the International Netherlands Group's ING Direct Cafes. Fitness centers seek to differentiate via the experience offered, from themed Crunch, to no-frills Curves, to large-scale Lifetime Fitness. Ian Schrager Company introduced the world to "boutique" hotels, followed soon by Kimpton Hotels, Joie de Vivre Hospitality, Starwood's W, and hundreds of independents represented by Design Hotels (based in Berlin). Blue Man Group and Cirque du Soleil offer truly new-to-the-world staged experiences. Museum experiences are being fundamentally rethought; visits to the International Spy Museum in Washington, D.C., the Harley-Davidson Museum in Milwaukee, and the Abraham Lincoln Presidential Library and Museum in Springfield, Illinois, clearly offer a new kind of encounter. The Internet offers new online experiences, from the U.S. Army's America's Army game at americasarmy.com to Linden Research's Second Life and Blizzard Entertainment's World of Warcraft. New experiences are available even at the end of life; Givnish Funeral Homes, outside Philadelphia, offers Life Celebration capabilities to other funeral directors throughout the United States. It is hard to find an industry still untouched by the shift to experiences.

Of course, no one has repealed the laws of supply and demand. Companies that fail to provide consistently engaging experiences, overprice their experiences relative to the value received, or overbuild their capacity to stage them will see demand or pricing pressure. For example, Discovery Zone, one stalwart of the birthday party circuit, went belly-up because of inconsistently staged events, poorly maintained games, and little consideration of the experience received by the adults, who, after all, pay for the event.[38] Planet Hollywood saw same-store sales plummet and had to significantly scale back its number of locations because it failed to refresh its experiences. As with most theme restaurants, repeat guests see (or do) little different from what they saw and did on previous visits. Even Disney succumbed to this problem when it let Tomorrowland grow horribly out of date over the past couple of decades; and the company had to invest billions to relaunch Disney's California Adventure Park after a lukewarm reception of the initial offering by Disney enthusiasts.

As the Experience Economy continues to unfold in the twenty-first century, more than a few experience stagers will find the going too tough to stay in business. Only the best of theme-based restaurants launched in the 1990s, for example, survived into the new millennium. But such dislocations occur as the result of any economic shift. Once, there were more than a hundred automakers in eastern Michigan, and more than forty cereal manufacturers in western Michigan. Now there are only the Big Three in Detroit (depending on how you want to count it these days) and the Kellogg Company in Battle Creek, all stalwarts of the Industrial Economy.

The growth of both the Industrial Economy and the Service Economy brought with it a proliferation of offerings that did not exist before imaginative companies invented and developed them. That's also how the Experience Economy will grow, as companies tough out what economist Joseph Schumpeter termed the "gales of creative destruction" that constitute business innovation. Those businesses that relegate themselves to the diminishing world of goods and services will be rendered irrelevant. To avoid this fate, you must learn to stage a rich, compelling experience.

CHAPTER 2

Setting the Stage

ON A HOT AUGUST NIGHT you find yourself in Evanston, Illinois, at the corner of Dempster and Elmwood. You spy a storefront named LAN Arena and, wondering what it might be, step inside. A T-shirted Gen Xer with "Commander Francisco" printed on his badge looks your way and mouths some words of greeting from atop his elevated platform. You nod in that general direction but decline his offer to explain the strange surroundings as you take a few more paces inside.

The walls are bare, the floor nearly empty. A faint odor of cement after a summer rain wafts its way into your nostrils. The tonal range looks decidedly grey. The sights and sounds soon draw your focus to the very heart of the place, in front of the Commander's platform, where finally you behold the domain he rules: fourteen PCs with large monitors, standard keyboards, and assorted gadgetry, half of them tethered to obviously quick-moving and presumably quick-witted people. You now identify the background noise that has been omnipresent from the moment you opened the door: the clicking and clacking of fingers on keys combined with the smooth sliding of joysticks. A yelp goes up from one of the six souls whose eyes focus on the screens before them: "Go away, you greasy-haired piece of monkey brains!" he yells, as you reflexively jump behind a pillar. Feeling foolish, you realize the taunt was aimed not at you but at an unseen combatant sparring with the truly greasy-haired piece of animated humanity before you. Another person mutters, "Who's in there? Careful! You're not getting off that easy!" A third shouts mild obscenities, punctuated by the occasional repeatable word.

As you walk around, desiring a closer look at both the human beings and their cybernetic appendages, you see that every PC has a nameplate: Toby, Fergie, Grape Ape, and—somehow you knew this was coming—Larry, Moe, and Curly. The screamer bangs away at Eastwood, the mutterer at one named Buddha. You glance back at Commander Francisco and notice for the first time that behind him are a number of shelves filled with row upon row of software boxes. Here, more names greet you: Diablo, Red Alert, Warcraft II, Command & Conquer. Ah! That's it! They're all playing some computer-based game against each other. "It's called Quake," the Commander announces, having watched your exploration of the place and now sensing your need to know. "It's sort of an electronic version of capture the flag."

You finally understand the attraction of this place and soon gain vicarious enjoyment from watching the players play. Three on three, the virtual opponents, physically seated less than twenty feet apart, battle in a virtual arena by means of a local area network, or LAN. You see the excitement in each player's face, the fluidity of human and machine working as one, and finally the joy that resounds in the one final cry of the victor as he vanquishes his last opponent. While disappointed in their loss, the also-rans all too happily begin anew. Hesitantly, anxiously, eagerly, you inform the Commander that you wish to join them. You sit down at a station and begin to experience the play for yourself.

This narrative, written in the second-person style endemic to certain kinds of computer games, more or less describes the real-life

LAN Arena as we first experienced it. It was the kind of place like many others that dotted the urban landscape in the late 1990s, where for a fee people played computer-based games against like-minded competitors. Commander Francisco Ramirez—who, in addition to being our host, was also one of three co-owners—explained that one could join in for $5 to $6 per hour and that regulars could select annual membership plans ranging between $25 and $100 to receive discounted rates, reserve a spot in the LAN Arena Directory, and play in occasional tournaments.

Despite the evident popularity of the LAN Arena, we couldn't help getting the feeling that the place resembled all the mom-and-pop video stores that mom-and-popped up across the country twenty-five or thirty years ago. The self-owned and -run local video store is now largely a historical curiosity—an interim solution—thanks to the creative destruction of alternative formats and innovative distribution and merchandising programs created by bigger enterprises. Not to mention industry consolidations, culminating in the wide swath cut by Blockbuster to gain the lion's share of the nascent industry's revenues. Then, of course, Blockbuster faced yet newer competition from outlet-free Netflix and its time-based pricing model, offering unlimited viewing experiences for a monthly fee in lieu of per-rental service charges (and pesky late fees).

Similarly, the LAN Arena format, with players seated together at a common site, proved only an interim solution before the play-at-home games of the past gave way to the play-in-cyberspace games of today. LAN Arena offered a ready-to-play gaming environment that was less costly and cumbersome than setting up the same arrangement at home, before the cost of faster hardware plummeted and broadband service became plentiful and free. Today, faster play is generally available on the Internet, and multiple players can readily participate simultaneously in the same Quake game or myriad others online. Indeed, the competitive landscape for gaming experiences knows few boundaries.[1]

Interestingly, as direct, online, from-home competitions came to dominate the gaming experience, "LAN parties" proliferated as pop-up events in cities around the world. Evidently the now-defunct LAN Arena was on to something. The social interaction, the game outside the game, weighs just as importantly in the enjoyment of software-enabled games as it does with the old table-top board games. Technology pundits anticipate that real-time audio, video, and tactile technologies will advance to the point that in a few years we'll be able to experience all interactions—yells and glares, teases and taunts, perhaps even pushes and shoves—*virtually* as well as we now do in reality. Evidently, no cyber game experience will be complete without its attendant virtual social experience.[2]

In the meantime, the staging of these LAN party experiences in physical venues has itself become a large-scale production. At about the same time LAN Arena opened in Evanston, id Software, the developers of Quake, launched QuakeCon. Now in its fifteenth year, the event features a QUAKE LIVE Masters Championship for advanced players (with a $50,000 purse for the winner), a four-on-four "Capture the Flag" competition, and an open tournament for less-skilled players—all held in an intimate 250-person arena, with others watching via streaming video. The competition comes complete with "shoutmasters" covering the action, culminating in a giant 3,000-person LAN party.

The future mix of virtual and physical action remains to be seen, and there is always the possibility that new social interfaces might even mask the interplay between the two. In any case, it is clear that not every company that stages these new experiences will be successful in the short term, much less the long term. Only a few will survive. What we don't know are which ones. Those that thrive will do so because they treat their economic offering as a rich experience—and not a glorified good or celebrated service—and will stage it in a way that engages the individual and leaves behind a memory. That means not making the mistake we see time and time again: equating experiences with mere entertainment.

Enriching the Experience

Because many exemplars of staged experiences come from what the popular press loosely calls the entertainment industry, it's easy to conclude that shifting up the Progression of Economic Value to stage experiences simply means adding entertainment to existing offerings. That would be a gross understatement. Remember that staging experiences is not about entertaining customers; it's about *engaging* them.

An experience may engage guests on any number of dimensions. Consider two of the most important, as depicted in the axes of figure 2-1. The first dimension (on the horizontal axis) corresponds to the level of *guest participation*. At one end of the spectrum lies *passive* participation, in which customers do not directly affect or influence the performance. Such participants include symphony goers, who experience the event purely as observers or listeners. At the other end of the spectrum lies *active* participation, in which customers personally affect the performance or event that yields the experience. Active participants include skiers, who participate in creating their own experience. But even people who turn out to watch a ski race are not completely passive; simply by being there, they contribute to the visual and aural event that others experience.

The second (vertical) dimension of experience describes the kind of *connection*, or *environmental relationship*, that unites customers with the event or performance. At one end of this spectrum

FIGURE 2-1

Experience realms

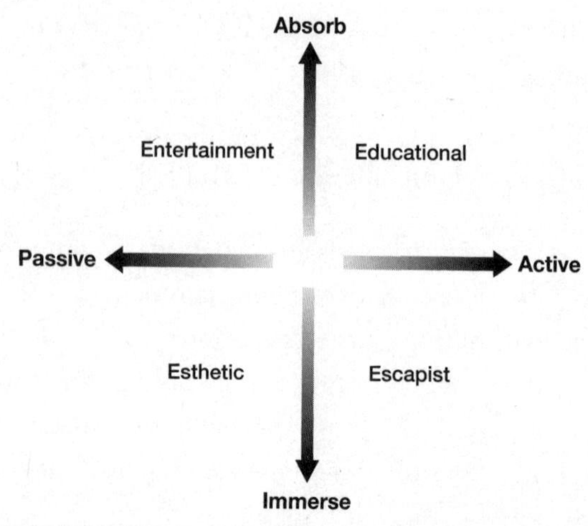

lies *absorption*—occupying a person's attention by bringing the experience into the mind from a distance—and at the other end is *immersion*—becoming physically (or virtually) a part of the experience itself. In other words, if the experience "goes into" guests, as when watching TV, then they are absorbing the experience. If, on the other hand, guests "go into" the experience, as when playing a virtual game, then they are immersed in the experience.

People viewing the Kentucky Derby from the grandstand absorb the event taking place before them from a distance. Meanwhile, people in the infield are immersed in the sights, sounds, and smells of the race itself as well as the activities of the other revelers around them. Students inside a lab during a physics experiment are immersed more than when they only listen to a lecture; seeing a film at the theatre with an audience, a large screen, and stereophonic sound immerses people in the experience far more than if they were watching the same film at home on the family room TV.

The coupling of these dimensions defines the four *realms* of an experience—entertainment, educational, escapist, and esthetic, as shown in figure 2-1—mutually compatible domains that often commingle to form uniquely personal encounters. The kind of experiences most people think of as entertainment occur when they *passively absorb* the experiences through their senses, as generally occurs when they view a performance, listen to music, or read for pleasure. But even though many experiences entertain, not all of them are, strictly speaking, *entertainment*, defined by the *Oxford English Dictionary* as "the action of occupying a person's attention agreeably; amusement."[3] Entertainment provides not only one of the oldest forms of experience (surely jokes have been around at least since the beginning of humankind) but also one of the most developed and, today, the most commonplace and familiar. (The "unproductive labourers" Adam Smith singled out were all entertainers: "players, buffoons, musicians, opera-singers, opera-dancers, &c.") As the Experience Economy gears up, people look in new and different directions for increasingly unusual experiences. At the same time, few of these experiences exclude at least momentary entertainment, making people smile, laugh, or otherwise enjoy themselves. But there are also opportunities for those enterprises staging these experiences to add to the mix components of the other three realms of experience: the educational, the escapist, and the esthetic.

The Educational

As with entertainment experiences, in educational experiences the guest (or student, if you prefer) absorbs the events unfolding before him. Unlike entertainment, however, education involves the active participation of the individual. To truly inform people and increase their knowledge or skills, educational events must actively engage the mind (for intellectual education) or the body (for physical training). As Stan Davis and Jim Botkin write in *The Monster Under the Bed*, "The industrial approach to education . . . [made] teachers the actors and students the passive recipients. In contrast, the emerging new model [of business-led education] takes the market perspective by making students the active players. The active focus will shift from the provider to the user, from educat-ors (teachers) to learn-ors (students), and the educating act will reside increasingly in the active learner, rather than the teacher-manager. In the new learning marketplace, customers, employees, and students are all active learners or, even more accurately, interactive learners."[4]

Judith Rodin, former president of the University of Pennsylvania, also recognized the active nature of education, as well as the fact that learning is not limited to the classroom. In her 1994 inaugural address she proclaimed, "We will design a new Penn undergraduate experience. It will involve not only curriculum, but new types of housing, student services, and mentoring, to create a seamless experience between the classroom and the residence, from the playing field to the laboratory. I am committed to having this in place for students entering Penn in the fall of 1997. That class—the Class of 2001—will be our first class to have an entirely new experience—the Penn Education of the Twenty-First Century."[5] Before leaving Penn in 2005 to head the Rockefeller Foundation, Rodin followed up her plan with a report outlining the progress made in successfully enhancing the educational value derived from all of campus life.

Although education is serious business, this doesn't mean that educational experiences can't be fun. The term *edutainment* was coined to connote an experience straddling the realms of education and entertainment.[6] Blending learning with fun occurs at each of the writing and tutoring centers affiliated with the nonprofit educational organization 826 National. Beginning with the first 826 location that opened in 2002 in San Francisco as 826 Valencia, each center features a uniquely themed storefront that acts as a portal of fun through which children (ages six through eighteen) must pass on their way to one-on-one tutoring, writing workshops, or other educational events. Each portal operates as a fully functioning retail store, exclusively selling merchandise in keeping with the location-specific motif (with proceeds helping fund the core learning sessions). At the original 826 Valencia, it's simply the Pirate Supply Store. Subsequent stores offer much richer edutainment: Brooklyn Superhero Supply Co. ("purveyors of high quality crimefighting merchandise") at 826 NYC; Echo Park Time Travel Mart at 826 LA; Liberty Street Robot Supply & Repair at 826 Michigan in Ann Arbor; The Boring Store at 826 Chicago, Greenwood Space Travel Supply Company at 826 Seattle; the Bigfoot Research Institute at 826 Boston; and the Museum of Unnatural History at 826 DC in Washington, D.C. By emphasizing creative and expository writing as the active measure of successful tutoring (many locations publish student material in bound book form) and by absorbing fun with each visit, students find that tutoring, formerly a dreaded experience, becomes much-desired learning.

The Escapist

Memorable encounters of a third kind—escapist experiences—involve much greater immersion than do entertainment or educational experiences. In fact, escapist experiences are the polar opposite of pure entertainment. Guests of escapist experiences are completely immersed in them as actively involved participants.[7] Examples of essentially escapist environments include generally artificial activities—trekking about in theme parks, gambling at casinos, playing computer-based games, chatting online, or even participating in a game of paintball in the local woods—as well as more natural ones, like the "thrilling escapes" featured in Peter Guttman's book *Adventures to Imagine*. Rather than play the passive role of couch potato, watching others act, people become actors, able to affect the actual performances.

One might enhance the inherent entertainment value of a movie, for example, not only with larger screens, bigger sound, cushier chairs, VIP rooms, and so forth, but also by having customers actually *participate* in the thrill of movement. Myriad companies now bring such experiences to a neighborhood near you via motion-based attractions.[8] Early stars of this genre include Tour of the Universe, a group flight through outer space from SimEx of Toronto; Magic Edge, a simulation of a military dogfight for multiple players in Mountain View, California, and Tokyo; and Disney's Star Tours, a simulation of a heroic battle for galactic domination based loosely on the *Star Wars* movies.

Most such escapist experiences are essentially motion simulator rides based on popular adventure or science fiction movies. Additional examples include Back to the Future: The Ride and Terminator 2: Battle Across Time hosted at Universal Studios in Orlando and Aladdin's Magic Carpet at Walt Disney World. These rides perfectly express the shift from the Service to the Experience Economy. It used to be, "You've read the book, now go see the movie!" Today, it's, "Now that you've seen the movie, go experience the ride!"[9]

Despite the appellation, guests participating in escapist experiences not only embark *from* but also voyage *to* a specific place and activity worthy of their time. For example, some vacationers, no longer content to only bask in the sun, go rollerblading, snowboarding, skysurfing, white-water kayaking, mountain climbing, or sports-car racing, or they take part in other extreme sports.[10] Others try their hand at the time-honored art of gambling not only to forget all their troubles and forget all their woes but also because they enjoy the visceral experience of risking their money in opulent surroundings for a chance at greater fortune. Others want to escape their fortunes to see what it's like conversing with the common man. Former Dallas Cowboys quarterback and TV commentator Troy Aikman, for instance, once told *Sports Illustrated* why he frequently visited America Online: "I like to go to the Texas Room and chat with people. It puts us on the same level. It's nice, too, having a normal conversation with somebody without them knowing who I am."[11] While celebrities may value an experience that turns them into ordinary folks, many escapist experiences, such as computer-based sports games, let the average person feel what it's like to be a superstar.

The Internet has indeed become a great place for such experiences, but many businesses still don't get it. They're heading into the commoditization trap, only selling their company's goods and services over the World Wide Web, when in fact most individuals surf the Internet for the experience itself. Surprisingly, Pete Higgins, vice president of Microsoft's Interactive Media Group, told *Business Week*, "So far, the Internet isn't a place for truly mindless entertainment."[12] But who wants it to be? The Internet is an inherently active medium—not passive, as television is—that provides a social experience for many people. Interactive entertainment is an oxymoron. The value people find online derives from actively connecting, conversing, and forming communities.

Formerly the domain of mom-and-pop outfits like The WELL, cyberspace was first brought to the masses by Prodigy, CompuServe, and America Online (mistakenly dubbed online "service" providers). AOL won the initial battle for members primarily because it understood that they wanted a social experience; they wanted to actively participate in the online environment growing up around them. While Prodigy at one point limited the amount of e-mail its members could send and CompuServe limited member identities to a string of impersonal numbers, AOL allowed its members to pick as many as five screen names (to suit the several moods or roles they might want to portray online).[13] AOL also actively encouraged the use of features that connect people: e-mail, chat rooms, instant messages, personal profiles, and "buddy lists," which let users know when their friends are also online. Even before AOL went to a flat-rate pricing scheme in late 1996, more than 25 percent of its 40 million connect-hours each month were spent in chat rooms, where members interacted with each other.[14] AOL proved no match for the social media that soon followed—MySpace, Facebook, Twitter, Foursquare, and myriad specialty sites such as ChatRoulette—let alone the explosion of "apps" providing other escapist experiences via smartphones.

For some people, the Internet provides a welcome respite from real life, an escape from the humdrum routine and the harried rush. For many others, we suspect digital life has become the new distracted reality from which they increasingly seek to escape to an alternative, unplugged existence.[15] It is still unclear how the near ubiquity of the Internet will ultimately alter the need most people have had for a physical place set apart from home and work, a "third place," in the words of sociologist Ray Oldenburg, where people can interact with others they have come to know as members of the same community.[16] These places—pubs, taverns, cafes, coffeehouses, and the like—once seemed to be on every street corner of every city, but the suburbanization of society has all too often left people too far apart to commune in this way.

Some people now look for community in cyberspace, while others use vacations at themed attractions to connect with large masses of people.[17] Still others find a middle ground at Starbucks or other such cafes.

The Esthetic

The fourth and last experiential realm we explore is the esthetic. In such experiences, individuals are immersed in an event or environment but have little or no effect on it, leaving the environment (but not themselves) essentially untouched. Esthetic experiences include standing on the rim of the Grand Canyon, beholding a work of art at a gallery or museum, and sitting at the Caffé Florian in Old World Venice. As mentioned earlier, sitting in the grandstand at the Kentucky Derby also qualifies. While guests partaking of an educational experience may want to *learn,* of an escapist experience want to *go* and *do,* of an entertainment experience want to *enjoy,* those partaking of an esthetic experience just want to *be.*[18]

At a Rainforest Cafe, for example, diners find themselves in the midst of dense vegetation, rising mist, cascading waterfalls, and even startling lightning and thunder. They encounter live tropical birds and fish as well as artificial butterflies, spiders, gorillas, and, if they look closely, a snapping baby crocodile.[19] Note that the Rainforest Cafe, which combines a dining room with a retail shop and bills itself as "A Wild Place to Shop and Eat," is not out to *simulate* the experience of being in a rain forest. Rather it aims to stage a certain esthetic experience that is the Rainforest Cafe.

Another wild place to shop can be found in Owatonna, Minnesota, at Cabela's, a 150,000-square-foot outfitter of hunting, fishing, and other outdoor gear. Rather than add elements of entertainment to the store, Dick and Jim Cabela turned it into an esthetic experience, centered (literally) on a thirty-five-foot-high mountain with a waterfall and featuring more than a hundred stuffed taxidermic animals, many of them shot by the two brothers or other family members. This part of the store represents four North American ecosystems. Elsewhere, two huge dioramas depict African scenes that include the so-called Big Five big-game targets: the elephant, lion, leopard, rhinoceros, and cape buffalo. Three aquariums hold a number of varieties of prized fish, while almost seven hundred kinds of animals are mounted in every department of the store. Truly, as Dick Cabela told the *St. Paul Pioneer Press*, "We're selling an experience."[20] So much so that more than thirty-five thousand people visited the refurbished store on the day it opened, and the company draws more than one million visitors every year.

The esthetic aspects of an experience may be completely natural, as when one tours a national park; primarily man-made, as when one dines at the Rainforest Cafe; or somewhere in between, as when one shops at Cabela's. There's no such thing as an artificial experience. Every experience created within the individual is real, whether the stimuli be natural or artificial. Extending this view, renowned architect Michael Benedikt discusses the role he believes architects play in connecting people to a "realness" within their created environments: "Such experiences, such privileged moments, can be profoundly moving; and precisely from such moments, I believe, we build our best and necessary sense of an independent yet meaningful reality. I should like to call them *direct esthetic experiences of the real* and to suggest the following: in our media-saturated times it falls to architecture to have the direct esthetic experience of the real at the center of its concerns."[21]

While architects may lead, it falls to everyone involved in the staging of esthetic experiences to connect individuals and the (immersive) reality they directly (albeit passively) experience, even when the environment seems less than "real." Benedikt would likely deem the Rainforest Cafe and similar venues "non-real" and insist that its architects address "the issue of authenticity by framing [displaying the inauthentic as inauthentic], by making fakery honest, as it were."[22] To stage compelling esthetic experiences, designers must acknowledge that any environment designed to create an experience is not real (the Rainforest Cafe, for instance, is *not* the rain forest). They should not try to fool their guests into believing it's something it is not.

Architecture critic Ada Louise Huxtable makes a similar distinction when she says, "It is becoming increasingly difficult to tell the real fake from the fake fake. All fakes are clearly not equal; there are good fakes and bad fakes. The standard is no longer real versus phony, but the relative merits of the imitation. What makes the good ones better is their improvement on reality."[23] To illustrate the difference, we'll consider two invented environments Huxtable spends considerable time critiquing: Universal CityWalk and almost anyplace Disney.[24]

CityWalk in Los Angeles is a collection of retail shops, restaurants, movie theatres, high-tech rides, and low-tech kiosks, each with a distinctive façade. Controlled exaggeration abounds, as in the four-story guitar adorning the Hard Rock Cafe. Visitors lazily stroll through a water fountain that shoots up at well-timed intervals. Guests pay an entrance fee for parking (nobody walks to anything in L.A., so here they pay admission to walk around) that's reimbursed only if they spend money at a dining or movie experience (purchases of goods merit no reimbursement). Part theme park and part public square, CityWalk primarily imparts an esthetic experience, Huxtable confirms, because it "is being used for its own sake."[25] The realness of its fakery evidences itself from the very moment you park your car in the ungarnished lot. The back of the buildings greet arriving guests, who thus see the unadorned undersides of the façades as they walk in. Outside you see the inside of the mask; inside you see its outside. Adjacent buildings, not associated with CityWalk, remain visible through alleys and other offshoots to the main drag. Its esthetic acknowledges its fakeness. Through framing, it's truly a *real* fake.

The esthetic of most Disney experiences, on the other hand, seeks to hide all things fake: no one gets to see behind the curtain. Parking lots smoothly flow into shuttle buses, welcoming booths, and turnstiles. Façades seamlessly integrate into one another, lest a guest detect the trickery in the dimensional downsizing. Mickey Mouse never takes off his mask, lest we see the pimply faced kid inside. It's the fake fake that Huxtable and other critics decry, Disney not being true to what they deem it really is.

Or is it *real* fake fake? Other critics laud Disney for creating wholly immersive environments, consistent and engaging within themselves. One writes, "From whatever angle, *nothing looks fake*. Fabricated, yes—fake, no. Disneyland isn't the mimicry of a thing; it's a thing . . . I'm convinced the genius of Disneyland isn't its fancifulness, but its literalism."[26] On the subject of Disney theme parks, many people (including we coauthors) disagree. But one thing remains clear: an esthetic experience must be true to itself or risk coming off as fake to its guests.

Experiencing the Richness

Companies can enhance the realness of any experience by blurring the boundaries between realms. While many experiences engage primarily through one of the four realms outlined earlier, most of them cross boundaries. British Airways, for example, stages a primarily esthetic experience: personnel pamper guests in an environment where they don't have to do anything for themselves. But Robert Ayling, successor to Sir Colin Marshall as CEO, had the company continually working on enhancing in-flight entertainment systems and integrating them with the overall flying esthetic. Ayling believed that more people would see movies in the air than in cinemas. "Long-haul airlines," he said, "will increasingly be seen not only as transport systems but as entertainment systems."[27] Virgin America has gone one step further, creating an animated cartoon to review safety instructions with passengers and installing mood lighting to alter the cabin ambiance during different times of the day.

American Express often mixes esthetic and educational elements in the Unique Experiences (AmEx's capitalization) it offers those enrolled in its Membership Rewards program.[28] In one such offer, Images of the Rain Forest—Photo Safari in Costa Rica, the company invited card members to join "celebrated nature photographers Jay Ireland and Georgienne Bradley for an unforgettable five-day photography workshop in Costa Rica's flourishing rain forest" and tempted them with the following description: "Surrounded by wildlife, you'll learn techniques and professional secrets that will enable you to capture astounding images. From cuddly Three-toed Sloths to majestic Great Egrets and comical Red-eyed Tree Frogs, you'll have countless opportunities to shoot professional quality images of exotic animals. You'll also enjoy enchanting views of the canals from the balcony surrounding your hotel, and be served first-class meals in the comfortable jungle setting. No matter what your photographic experience, this adventure promises to be unforgettable."

To make retailing more unforgettable, most store executives and shopping mall developers talk about making the shopping experience more entertaining, but leading-edge companies also incorporate elements from the other experiential realms. For example, to engage the locals and tourists at the six-block retail and entertainment district Bugis Junction in Singapore, design firm CommArts of Boulder, Colorado, mined the historical trading culture of Singapore to create what cochairman Henry Beer calls "an esthetically pleasing built environment designed to connect the project deeply to the resident culture of Singapore." Seaside architecture, sails, chronometers, and kindred elements fulfill the dominant motif, while bright signage informs and educates guests on the history of the native seafaring merchants known as the Bugis people. Similarly, for the Ontario Mills retail project, CommArts laid out streets and neighborhoods that provide a distinctive esthetic experience drawn from the rich heritage of Southern California. Unlike a traditional mall, Ontario Mills is not anchored by large department stores selling goods but instead by businesses staging large experiences—a thirty-screen AMC movie house, a Dave & Buster's arcade and restaurant, a Rainforest Cafe, and the Improv Comedy Club & Dinner Theatre. One of its wings houses Steven Spielberg's Gameworks, and another features a Build-A-Bear Workshop. As Beer related to us, "Competition for the retail dollar demands that we create a rich retail theatre that turns products into experiences."

The richest experiences encompass aspects of all four realms. These center on the "sweet spot" in the middle of the framework.[29] Consider the world's largest flower park, Keukenhof, located in the South Holland region of The Netherlands. The park's success results not from any one element but from the collective multi-realm experience it allows each visitor to enjoy traversing through the seventy acres of tulip fields, landscaped gardens, and indoor flower show pavilions. Featuring more than sixteen thousand varieties of flowers (including one thousand varieties of tulips alone, with more than six million bulbs hand-planted each year) and eighty-seven varieties of trees (twenty-five hundred in all), the venue deserves its reputation as "the garden of Europe." The Dutch so meticulously manicure the garden that it offers a great place to just hang out and behold the flowers.

(Some claim Keukenhof is the most photographed place on earth.) This esthetic value is enhanced through the placement of more than one hundred art statues as well as a half-dozen "inspirational gardens" that create a special sense of intimacy through the use of enveloping hedges, wooden fences, and walls. The escapist value of walking the fifteen kilometers of footpaths gets an uptick through the careful placement of a handful of elements designed to encourage visitors to interact with one another, such as a maze featuring three-meter-high shrubs and an elevated tree house in the center from which one can look down, see the pattern, and shout out (correct or incorrect) instructions. Small educational signs display the names and other horticultural information for all the varieties of flowers so that guests can learn about the varieties (taking notes for ordering bulbs and seeds later in the flower shop); tours and other programs provide lessons on the Dutch bulb-growing industry and the history of the Keukenhof chateau. For entertainment, guests periodically encounter small musical acts and eventually find their way to a pavilion featuring a water show, in which a fountain gyrates to synchronized music. These and other elements combine to create a truly compelling experience, drawing from all four experiential realms.

To design a rich, compelling, and engaging experience, you don't want to incorporate only one realm. Instead, like those who designed Keukenhof, you want to use the experiential framework depicted in figure 2-1 as a set of prompts that help you creatively explore the aspects of each realm that might enhance the particular experience you wish to stage. When designing your experience, you should consider the following questions:

- What can be done to enhance the *esthetic* value of the experience? What would make your guests want to come in, sit down, and just hang out? Think about what you can do to make the environment more inviting and comfortable. You want to create an atmosphere in which your guests feel free "to be."

- Once your guests are there, what should they do? The *escapist* aspect of an experience draws in your guests further, immersing them in various activities. Focus on what you should encourage guests "to do" if they are to become active participants in the experience. Further, what would cause them "to go" from one sense of reality to another?

- The *educational* aspect of an experience, like the escapist, is essentially active. Learning, as it is now largely understood, requires the full participation of the learner. What do you want your guests "to learn" from the experience? What interaction or activities will help engage them in the exploration of certain knowledge and skills?

- *Entertainment*, like the esthetic, is a passive aspect of an experience. When your guests are entertained, they're not really doing anything except responding to (enjoying, laughing at, etc.) the experience. What entertainment would help your guests "to enjoy" the experience better? How can you make the time more fun and more enjoyable?

Addressing these design issues sets the stage for service providers to begin competing on the basis of an experience. Those that have already forayed into the world of experiences will gain from enriching their offerings in light of these four realms—as the means both to enhance current experiences and to envision whole new ones.

Consider ski resorts. The locale of the mountain drives the quintessentially escapist nature of the skiing itself. Almost all resorts offer lessons to provide educational value. In addition to lodges for après-ski experiences, many resorts have incorporated "ski-to" places as mid-mountain havens where guests can take a break from skiing, kick back—say, on comfortable Adirondack chairs—throw off the goggles, and catch some rays. But few resorts recognize the one place where the entertainment element is inherently part of the skiing experience and seek to enhance its value: the ski lift! It's the place where people relive their runs, tell jokes and stories, and look below at fellow skiers. The commodity mindset mistakenly thinks the ski lift merely performs the function of transporting people from the bottom to the top of the mountain. An experience mindset—leveraging the four realms—would look for ways to add fun to the lift experience, perhaps mimicking hotelier Ian Schrager, who often turned his hotel elevators into unique experiences.

Schrager deserves credit for kick-starting the renewed interest in design in the hotel and lodging industry. Before Schrager, hotel lobbies offered little esthetic value and served largely as places for guests to meet other parties before leaving the premises. Schrager turned his lobby spaces into hip lounges that kept guests from wanting to wander away. And thanks to Starwood's Westin Hotels and its "Heavenly Bed," almost every hotel chain has reinvented its beds to address the age-old problem of getting to sleep in a strange place, enhancing the escapist value of a stay. The in-room experience has also seen vast improvements in offering greater entertainment value with the introduction of flat-screen televisions. What opportunity awaits to improve the educational experience? Perhaps reinventing concierge services, given that guests now have access to a great deal of information via in-room Internet access or their own handheld devices.

Similarly, medical providers should rethink the educational element of treatment, lest the ever-increasing availability of information online further frustrate doctors and patients as they communicate past each other. And what hospital or doctor's office wouldn't benefit from fundamentally rethinking the "waiting room" paradigm in order to increase the esthetic value of the welcoming experience? What medical procedure wouldn't be received by patients more positively if certain escapist rituals were introduced to help patients prepare for surgery? (Take a cue from refractive eye surgeon Roy Rubinfeld of Washington Eye Physicians & Surgeons in Chevy Chase, Maryland, who joins staff and patient in a shot-glass toast of carrot juice before entering the surgery room!) The suggestion of adding entertainment value to the experience should not be construed as wanting to turn every doctor into Patch Adams; in moments of life and death, however, it often pays to lighten up. (Recall Ronald Reagan's comment in the hospital after being shot: "I forgot to duck.")

Consider finally the big business of professional sports. Many franchises have had new stadia built to improve the esthetic value of the fan experience. Scoreboards offer greater entertainment. League websites are replete with searchable and sortable statistics that fans actively explore to learn how their teams and favorite (or fantasy) players are doing. Successful teams not only pack in the crowds at live games but also generate revenues from electronic broadcasts and online subscriptions. To no one's surprise, the New York Yankees lead the way, not only with its new Yankee Stadium but also with its YES cable network. What's next in creating new revenue streams? Consider how new escapist experiences might be welcomed by diehard fans. Teams generate revenue from ticket sales for home games as well as advertising sales on broadcasts of away games enjoyed from home. Maybe there's a third-place opportunity for sports. Couldn't some teams charge fans to come to a facility designed explicitly for watching away games? On occasion, teams allow fans to watch away playoff games in home arenas. But these venues are built for taking in live events and not mediated action. Like LAN parties, third-place arenas for away games could mix some of the excitement of being together with other fans with access to certain technological interactions with games that simply are not available from home. The design of such experiences should aim to offer distinctive new places for experiencing away games.

When all four realms abide within a single setting, then and only then does *plain space* become a *distinctive place* for staging a new or improved experience. Occurring over a period of time, staged experiences require a sense of place to entice guests to *spend more time* engaged in the offering. Time-conscious consumers and businesspeople want to spend less and less time with providers of goods and services, who seem all too willing to oblige. Think of fast-food chains and corporate call centers striving to minimize the *seconds* per service transaction. The obvious destination: not spending *any* time with customers, who learn to spend their time elsewhere. That is the prevailing attitude in banking, for example, an attitude that led directly to widespread commoditization.

So where will your customers spend their hard-earned time? In places deserving of more time, where people can simply be, go and do, learn, and enjoy. To understand the nature of such places, consider what turns a house into a home, and turns any space into a place. In *Home: A Short History of an Idea*, Witold Rybczynski, professor of urbanism at the University of Pennsylvania, examines five centuries' worth of designed environments, from the Middle Ages to Ralph Lauren Home Furnishings. Among the multiple cultures that Rybczynski examines, he calls particular attention to the desire and ability of the Dutch during their Golden Age to successfully "define the home as a separate, special place."[30] For the Dutch, "'Home' meant the house, but also everything that was in it and around it, as well as the people, and the sense of satisfaction and contentment that all these conveyed. You could walk out of the house, but you always returned home."[31] In such Dutch homes, furnishings strictly revolved around the use of each room, thereby defining the sense of place. Outside the home, gardens and other landscaping—however modest, given Holland's relatively small size—skillfully signaled the passage from the plain space outdoors to the distinctive place indoors. Such welcoming formed the basis for communing with family and friends.

The sweet spot for any compelling experience—incorporating entertainment, educational, escapist, and esthetic elements into otherwise generic space—is similarly a mnemonic place, a tool aiding in the creation of memories, distinct from the normally uneventful world of goods and services. Its very design invites you to enter, and to return again and again. Its space is layered with amenities—props—that correspond with the way the space is used, and it is rid of any features that do not follow this function. Engaging experiences bring these four realms together in compelling ways. We've already mentioned edutainment as one combination of realms aimed at achieving a certain experiential aim:

Edutainment = Education + Entertainment
(holding attention)

Consider, too, the five other dimensions of an engaging experience that emerge from combining realms:

Eduscapist = Education + Escapist (changing context)
Edusthetic = Education + Esthetic (fostering appreciation)
Escasthetic = Escapist + Esthetic (altering state)
Entersthetic = Entertainment + Esthetic (having presence)
Escatainment = Escapist + Entertainment (creating catharsis)

The terms vary in how trippingly they fall from the tongue (although *edutainment* flows smoothly, primarily through familiarity and repetition), but each maps out rich territory for understanding how to set the stage for compelling experiences.[32] Holding attention, changing context, fostering appreciation, altering states, having presence, and creating catharsis—these lie at the heart of orchestrating compelling theatrical performances. When every business is a stage, these states need to be mastered.

CHAPTER 3

The Show Must Go On

For his older brother Nicky's birthday, Conrad purchased a rather unusual gift. Feeling Nicky had become too stuffy and set in his executive ways, Conrad contracted with Consumer Recreation Services (CRS) to stage a rather elaborate experience. No present needed unwrapping as Conrad simply handed his brother a CRS-furnished card, inviting Nicholas Van Orton to participate in "The Game." Once he accepted the offer, Nicky found himself involved in a world all its own, with intriguing characters drawing him into seemingly life-threatening situations, curiously assimilated into his day-to-day routines. Every time he thought he had it figured out, a new twist emerged until the events finally spiraled into a fast-paced climax. To pull off "The Game," CRS had to put on a well-orchestrated show. No company, not even Disney, has mastered such intricate experience orchestration—staging rich, compelling, integrated, engaging, and memorable events—as well as CRS, the fictional business depicted in the movie thriller *The Game*, starring Michael Douglas as Nicholas and Sean Penn as Conrad. But the day has arrived when this type of staging will form the bulk of real commercial activity.

How so? To quote a line from the Broadway musical *Rent*, "Real life's getting more like fiction each day." Look around. So-called reality TV dominates the airwaves. The significance of this new genre of television programming lies in how it mirrors the vast array of experiences consumed in the marketplace. Consider the parallels: *The Bachelor* (e-Harmony, match.com), HGTV shows galore (home improvement and decorating), *Fear Factor* (extreme sports), *The Amazing Race* (adventure travel and ever-new forms of tourism), *Iron Chef* (cooking schools and foodie festivals), *Man Versus Food* (competitive eating), *The Biggest Loser* (fitness centers and diet programs), *Extreme Makeover* (cosmetic surgery), *Nanny 911* (life coaching), and, of course, *American Idol* (karaoke, Guitar Hero, and *American Idol* auditions!). Watch old footage of game highlights from the National Basketball Association, and compare its matter-of-fact action to today's sport, with its colorfully decorated floors, lavish pregame light shows, and poster-boy personalities. The NBA first gave us Dennis Rodman. The NFL followed with "T.O." and "OchoCinco," bedfellows in the personification of real-life fiction, tweeting their day-to-day lives. All major sports leagues find their in-stadium events having to compete with the at-home viewing experiences enabled by new television technologies. Furthermore, streaming video now makes it possible to display every everyday event at ordinary places—from repair shops to maternity wards—on the World Wide Web, where they can be viewed by anyone anywhere in the world. (Perhaps real life is less like *The Game* than *The Truman Show*—the film in which Jim Carrey plays a real person who unknowingly lives in a made-for-TV world.)

Experience orchestration has become as much a part of doing business as product and process design. The evidence is everywhere. In restaurants and retail stores, classrooms and parking garages, hotels and hospitals, leading companies set the stage for others now joining the Experience Economy. No longer in the embryonic phase of development, pioneering experience staging has resulted in practices that provide the starting point from which still further refinements will surely emerge. Elvis has left the building, and it's showtime!

Theme the Experience

Just hear the name of any theme restaurant—Hard Rock Cafe, House of Blues, or the Medieval Times, to name a few—and you know what to expect when you enter. The proprietors have taken the first, crucial step toward staging an experience by envisioning a well-defined *theme.*[1] A poorly conceived theme, on the other hand, gives customers nothing around which to organize their impressions, and the experience yields no lasting memory. An incoherent theme is like Gertrude Stein's Oakland, California: "There is no there there."

Of course, such theming can take diversely clever forms. Darden Restaurants, the world's largest full-service restaurant company, operates a vast array of differently themed chains: Red Lobster, Olive Garden, Longhorn Steakhouse, Capital Grille, Bahama Breeze, and Seasons 52, each with its own distinctive design inspiration. The Darden restaurant brand Seasons 52, most notably, simply leverages the calendar as its theme. The chain offers a "seasonally inspired" menu that changes four times a year; it runs specials fifty-two times a year (unlike daily specials, weekly specials are more likely to encourage diners to later recommend a dish to family and friends), and desserts ("mini-indulgences") contain only 365 (or so) calories. Independent fine-dining establishments often employ even more sophisticated theming.

Chef Homaro Cantu's postmodern Moto Restaurant, located in the meatpacking and produce district of Chicago, offers themed platings and wine pairings, among other technology-driven gastronomic fare (for example, one literally eats the "edible paper" menu). Well-orchestrated themes do not exist in name only (as did old high school proms in the gym) but instead act as the dominant idea, organizing principle, or underlying concept for every element in the experience.

Retailers often offend this principle. They talk of "the shopping experience" but fail to create a theme that ties disparate merchandising presentations together into a cohesively and comprehensively staged way. Home appliance and electronics retailers, for example, show little thematic imagination. Row upon row of washers and dryers, and wall after wall of refrigerators, merely highlight the sameness of different companies' stores. Shouldn't there have been something distinctive about an establishment called Circuit City? (Its array of merchandise took its thematic footprint from headstones at a cemetery, adumbrating its eventual demise.)

One retailer in the forefront of leveraging the experience of shopping was Leonard Riggio. When the Barnes & Noble CEO began to expand the chain of bookstores into superstores, he hit on the simple theme of "theatres." Riggio realized that people visited bookstores for much the same reason they go to the theatre: for the social experience.[2] So he changed everything about the stores to express this theme: the architecture, the way salespeople acted, the decor and furnishings. And of course he added cafes as an "intermission" from mingling, browsing, and buying. With online bookseller Amazon.com now the dominant force in the industry, offering reader reviews and forwardable e-mail confirmations, yet more needs to be done to turn the bookstores (still merely selling goods) into true book-recommending and book-reading venues (selling experiences). The rise of e-readers only intensifies the need to invent yet new themes in physical space if bookstores wish to successfully compete.

Consider the history of Forum Shops in Las Vegas, a mall initially conceived by developer Sheldon Gordon (of Gordon Group Holdings) and developed along with Indianapolis-based real estate company Simon Property Group. Triggering the rise of retailing as a new revenue stream for Vegas resorts, the Forum Shops opened in 1992. The mall displays its distinctive theme—an ancient Roman marketplace—in every detail, fulfilling this motif through a panoply of architectural effects. These include marble floors, stark white pillars, "outdoor" cafes, living trees, flowing fountains, and even a painted blue sky with fluffy white clouds that shifts from day to night every hour. Every mall entrance and every storefront, no matter the brand, must conform to the overarching theme. One telling detail we think brings it all together: the channels lining both sides of the hallways, a few feet from the store entrances, as if the shopkeepers cleaned their stores every morning with water buckets and then threw out the water to make its way to the Adriatic Sea. The theme implies opulence, and after a 1997 phase II expansion doubled the mall's size, sales grew to more than $1,000 per square foot (versus less than $300 at a typical mall). A phase III expansion in 2004, which added a four-thousand-seat "Colosseum" for show performances as well as four spiral escalators, continues the theming tradition.

Walt Disney's idea for Disneyland grew out of his dissatisfaction with amusement parks—themeless collections of rides, games, and refreshments geared to the young. As he related to biographer Bob Thomas, "It all started when my daughters were very young, and I took them to amusement parks on Sunday. I sat on a bench eating peanuts and looking all around me. I said to myself, dammit, why can't there be a better place to take your children, where you can have fun together?"[3] And from these first thoughts Disney conceived the original idea of Disneyland—in his words, "a cartoon that immerses the audience." It developed into a cohesive orchestration of *theme rides*—such as the King Arthur Carousel, Peter Pan's Flight, and the Mark Twain paddle-boat (each "like nothing you've ever seen in an amusement park before").[4] These rides operated within *theme areas*—such as Fanta-syland and Frontierland—within the very first *theme park* any-where in the world, what its first brochure called "a new experience in entertainment."[5] What was the overarching theme of the Disneyland experience? Disney's 1953 proposal to potential financial backers begins with a very simple and engaging theme and then goes on to elaborate the meaning of this theme in very real, and soon realized, terms:

> *The idea of Disneyland is a simple one. It will be a place for people to find happiness and knowledge.*
>
> *It will be a place for parents and children to share pleasant times in one another's company: a place for teachers and pupils to discover greater ways of understanding and education. Here the older genera-tion can recapture the nostalgia of days gone by, and the younger generation can savor the challenge of the future.*[6]

"A place for people to find happiness and knowledge" conjured such a wonderful image that Disney quickly found financial back-ers. In less than two years the *themed* park opened to far more visitors than anyone had imagined.

As a model, consider an often-used theme in novels and films: crime doesn't pay. Three simple words say it all. Or consider the television tavern *Cheers*, "where everybody knows your name." Companies that stage experiences must seek equally crisp thematic constructions. Of course, businesses wishing to impart very different experiences require very different themes. The Geek Squad serves as a powerfully simple and appropriately geeky name for the Minnesota-based computer support business. It might appear that, like many theme restaurants, the Geek Squad's theme is stated right in its name. Not so. Rather, founder and Chief Inspector Robert Stephens says the organizing principle for everything the business strives to fulfill is "comedy with a straight face."[7] Using this theme allows "Special Agents" to maintain a straitlaced demeanor (as if they had walked off the screen of a modern-day episode of *Dragnet*) while engaging clients with Geek-based humor (as when flashing an identification badge: "Hi, I'm Special Agent Seventy-three here for your computer … Step away from the computer, ma'am"). They still perform the necessary installation or repair, but the costuming and props—white short-sleeve shirts, black clip-on ties, black pants, and company-issued shoes, VW beetles painted as black-and-white squad cars dubbed Geekmobiles—direct the enveloping geek performance.

The Geek Squad also provides a study in the difference between a theme and a motif. Dictionaries treat the two words nearly synonymously. Think of a *motif*, however, as the outward manifestation of a theme. The motif and theme can be one and the same (as is typically the case with Disney, when it explicitly uses movies or updated fairy tales as themes for its rides) but need not be. The Geek Squad's motif evidences itself in its name, logo, vehicles, badges, and attire; it all winks at the notion of *law enforcement*. But this motif is only the means through which the underlying theme tells a story. Indeed, at its best, theming means scripting a story that would seem incomplete without guests' engagement in the experience.[8] As designer Randy White of White Hutchinson Leisure & Learning Group says, "Storyline-based themes are powerful.

They draw guests into a fanciful, imaginary world and have the potential to touch the eye, mind and head of visitors."[9] Such theming can be scaled; in an otherwise mom-and-pop service industry, thanks to its 2002 purchase by Best Buy the Geek Squad has grown to more than twenty-four thousand agents in its "24-Hour Computer Support Task Force." It did so by treating each customer interaction as an opportunity to (comically) tell the Geek Squad story (with a straight face). Any number of other highly fragmented service industries—car washes, dry cleaners, landscapers, nail salons, even funeral homes—represent opportunities to similarly build scalable businesses through theming.

Developing an appropriate theme for such experiences is certainly challenging. One place to start is with general categories of themes. In his insightful, albeit academic, book *The Theming of America*, sociology professor Mark Gottdiener identifies ten themes that often materialize in the "built environments" that he calls staged experiences: (1) status, (2) tropical paradise, (3) the Wild West, (4) classical civilization, (5) nostalgia, (6) Arabian fantasy, (7) urban motif, (8) fortress architecture and surveillance, (9) modernism and progress, and (10) representations of the unrepresentable (such as the Vietnam Veterans Memorial Wall).[10] Marketing professors Bernd Schmitt and Alex Simonson, in their instructive book *Marketing Aesthetics*, offer nine more "domains" in which themes can be found: (1) history, (2) religion, (3) fashion, (4) politics, (5) psychology, (6) philosophy, (7) the physical world, (8) popular culture, and (9) the arts.[11]

Of course, these general categories only point out possible directions for discovering a specific theme. The Library Hotel in New York City, for example, took as its theme another classification system (and a set of domains far exceeding Gottdiener's or Schmitt and Simonson's lists)—namely, the Dewey Decimal System. In this architecture of theming, the hotel organizes each of the ten guest room floors based on one of ten major Dewey Decimal System categories: Social Sciences, Languages, Math & Sciences, Technology, The Arts, Literature, History, General Knowledge, Philosophy, and Religion. Rooms on each floor break down each category into different topics, with corresponding room numbers. For example, the six rooms on the seventh floor ("The Arts") are numbered 700.006 (Fashion design), 700.005 (Music), 700.004 (Photography), 700.003 (Performing arts), 700.002 (Paintings), and 700.001 (Architecture). Each guest room's bookshelf is stocked with its own collection of topic-specific books, a corresponding coffee table volume, and topic-inspired artwork.

Every experience has a theme. Whether or not themed intentionally, whether or not designed well, and whether or not executed thoroughly and rigorously, a theme always emerges. Discovering a suitable theme is central to experience design. No matter what list or category prompts the discovery, the key lies in determining what theme will actually prove to be compelling and captivating. Five principles are paramount in developing such a theme.

First, an engaging theme must alter a guest's sense of reality. Each of Gottdiener's themes alters a dimension of the human experience, be it temporal age, geographic location, environmental condition (familiar/foreign, risky/safe), social affiliation, or self-image. Creating a reality other than the everyday—for doing, learning, enjoying, and being—underlies any successful theme and is at the heart of establishing a sense of place.

Second, the richest venues possess themes that *fully* alter one's sense of reality by affecting the experience of space, matter, and time. Parking garages are a space we've all experienced. Typical parking lines occupy space in one dimension and serve only to identify a stall—usually when drivers pull in, more than when they return. Signs provide a two-dimensional view, helping one see where one has parked. The themed design of the Standard Parking garage at Chicago's O'Hare airport, however, offers a place to *experience* parking spots in full 3-D perspective. Indeed, the intent is to bring energy and motion into the process of locating one's car. As a result, returning guests do not waste time wandering around looking for their cars.

Time feels different for children (and more than a few parents) at Disneyland's revamped Tomorrowland, which seeks to alter one's sense of the future. The same altered sense of the future can be experienced in various B2B settings, such as through the parade of five- to fifteen-minute talks at a TED Conference, with its three-word theme: technology, entertainment, design. The Hard Rock Cafe attempts to manipulate the past, as do many museums and corporate briefing centers. In an interesting twist of the clock, The Little Gym (decorated in a primary color motif) overcomes any risk of dissatisfaction with its gymnastics instruction for small children by theming time itself. Rather than present lessons as themeless repetitions of tumbling drills, climbing exercises, and other apparatus use, it themes each program (such as "Funny Bugs") as well as each class (e.g., "Upside Down Week"); the aim is to hold gymnasts' interest week-to-week while essentially going over the same underlying routines. Google themes its very own logo on its home page based on events that happened on this particular date in history. And in Southern California, the Cerritos Public Library bills itself as "the world's first experience library," employing the theme of "journey through time" to alter the décor and furnishings of each room. In a town of fifty thousand residents, the library averages more than three thousand visitors daily.

Likewise, matter can be neither slighted nor ignored in the formation of a compelling theme. Themes may suggest alternative sizes, shapes, and substances of things. Cabela's and rival Bass Pro Shops' outdoor themes display the objects of an outdoor enthusiast's desire, through taxidermy and other backdrops, and in the process bring the hunter closer to the hunted. Marriott Vacation Club International places a large pirate ship, complete with water-firing cannons and waterslide planks, in its resort pool at its Horizons resort in Orlando. It supports the pirate motif and the underlying theme of "stuff in pool" by offering all sorts of things that work together to enhance the family experience, from "Captain Horizon" leading squirt-gun fights on the hour to VIP welcome packages placed in rooms as treasure chests. In a more adult setting, Marriott's joint venture with Ian Schrager, the new Edition "lifestyle" hotels, opened its first venue in late 2010 in Waikiki Beach. The resort includes an outdoor movie theatre, surfing and swimwear "boot camps," and a hidden lobby bar accessible to guests only through a secret passageway.

And space matters. Billion-dollar airlines typically take few steps to alter the sensation of crammed space experienced by the coach traveler. Mike Vance, creativity expert and former dean of Disney University, relates in speeches how he travels with personal items in a bag he calls his "Kitchen of the Mind"—family pictures, pieces of paper, and assorted knickknacks that he uses to decorate his seat back, tray table, and window shade, especially on long flights. Flight attendants look at Vance as if he, and not the themeless airline, has a problem.[12] Thus travelers welcomed the arrival of Virgin America to the United States, with its mood lighting and entertainment system that create a foreign feel for its version of domestic U.S. air travel. One feature that should not be overlooked is its contribution to this radically designed cabin space: the wall that hides the flight attendant jump seats and food prep areas has been eliminated, placing flight attendants in full view throughout the entire flight. As a result, the dynamic between passengers and crew has been vastly improved, largely because the crew now must act onstage, all the time, as a unified ensemble.

Third, engaging themes integrate space, matter, and time into a cohesive, realistic whole. To see how, consider a work of theology. In his apologetic for the Christian faith, Henry M. Morris states, "It is not that the universe is a *triad* of three distinct entities [time, space, and matter] which, when added together, comprise the whole. Rather each of the three is itself the whole, and the universe is a true trinity, not a triad. Space is infinite and time is endless, and everywhere throughout space and time events happen, processes function, phenomena exist. The tri-universe is remarkably analogous to the nature of its Creator."[13]

Therein lies the power of storytelling and other narratives as a vehicle to script themes. Great books and good movies engage their audiences when they create completely new realities, altering every detail of the reading and cinematic experience. Lori's Diner, a small chain of restaurants in San Francisco, creates an authentic-looking 1950s diner, complete with vintage jukeboxes, pinball machines, booths, waiter and waitress uniforms—occasionally even a Fonz-like character outside who beckons passersby to enter into this past world.[14] So why not borrow this principle for bank branches and car-rental shuttle buses, conference sessions, and other B2B marketing events?

Fourth, creating multiple places within a place strengthens themes. At the now-defunct Discovery Zone, almost every corner of the place was visible from any other vantage point. See-through nets separated one section from another, with the so-called ball pit attraction often at the center of activity. Even if this setting was meant to help parents keep track of their youngsters' whereabouts, it called to mind Gottdiener's fortress architecture and surveillance theme more than a place for imaginative exploration and play. Consider instead the American Girl Place. The merchandise is secondary to the overall experience, which is wonderfully staged by offering multiple places within the place. A visit starts with the library, where all the books written about each doll are displayed. A dozen or more animated screens display each doll's character. The restaurant, simply called "Cafe," provides yet another place, and its doors remain closed until the appointed seating times for brunch, lunch, afternoon tea, and dinner. A photo studio provides a place for girls to have their pictures taken for customized covers of *American Girl* magazine. The studio comes complete with a separate area to receive a preparatory make-up session. Then there is the hair salon, where girls can have their dolls' hair styled or, for older dolls, restored to its original condition.

Finally, a theme should fit the character of the enterprise staging the experience. In 1947 Chicago developer Arthur Rubloff coined the three-word phrase "Chicago's Magnificent Mile" to describe the famous stretch of commercial property along greater North Michigan Avenue in downtown Chicago. It is a magnificently constructed theme, enduring for generations because it befits not only the *walking* that shoppers must do to shop and eat there, but also the luxury and opulence on display. Rubloff later formed The Greater North Michigan Avenue Association, which was instrumental in hosting "Cows on Parade" in 1999. Chicago was the first U.S. city to import this cow parade concept from Switzerland, commissioning local artists to paint three hundred life-sized cow statues that were placed throughout the city. The public art exhibit accounted for hundreds of millions of incremental tourist dollars as people flocked to Chicago to see and to be photographed with the cows. The cow theme was ideal, given

Chicago's mid-nineteenth-century history as the only rail distribution hub for transporting livestock from the West to the rest of the nation. Other cities copied the themed exhibition, with mixed success (guitars in Cleveland, flying pigs in Cincinnati, and so forth) depending largely on how well the theme tied to the character of the city.

An effective theme must be concise and compelling. Too much detail clutters its effectiveness in serving as an organizing principle for staging the experience. The theme is not a corporate mission statement nor a marketing tagline. It needn't be publicly articulated—just as the term "Trinity" appears nowhere in the texts of Scripture—and yet its presence must be clearly felt. The theme must drive all the design elements and staged events of the experience toward a unified storyline that wholly captivates the customer. That is the essence of the theme; all the rest simply lends support.

Harmonize Impressions with Positive Cues

The theme forms the foundation of an experience, but you must render the experience with indelible *impressions*. Impressions are the "takeaways" of the experience—what you want customers to have topmost in their minds when they leave the experience. The congruent integration of a number of impressions affects the individual and thereby helps fulfill the theme. Thinking about impressions begins with asking yourself how you would like guests to describe the experience: "That made me feel ..." or "That was ..." Schmitt and Simonson again provide a useful list, this one delineating six "dimensions of overall impressions":

1. *Time:* Traditional, contemporary, or futuristic representations of the theme

2. *Space:* City/country, East/West (to which we might add North/South), home/business, and indoor/outdoor representations

3. *Technology:* Handmade/machine-made and natural/artificial representations

4. *Authenticity:* Original or imitative representations

5. *Sophistication:* Yielding refined/unrefined or luxurious/cheap representations

6. *Scale:* Representing the theme as grand or small.[15]

Experience orchestrators can use these dimensions to think creatively about the many possibilities for rendering a theme with indelible impressions. The connection to space-matter-time is obvious.

Yet this list only begins to tap the relationship between impressions and the theme they support. For what may be the most comprehensive list of impressions imaginable, no source can exceed Peter Mark Roget's synopsis of categories. *Roget's International Thesaurus* (fourth edition) offers 1,042 categorized entries from "Existence" to "Religious Buildings" across 8 classes and 176 subclasses and, should you want the detail within the *Thesaurus* itself, 250,000 words and phrases.[16] It's the richest possible source for exploring the exact words to denote the specific impressions you want guests to take away from the experience.

Words alone obviously are not enough to create the desired impressions. Companies must introduce cues that together affirm the nature of the desired experience for the guest. *Cues* are signals, found in the environment or in the behavior of workers, that create a set of impressions. Each cue must support the theme, and none should be inconsistent with it.

Joie de Vivre (JDV) Hospitality of San Francisco employs a brilliant technique for harmonizing impressions with positive cues when it themes its portfolio of hotels, restaurants, and spas. Founder Chip Conley began his hospitality business by purchasing a cheap, rundown motel in the Tenderloin district of San Francisco. Conley wanted to create a unique hotel experience, but he didn't have the money—beyond that necessary to buy and remodel the property—to conduct market research to identify who might be attracted to the venue. So he seized on an industry that could provide such insights—magazines—and themed his Phoenix Hotel after *Rolling Stone* magazine. He pored over back issues to determine five impressions that the rock 'n' roll rag imparted to its readers: adventurous, hip, irreverent, funky, and young-at-heart. Conley then redesigned the entire place (much of it cosmetically and therefore inexpensively) to bring these impressions to life as a consistent, coherent, and compelling whole wrapped around the magazine theme. JDV turned the swimming pool into a "dive-in" for partying, colorfully decorated the guest rooms (including that little old place, room 3-2-1, as the "Love Shack"), and slapped bumper stickers from local rock bands on the housekeeping carts. "Listening posts" were set up for staff to pick up ideas from guests for additional cues that might enhance the experience. Note that JDV did not name the hotel after the magazine, advertise the connection, nor even tell guests the theme. Rather, it introduced cues to create the desired impressions, and, amazingly, without revealing its theme, the Phoenix Hotel became the happening place to stay in San Francisco for touring bands and their road crews. JDV Hospitality uses this same "pick a magazine" technique for each of its dozens of California venues.

Different kinds of experiences, of course, often rely on radically different kinds of impression-forming cues. At East Jefferson General Hospital in Metairie, Louisiana, just outside New Orleans, CEO Peter Betts (now retired) and his management team redesigned the hospital around the impressions of warmth, caring, and professionalism. The hospital conveys these three key impressions by means of having team members wear easily read name tags that list professional titles and degrees, and they knock before entering a patient's room, among other things. The hospital designates any area accessible to guests—including not only patients but also family members, clergy, and any other visitors—as onstage and all others as offstage. It then confines unpleasant activities (such as transporting blood) and "hall conversations" to offstage areas and carefully crafts all onstage areas with appropriate cues that enhance the experience. Toward this end, painted murals cover the ceilings of rehabilitation rooms where patients frequently exercise on their backs, and different kinds of flooring identify distinct locations (lobbies are carpeted, paths to dining areas are slate, and paths to conference rooms are terrazzo).[17]

Lewis Carbone, chief experience officer of Minneapolis-based Experience Engineering, developed a useful construct for engineering preference-creating experiences. Carbone divides cues—or "clues," as he calls them—into "mechanics" and "humanics," or what might be called the inanimate and the animate. The former are "the sights, smells, tastes, sounds, and textures generated by *things*, for example, landscaping, graphics, scents, recorded music, handrail surfaces, and so on. In contrast, 'humanics' clues emanate from *people*. They are engineered by defining and choreographing the desired behavior of employees involved in the customer encounter."[18]

At Disney, to avoid any possible association with rowdy local carnivals or run-down amusement parks, management set the impression of cleanliness as a cardinal principle. The designers translated this concern into two key cues: the mechanics of making sure a trash receptacle is always within sight of any guest, and the humanics of assigning a large number of cast members whose sole role is to pick up any trash that does not make it into a receptacle. Well, not quite the sole role: they're also to make eye contact and smile whenever they're within ten feet of any guest to reinforce the "happiness" impression.

The cues trigger impressions that fulfill the theme in the customer's mind. An experience can be unpleasant merely because an architectural feature has been overlooked or underappreciated or is not coordinated with the overall theme. Unplanned or inconsistent visual and aural cues can leave a customer confused or lost. Have you ever been unsure of how to find your hotel room, even after the front-desk staff has provided detailed directions? Better, clearer cues along the way would have enhanced your experience.

Eliminate Negative Cues

Ensuring the integrity of the experience requires more than layering on positive cues. Experience stagers also must eliminate anything that detracts from fulfilling the theme. Guests at most constructed spaces—malls, offices, buildings, or airplanes—find them littered with meaningless or trivial messages. While customers sometimes do need instructions, too often service providers say it poorly or choose an inappropriate medium, such as the sign we encountered on a chair in a Wyndham Garden Hotel room some years ago: "For your comfort, this chair reclines." (The better cue of having the chair reclined upon arrival would have rendered the signage unnecessary.) Cognitive psychologist and industrial design critic Donald Norman gives a "rule of thumb for spotting bad design: Look for posted instructions."[19] In other words, any instructional signage is a sign of poor design. It serves only to form a poor impression.

Seemingly minor cues can impair any experience. At most restaurants, for example, a host droning, "Your table is ready" cues customers to expect the usual meal service. That phrase is now so familiar it forms no impression. At a Rainforest Cafe, however, the host sets the stage for what lies ahead by proclaiming for all to hear, "The Smith party, your adventure is about to begin!" Should the Smith party fail to appear after the third call, the host informs the other guests that the Smith's "safari has left without them." After we stated "Three, please" to a host at Ed Debevic's in Chicago, he snaked our party in and around tables until we finally inquired about our table. His smart-alecky response: "Oh, you didn't say anything about a *table*." (Ed Debevic's harmonizes its cues around a set of impressions that can best be described as nasty, rude, mean spirited, obnoxious, and ill tempered; it works because of how well the company humorously harmonizes the cues. Our party should have picked up on the initial cue: our host sported a name tag bearing the stage name "Smiley.")

To avoid giving cues at odds with its good-tempered themes, Disney cast members always act their parts, never stepping out of character while onstage. Only when offstage, in an area prohibited to customers, can cast members talk freely among themselves. Many historical villages, such as Old Sturbridge Village and Plimoth Plantation, both in Massachusetts, also require employees to stay in character (eighteenth-century farmers and the like at Sturbridge; Pilgrims and Indians at Plimoth). Others, such as Colonial Williamsburg and Jamestown in Virginia, significantly diminish the integrity of their experiences by allowing period-costumed employees to talk the talk of their present-day guests.

The idea of "role-appropriate" clothing and behavior can also apply to people with workaday jobs. At East Jefferson General Hospital, all team members must personify "the EJ Look"—a set of dress standards that eliminates potentially negative cues. Not allowed, for example, are casual shirts without ties on men, extra-long fingernails and certain shades of polish on women, and strong colognes or perfumes on either. The EJ Look helps the staff create the hospital's desired impression of professionalism and has proved so effective that people they meet out and about in the community often immediately identify them as being from East Jefferson.

Presenting too many cues, particularly when put together haphazardly—such as overservicing in the name of customer intimacy—can also ruin an experience. As a writer for *Fortune* put it in extolling the virtues of staying in chartered homes instead of hotels while traveling, "There are no check-ins, no checkouts, no bills to puzzle over, no inflated telephone charges (you dial direct and an itemized list of calls is sent to you later), and only a two- or three-night minimum. Even better, no *service-industry intrusions*: no bellman waiting to be acknowledged or tipped, no maids lurking in your room watching TV, no agents sneaking in at night to hide chocolates in the bed."[20] Lest they slowly lose their clientele to the better experience of an away-from-home home, hotel chains should work harder to eliminate negative cues: stop cluttering end tables, dressers, and desktops with tent cards and other service communication; assign offstage personnel to answer phones so that front-desk staff won't have to interrupt face-to-face conversations with paying guests to field telephone calls; make sure bellmen and maids perform their tasks unobtrusively; and so forth. Only then will their guests be made to feel truly at home.

Mix in Memorabilia

People have always purchased certain goods primarily for the memories they convey. Vacationers buy postcards to evoke treasured sights, golfers purchase shirts or caps with embroidered logos to recall particular courses or rounds, and teenagers collect T-shirts to remember rock concerts. They purchase such memorabilia as tangible artifacts of the experiences they want to remember.

Such items are often among people's most cherished possessions, worth far more to them than the manufacturing cost of the artifact. Take something as simple as a ticket stub, a natural by-product of many an experience. Perhaps you have some tucked away in the bottom of a jewelry box (with other valuable items), or your children have some carefully mounted and displayed in their bedrooms. Why do we keep these torn scraps of paper? It's because they represent a cherished experience. Your first Major League baseball game, a favorite musical, a meaningful date at the movies—all events that run the risk of fading away without a physical reminder.

Of course, that's not the only—perhaps not even the primary—reason we purchase memorabilia. Greater still may be our desire to show others what we have experienced to generate conversation and, not a small factor perhaps, envy.[21] This factor provides more food for the thoughtful experience stager. As Bruno Giussani, European director of TED Conferences, related to us, "Memorabilia are a way to 'socialize' the experience, to transmit parts of it to others—and for companies entering the Experience Economy, they are means to entice new guests."

People already spend tens of billions of dollars every year on this class of goods, which generally sells at price points far higher than those commanded by similar items that don't commemorate an experience locale or event. A Rolling Stones concertgoer will pay a large premium for an official T-shirt emblazoned with the date and city of the concert. That's because the price point functions less as an indicator of the cost of the goods than of the value the buyer attaches to remembering the experience. In addition to gaining a premium over run-of-the-mill T-shirts, the Hard Rock Cafe induces guests to make multiple purchases simply by printing the location of each particular cafe on its T-shirts.

Selling memorabilia associated with an experience provides one approach to extending an experience; giving away items inherently part of the experience is another. Mixing the memorabilia into the experience to be used by guests affords a richer opportunity to attach a memory to the physical artifact. Thus hotels print artwork on electronic key cards and design alternative slogans for "Do Not Disturb" signs. Some forgo text altogether, as the JW Marriott Desert Springs Resort & Spa has done; its door hanger is simply a pink flamingo with no text, harmonizing with the pink flamingos that grace the grounds. The Cafe restaurants in American Girl Place venues provide an exemplary illustration. Rolled napkins are placed inside hair scrunchies (colored black-and-white, either striped or polka-dotted, to harmonize with the room's décor). Once these perks are discovered, the young patrons immediately inquire as to whether they may keep them—only to be assured that the complimentary item is theirs to take home. (American Girl also sells memorabilia for its Cafe experience: dolls sit in twelve-inch-high chairs called "treat seats" during meals; they sell for $25!) Thomas Keller's French Laundry restaurant in Yountville, California, also mixes in napkin-holding memorabilia in the form of an embossed clothespin.

Companies should get creative and seek to develop wholly new forms of memorabilia. When the Ritz-Carlton in Naples,

Florida, installed a new computerized safety system with key cards, management decided to give away the old doorknobs to past guests instead of selling or tossing them out. Each of the 463 knobs was engraved with the classic Ritz-Carlton lion and crown insignia, converted into a distinctive paperweight, and given to those guests—among the more than six thousand people who requested one—whose story of an experience at the Ritz most touched the hearts of the associates who read each appeal. The limited-supply doorknobs became a tangible reminder of a memorable stay, and, Ritz-Carlton certainly hoped, a cue to relive that experience in the future. The sense of obligation created within guests was worth far more than the Ritz would have gotten by selling the doorknobs.

Moreover, companies should develop memorable methods of mixing in the memorabilia so that the very means by which guests obtain the items becomes a signature moment, such as when young girls discover the hair scrunchie at the American Girl Place's Cafe. The City of Calgary does this in a remarkable way when it awards a tall, white Bailey cowboy hat to visiting meeting planners and speakers. Recipients raise their right hands when sworn in as "honorary Calgarians," repeating an amusing oath ("I promise to wear my hat at all times … even when I sleep …") before also receiving a certificate that bears an image of the hat as well as the date. Similarly, the Geek Squad pays attention to how agents bestow Geek Squad T-shirts on paying customers; they toss the shirts as a final act before zipping off to their next appointment.

With the proper stage setting, any business can mix memorabilia into its offerings. If service businesses such as banks, grocery stores, and insurance companies find no demand for memorabilia, it's because they do not offer anything anyone wants to remember. Should these businesses offer themed experiences layered with positive cues and devoid of negative ones, their guests will want and pay for memorabilia to commemorate their experiences. (If guests don't want to do this, it probably means the experience wasn't all that great.) If airlines truly were in the experience-staging business, more passengers would actually shop in those seat-pocket catalogs for mementos. Likewise, mortgage loans would inspire household keepsakes; grocery checkout lanes would stock souvenirs in lieu of nickel-and-dime impulse items; and perhaps even insurance policy certificates would be suitable for framing.

Engage the Five Senses

The sensory stimulants that accompany an experience should support and enhance its theme. The more effectively an experience engages the senses, the more memorable it will be. Smart shoe shine operators augment the smell of polish with crisp snaps of the cloth, scents and sounds that don't make the shoes any shinier but do make the experience more engaging. Savvy hair stylists shampoo and apply lotions not simply for styling reasons but because they add more tactile sensations to the patron's experience. Similarly, better grocers pipe bakery smells into the aisles, and some use sight and sound to simulate thunderstorms when misting their produce to better engage food shoppers. Indeed, in almost any situation the easiest way to sensorialize a service is to add taste sensations by serving food and drink.

West Point Market in Akron, Ohio, founded by Russ Vernon, was one of the first to serve specialty foods in a grocery store. Retail guru Leonard Berry of Texas A&M University describes this upscale market as "a sea of colors, an adventure in discovery, a store of temptation with its killer brownies, walnut nasties, and peanut-butter krazies."[22] Berry quotes Kaye Lowe, director of public relations, as saying, "We don't hesitate to let customers taste a product. Some people come in on a Saturday and eat their way around the store. Russ's favorite saying is: 'Come see the sights, smell the delights, and taste the wonders of WPM.'"[23]

Services turn into engaging experiences when layered with sensory phenomena, as can be seen in the very earliest stages of life. Consider the task of feeding an infant. One evening during dinner, then eleven-month-old Evan Gilmore pushed aside his mother's hand, refusing the food she offered. So Daddy took over. In an act performed by countless parents before, the spoon no longer went directly from jar to mouth. Instead, it was taken two feet back and raised high in the air. With herky-jerky movements, the flying machine descended, accompanied by the sputtering motor-mouthed improvisations of Air Traffic Papa. Tightly clinched baby lips soon opened as wide as a hangar to receive a spoonful from each flight.

Believe it or not, this airplane game conveys the essence of what any dining establishment does to turn ordinary food service into a scintillating experience for paying adults: designing exactly the right *sensations* as cues that convey the theme for which the guests have come. With young Evan, everything fit the "flying food" theme and gave the impression that a safe landing was required. The experience stager eliminates negative cues (such as a sternly stated "Eat your food"), while tuning each positive cue (visually, aurally, tactilely, flavorfully, aromatically) to integrate the impressions into a believable and appealing theme.

To enhance its theme, the mist at the Rainforest Cafe appeals serially to all five senses. You first encounter it as a sound: sss-sss-zzz. Then you see the mist rising from the rocks and feel it, soft and cool, against your skin. Finally, you smell its tropical essence and taste (or imagine that you do) its freshness. It's impossible not to be affected by this one, simple, sensory-filled cue.

Some cues heighten an experience through a single sense by means of striking simplicity. The Cleveland Bicentennial Commission spent $4 million to illuminate eight automobile and railroad bridges over the Cuyahoga River near a nightspot area called The Flats. No one pays a toll to view or even cross these illuminated bridges, but the dramatically lighted structures are a prop that city managers now use to attract tourist dollars by making a nighttime trip to downtown Cleveland a more memorable experience.

Similarly, a single, simple sensation can completely detract from an experience. Think of the recorded or mechanical voices now heard everywhere—fronting voice mail systems, beginning a telemarketing pitch, guiding passengers in boarding and exiting shuttles, informing you of how to work a seat belt on an airplane, even giving you a wake-up call at a hotel. People quickly drown out this monotonous droning because companies don't bother to explore alternative creative ways of yielding the same benefits without the negative sensory cues. Here, the four realms of an experience presented in chapter 2 can be tapped to invent schemes to enrich the senses. How could an automated voice entertain—by using humor? How might it not only inform but also educate? How might it induce action to create an escapist experience? And how might the sounds of—or behind—the voice be so esthetically pleasing that guests just want to listen to it?

Adding sensory phenomena requires businesses to employ technicians who know how to affect our senses.[24] Experience-based enterprises require architectural and musical skills not only to design buildings and select music but also to fill the experience with sensations that make sense. (In the future, hotels will provide "sensory specialists," and not AV technicians, for meetings.) Not all sensations are good ones, and some combinations don't work. Barnes & Noble may have discovered that the aroma and taste of coffee go well with a freshly cracked book, but Duds 'n Suds went bust attempting to combine a coin-operated laundromat and a bar. Apparently, the smells of phosphates and hops aren't complementary.

Companies that want to stage compelling experiences should begin with all five principles outlined earlier to explore the possibilities that await them. They must determine the theme of the experience as well as the impressions that will convey that theme to guests. Many times, experience stagers develop a list of impressions they wish guests to take away and then think creatively about different themes and story lines that will bring the impressions together in one cohesive narrative. Then they winnow the impressions to a manageable number—only and exactly those that truly denote the cogent theme. Next, they focus on the animate and inanimate cues that could connote each impression, following the simple guidelines of accentuating the positive and eliminating the negative. They then must meticulously map out the effect each cue will have on the five senses—sight, sound, touch, taste, and smell—taking care not to overwhelm guests with too much sensory input. Finally, they add memorabilia to the total mix, extending the experience in the customer's mind over time.

All five principles—and not only the first one—together constitute the act of theming, or better, THEME-ing:

- Theme the experience
- Harmonize impressions with positive cues
- Eliminate negative cues
- Mix in memorabilia
- Engage the five senses

Of course, embracing these principles remains, for now, an evolving art form. But those companies that figure out how to design experiences that are compelling, engaging, memorable—and rich—will be the ones that succeed in the Experience Economy.

You Are What You Charge For

The transition to an economy in which experiences fuel the engine of growth is undergoing many of the same changes encountered in the earlier transition from the Industrial to the Service Economy. This transition begins when companies *give away* experiences in order to sell existing offerings better, just as IBM and others initially gave away services in order to sell their goods. Service providers, consciously or not, recognize the value clients place on the experience, but rather than charge separately for it, they surround their core services with experiential effects. Most restaurants, for example, still charge for the food even though customers come in for the overall experience. This à la carte pricing reflects a lingering food service mindset: charging for the activity of making individual items. Prix fixe (or table d'hôte) pricing, on the other hand, explicitly charges for the dining experience, a practice on the rise. At Moto Restaurant, for example, diners pay $135 for ten courses or $195 for the Grand Moto Tour of twenty (plus) courses; wine progressions range from $45 to $95. American Girl Place's Cafe charges a flat fee of $19 to $26, including gratuity, for its dining experiences—the exact price depending on location and meal occasion.

Ultimately, a business defines itself by what it collects revenue for, and it collects revenue only for what it decides to charge for. You're not truly selling a particular economic offering unless you explicitly ask your customers to pay for that exact offering.

For experiences, that means *charging for the time customers spend with you*, such as charging an admission fee. Appealing to a buyer's five senses, mixing in memorabilia, minding your impressions and cues, and theming may create a greater preference for your offering versus that of its commoditized competitors, but unless you explicitly charge customers for using it—not for owning it—in a *place* or *event* you control, your offering is not an *economic* experience. You may design the most engaging experience for your service offering or within your retail establishment, but unless you charge people specifically for watching or participating in the activities performed—just for entering your place, as do concert halls, theme parks, sports arenas, motion-based attractions, and other experience venues—you're not staging an economic experience.[25]

Even if you reject for now the idea of charging admission—out of fear, uncertainty, or doubt—it should still be your design criterion. Ask yourself, What would we do differently if we charged admission? This exercise will force you to discover which experience will engage guests in a more powerful way. Bottom line: your experience will never be worth an admission fee until you explore how to stop giving it away for free.

Think about a pure retailer that already borders on the experiential. The next time you go to a Brookstone, watch customers meander around the store and play with the latest high-tech devices. Many wouldn't dream of actually having most of these physical goods at home or in the office. But notice how many enjoy playing with the gee-whiz gadgets, listening to miniaturized hi-fi equipment, sitting and lying on massage chairs and tables, and then *leave without paying for what they valued*—namely, the experience.[26] Lacking admission fee revenue, one can only wonder whether the Brookstone chain will soon follow Sharper Image in selling only via catalogs and online.

Could such an establishment really charge admission? Today, few people would pay just to get into the store (or its website), although surely not enough (not, at least, as the company currently manages its stores) to sustain the enterprise on admission fees. But if Brookstone decided to charge an admission fee, it would *force* the company to stage better experiences to attract guests, especially on a repeat basis. The merchandise mix would need to change more regularly, perhaps daily, even hourly. Demonstrations, showcases, contests, and a plethora of other experiential attractions would add to the experience. Membership fees could provide access to trial use of new items or loaned "item-of-the month" merchandise. Indeed, it would no longer be another mere store but an escape from the reality of shopping elsewhere in the mall. As a result, the retailer might very well sell more goods.

Or consider Niketown. Its original design was steeped in such experiential elements as exhibits that chronicled past shoe models, displayed *Sports Illustrated* magazine covers featuring athletes wearing Nikes, a usable half-court basketball floor, and video clips of everyday athletes viewed in an intimate theatre. Indeed, according to a company press release for the opening of the first Niketown in Chicago, that store was "built as a theater, where our consumers are the audience participating in the production."[27] Through these flagship stores Nike built its brand and stimulated buying at other non-Nike retail outlets, all the while maintaining that its own locations were meant to be noncompetitive with other retail channels.

If so, then why not explicitly charge people to enter Niketown? An admission fee would force the company to stage compelling events inside, such as letting guests actually use the basketball court, perhaps to go at it one-on-one with past NBA stars or to play a game of h-o-r-s-e against a WNBA player. Customized

Nike T-shirts, commemorating the date and score of such events—complete with an action photo of the winning hoop—could be purchased afterward. There also could be interactive kiosks for educational and entertaining exploration of past athletic triumphs. We're convinced Nike could generate as much admission-based revenue per hour at Niketown as American Girl does at its venues. Instead, sans admission fees, the Nike stores have increasingly become houses of merchandise. Gone are the basketball courts, the educational videos, and other immersive experiences, and in their place, more rows of shoes and racks of apparel.

Granted, an admission fee would make it more difficult to lure *first-time* guests ("You mean I have to pay to get in there?"), but it would be easier to get them to come back. And there's another benefit of charging admission. For those experience stagers struggling to attract guests for return visits, such as eatertainment restaurants, the admission fee alters the buyer's evaluation of the value of the total offering. For when restaurants try to recover all the costs of staging an experience from the food alone, people quickly get used to accessing the experience for free and then begin to view the food as grossly overpriced. So why go back? With an admission fee, guests rightly perceive each offering they consume—goods, services, and experiences—as reasonably priced in its own right. The same principle applies to direct manufacturers, website operators, insurance agents, financial brokers, business-to-business marketers, and any other cueless business that wraps free experiences around costly goods or services. The demise of many retailers—Imaginarium, Just for Feet, The Nature Company, Oshman's, and Warner Bros., to name a few—testifies to the fate of those who neglect to consider charging admission, as do the struggles of yet additional retailers—FAO Schwarz, Eddie Bauer, Guitar Center, Linens 'n Things, and, of course, Disney itself.

Disney's initial foray into specialty retailing outside its primary properties disappointed. Other than the Disney videos playing in the background, its mall stores pretty much looked and felt like everyone else's mall stores, and the blame lay squarely on Disney's failure to charge admission. Because no one paid to get in the door, Disney provided a pedestrian shopping trip rather than a magical adventure. Even when Disney put concerted effort into the architecture and furnishings—such as at its store in midtown Manhattan, where on entering you seemed to have been transported, for a moment, to Walt Disney World itself—the experience giant never harmonized all the cues. The elevator, for example, appeared both inside and out to be an entrance into Snow White's castle, but once you boarded, you were exposed to blaring rock music that had nothing to do with the medieval surroundings. And everywhere you found costumed employees (here, they did not earn the term "cast members") totally out of character, talking among themselves. Perhaps this was not Disney's intention. Perhaps it was merely poor execution. But that execution stemmed directly from the lack of an admission fee—even one reimbursable later for merchandise—and it certainly diminished the Disney brand by failing to live up to the company's high experiential expertise. Disney eventually got out of the retail store business, returning only when its licensee The Children's Place went bankrupt, and now is finally adding in such experiential elements as a "magic mirror" and store-opening ceremony.

Perhaps the right way to start charging admission is to do so for only a particular portion of a place, or for certain times in a place. Apple Retail Stores—where enthusiasts as well as prospects go to "Gather. Learn. Create."—charge for certain times in the store with its One to One offering. With a $99 membership, customers not only get system setup and file transfer services, but also can book one-hour training sessions or two-hour "personal project" sessions with individual trainers. During every moment at an Apple store when these sessions are held—and Apple trainers hold a lot of them—a portion of the space and a certain amount of time generates experience-based revenue apart from the sale of goods and services.

At four fun-filled Jordan's Furniture locations across New England, the company stages myriad experiences (including audio-animatronic replicas of the third-generation owners, brothers Barry and Eliot Tatelman; a Bourbon-Street-theme Mardi Gras atmosphere; and an IMAX theatre). Jordon's, now owned by Warren Buffett's Berkshire Hathaway, still gives these away, but at its Avon, Massachusetts, store it charges admission to the Motion Odyssey Machine, which takes audiences on a thrill ride simulating a roller coaster, a dune buggy, an out-of-control truck, and so forth, complete with wind and water effects. As Barry Tatelman often said, "There's no business that's not show business."

In the full-fledged Experience Economy, we will see not only portions of retail stores but entire shopping malls charge admission before a person is allowed to set foot in a store.[28] In fact, such shopping malls already exist. Disney's archrival Universal Studios, for example, charges admission (in the form of a parking fee) to CityWalk. But the Minnesota Renaissance Festival, the Gilroy Garlic Festival in California, the Kitchener-Waterloo Oktoberfest in Ontario, Canada, and a host of other seasonal festivals charge admission for what are really outdoor shopping malls. Consumers find these festivals to be worth the entrance fees, because their owners explicitly script distinctive experiences around particularly enticing themes and then stage a wealth of activities that captivate guests before, after, and while they shop.

At the Minnesota Renaissance Festival, for example, handsome knights and fair maidens greet visitors to the twenty-two-acre domain of King Henry and Queen Katherine outside Minneapolis, hand them a *News of the Realm* guide on simulated parchment, and invite them to enjoy the day's festivities. Throughout the day various merrymakers in Renaissance costume—magicians, jugglers, peddlers, singers, dance troupes, and even a pair of bumbling commoners known as Puke & Snot—frequently accost guests (many of whom also clothe themselves in period costume) with the express intent of ensuring that they, their companions, and everyone else within earshot have a wonderful time. Among the numerous categories of activities in which guests delight—and that could apply to any experience—are the following:

- Period demonstrations (armor making, glass blowing, bookbinding, and so forth)
- Crafts that guests perform themselves (brass rubbing, candle making, calligraphy)
- Games, contests, and other challenges for which prizes are awarded (archery, giant maze, Jacob's ladder)
- Human- and animal-powered (never electric) rides (elephants, ponies, cabriolet)
- Food (turkey legs, apple dumplings, Florentine ice)
- Drink (beer and wine but also—in an admitted concession to modern concessions—soda and coffee)
- Shows, ceremonies, parades, and various and sundry revelry (magicians, puppetry, jousts), some of which require an additional fee

Not to mention the hundreds of Renaissance-themed shops (make that *shoppes*), all selling handcrafted goods appropriate to the period, such as jewelry, pottery, glass, candles, musical instruments, toys, apparel, plants, perfumes, wall hangings, and sculptures, or services such as face painting, astrology readings, portraits, and caricatures. With nearly every guest leaving with one or more bags of goodies, the Renaissance Festival experience clearly siphons off shopping dollars that otherwise would be spent at traditional malls and other retail outlets.

Fortunately for their conventional competitors, the proprietors of such festivals do not hold them year-round … yet. The Minnesota Renaissance Festival, for example, opens its gates weekends and Labor Day from mid-August to the end of September. Because of its intensity and unusual nature, most people do not repeat this kind of experience often enough to make staging it every day worthwhile. However, with appropriately malleable grounds and facilities, consumers could be enticed over and over again if different experiences were rotated through the same place. Mid-America Festivals, the company that runs the Minnesota Renaissance Festival as well as similar endeavors in other states, added Halloween-theme experiences (Trail of Terror, Gargoyle Manor, and BooBash) at the same locale, as well as a Christmas-theme gourmet dinner and entertainment called the Fezziwig Feast. Shopping malls that wish to embrace the Experience Economy must learn how to stage revolving productions, just as theatres did long ago, that entice people to pay an admission fee again and again.

Do you think people would be crazy to pay for the experience of shopping at their local mall? Imagine the reaction if, decades ago—just after World War II, let's say, when the U.S. economy was booming, flush with returning GIs buying houses in the suburbs and filling their garages with new cars and their kitchens with the latest in household gadgets—you had told people that in the near future the typical family would pay someone else to change the oil in their car, make their kids' birthday cakes, clean their shirts, mow their lawn, or deliver a host of other now-commonplace services. No doubt they would have said you were insane! Or imagine going back hundreds of years and telling rural farmers that in the centuries hence the vast majority of people would no longer farm their own land, build their own houses, kill animals for their own meals, chop their own wood, or even make their own clothes or furniture. Again, you would have been thought crazy.

The history of all economic progress consists of charging a fee for what once was free. In the full-fledged Experience Economy, instead of relying purely on our own wherewithal to experience the new and wondrous—as has been done for ages—we increasingly pay companies to stage experiences for us, just as we pay companies for services we once delivered ourselves, goods we once made ourselves, and commodities we once extracted ourselves. We find ourselves paying to spend more and more time in various places or events.

Admission to such experiences need not be limited to paying to enter, although such entry fees will certainly continue as one form of admission fee. In addition to paying at the start of experiences, customers may pay by occurrence or per period of time. And for each measurement (at start, by occurrence, and per period), paying guests may be admitted either for specific occasions or on an open basis. As shown in figure 3-1, six forms of admission therefore are available to experience stagers:

- *Entry fee:* Payment to enter a venue or event, such as going to a movie, seeing a stage performance, attending a sporting event, or walking a trade show floor

- *Per-event fee:* Payment to participate in an event, such as playing an arcade game, placing a wager, taking part in a competitive contest, or partaking in a conference or seminar
- *Per-period fee:* Payment for a set time—per minute, per hour, per day, per week, per month, per quarter, per year—at, for, in, or with offerings, such as satellite TV, Internet use, or club or association dues
- *Initiation fee:* Initial payment to affiliate with an experience, such as joining a country club, social club, website, or social network
- *Access fee:* Payment to obtain entrance, participation, time, affiliation, or membership, such as a backstage pass, beginner fee, test period, "professional seat license," or trial membership
- *Membership fee:* Payment to be enrolled or included in a group's experiences, such as in a club, league, forum, co-op, or other association, whether for a group or an individual

Entry fees are paid before an experience just to get in; per-event fees are paid during an experience (or at the end of it) to get involved; and per-period fees are paid over time to yet again experience an offering. Initiation fees are paid to join and be received; access fees are paid to pass through and experience an exclusive offering; and membership fees are paid to continue and belong.

Remember: *you are what you charge for.* Knowing these varied admission fee possibilities opens up new opportunities for differently structuring economic relationships with customers—and thus alters the perceived value of one's offerings. For example,

FIGURE 3-1

Forms of admission

Admittance		On start	By occurrence	By period
	Specific	Entry fee	Per-event fee	Per-period fee
	Open	Initiation fee	Access fee	Membership fee

Measurement

hotels that require guests to check out by a certain time in the morning still embrace a service mindset evidenced in the form of a *room rate*, wherein customers essentially pay for a collection of activities performed directly or (often) indirectly on their behalf. The requirement often frustrates guests. Hotels can shift to an experience mindset by charging per-period in the form of a *day rate*, allowing guests to stay in full twenty-four intervals before checking out. (Or alternatively, charge *hour rates*, as "hotel cabin" chains like YO! Company's YOtel now do.) Any business can differentiate itself by considering alternative approaches; any number of the six forms of admission could be combined to effect greater loyalty.

Charging explicitly for experiences, versus merely for goods and services, can lead to fundamentally altering the financial winners in an industry. Think movies. Blockbuster once dominated the movie rental industry, charging for each film rented, and fining customers (yes, *fining* customers!) for late returns. Enter Netflix. It offered an alternative pricing model, one based on charging explicitly for movie-viewing experiences (not movie-renting services). Netflix customers simply pay a monthly (per-period) fee, with unlimited movie rentals subsumed within the offering. Granted, Netflix also reinvented the underlying delivery service and is eagerly reinventing it again. Why? It's because by charging for time (each month) and not for the service (each rental), Netflix treats new technological platforms not as a threat to service revenues but as the means to lower delivery costs supporting its experience revenues.

Consider other such per-period possibilities. Imagine paying a company an annual fee to carefully manage an ever-changing mix of toys as part of a child development offering—instead of family and friends showering children with too many (inevitably unused) toys. Imagine a similar wardrobe management offering for adults, routinely providing expertise in the selection, maintenance, and replacement of garments—instead of closets packed with too many seldom-worn articles of clothing. Such subscription-based wardrobes could be customized based on color analysis, individual levels of fashion consciousness, and actual wear and tear. Or think about grocery stores, which charge for individual packaged goods and other foodstuffs. In a time when many people are overweight, couldn't a grocer offer to charge a per-period fee for a maximum number of calories to be taken home from the store each week? Almost any industry would benefit from seeking to differentiate based on for-fee experiences.

Charging admission does not necessarily mean, however, that companies stop selling their goods and services. (Still, some will indeed give away their lower-level offerings to better sell their high-margin experiences, just as telephone companies today give away cell phones to consumers who sign up for their wireless service.) The Walt Disney Company derives an awful lot of profit at its theme parks from photographic, food, and other services, as well as from all the goods it sells as memorabilia. But without the staged experiences (not only of the theme parks but also cartoons, movies, and TV shows) there would be nothing to remember—Disney would have no characters to exploit. While historically Disney started with the experience and then added lower-level offerings, the principle holds for those starting with goods and services that shift up to experiences. In the Experience Economy, experiences drive the economy and therefore generate much of the base demand for goods and services. So explore the experiences you could stage that would be so engaging that your current customers would actually pay admission and then pay extra for your services while they are so engaged, or pay more for your goods as memorabilia. In doing so, you would be following the lead of not only Disney but also the Minnesota Renaissance Festival, American Girl Places, prix fixe restaurants, and a host of other companies that have already entered the Experience Economy.

The same principle applies to business-to-business companies: staging experiences for their customers will drive demand for their current goods and services. The business equivalent of a shopping mall is, after all, a trade show—a place to find, learn about, and, if a need is met, purchase offerings. Trade show operators already charge admission (and could charge even more, if they staged better experiences); individual companies can do the same thing. If a company designs a worthwhile experience, customers will gladly pay the company to, essentially, sell to them.

Again, all the forms of admission fees are fair game for alternatively structuring B2B relationships. R&D-intensive companies could charge for membership and access to ongoing research findings and development intelligence. New experience-based revenue streams would emerge, replacing the paradigm of recovering costs only when a new good or service output eventually materializes. After all, new goods and services, once on the market, will only be reverse-engineered or otherwise copied and offered at a lower price. Charging admission to R&D may well provide the needed remedy for the tenuous cost issues causing turbulence (illegal imports, counterfeiting, medical tourism, and so forth) in the pharmaceutical, medical device, and other healthcare industries.

Will every company be able to charge admission? No, only those that properly set the stage by designing rich experiences that cross into all four realms: the entertainment, the educational, the escapist, and the esthetic. And only those that use the THEME-ing principles outlined earlier to create engaging, memorable encounters. Charging admission is the final step; first you must design an experience worth paying for.

But launching experiences worthy of charging admission is precisely what is needed in order to grow revenues, create jobs, increase wealth, and ensure continued economic prosperity now and in the future. Charging for goods and services is no longer enough. Instead of bombarding children with too many toys, we need new toy management and child development firms—operating essentially as the Netflix of toy-playing. Instead of closets and drawers full of too many clothes, we need wardrobe management offerings. We need new models for charging for nutritional foods. Fundamentally, we need to stop protecting old Mass Production businesses and start encouraging new customizing ventures. That show must go on.

CHAPTER 4

Get Your Act Together

REMEMBER THE LAST TIME YOU received particularly poor service, perhaps at a restaurant, automotive shop, or airline counter? For many, such ordeals create our most lasting recollections of a company—and often our best cocktail-hour stories. We forget consistently dependable service while remembering the occasional mishap. Companies that falter on the service front discover the hard way that the easiest way to turn a service into an experience is to provide poor service, thus creating a memorable encounter of the most unpleasant kind.

The surest way to provide poor service is to walk every client through the same rote, impersonal routine, never varying, no matter who the individual client is or what he really needs. Customers have been receiving such treatment ever since service providers embraced the same principles of Mass Production that manufacturers used to dramatically lower costs. And it has become even worse as the forces of commoditization that hit manufacturing now attack services as well. So service providers reengineer their call centers to reduce call time and downsize already harried frontline staff or outsource the work to save on fixed costs and overhead. The end result? Their employees spend less time with clients, and the time they do spend no longer delivers the same level of service. By focusing on costs at the expense of what clients want, these companies commoditize themselves. Why should customers pay a higher price for demonstrably poorer service?

But the inverse principle also holds true: customizing a service can be a sure route to staging a positive experience. Certainly, customization is not the be-all and end-all; rather, companies should use it to create customer-unique value, the portal through which experiences reach individual customers. An economic offering confers customer-unique value, at its ideal, when it is

- *Specific to individual customers*: Brought into being at a particular moment for this precise customer
- *Particular in its characteristics*: Designed to meet this customer's individual needs (although some other customer may have the same needs and may therefore purchase the same offering)
- *Singular in its purpose to benefit this customer*: Not trying to be any more or less than, but rather only and exactly, what the customer desires

When a company provides such customer-unique value, it takes an invaluable first step toward creating memorable interactions that stand apart from the routine transactions mass producers foist on their customers.

Progressive Insurance of Cleveland, for example, gives adjusters "immediate response vehicles" (IRVs) outfitted with a personal computer, wireless uplink to its mainframe computers, and everything else they may need for the *singular* purpose of efficiently resolving a claim from the site of an accident. While the other party may wait days or weeks for his insurance company's cost-conscious adjuster to fit him into the schedule, the Progressive claimant finds his *particular* needs handled right then and there—receiving not only a check but also a cup of coffee and, if need be, a few minutes to sit down and relax in the IRV and call to reassure his family (or arrange for a ride). Because Progressive customizes its claims service to the *specific* individual insured, its offering goes beyond the expected service to provide an experience appropriate to the physical and emotional needs of the claimant. And in doing all this, the company actually lowered its costs.

Automatic Shifting

The same effect works for goods: customizing a good automatically turns it into a service. Look at Dell. Ever since Michael Dell founded the company in his University of Texas dorm room in 1984 he focused on producing computers on demand to individual customer order. Until recently, the company never produced anything to put in finished goods inventory but instead made its personal computers (and, increasingly, servers, switches, consumer electronic devices, and so forth) only when a real, live, breathing customer provided the exact desired specifications. Via its web-based configurator or a telephone call center, or (for large corporate customers) directly to a salesperson, Dell collaborates with its customers to define the particular computing goods to meet their own individual needs.

In the fast-moving computer industry, Dell lowers its costs over inventory-laden mass producers because of what the company calls its "cash conversion cycle"—the time between when it pays its suppliers and when its customers pay it. For most manufacturers that's days, weeks, even months. (Think of all the "tired iron" that automakers push out to their dealers, where the industry standard is a sixty-day supply.) For Dell, in fiscal year 2010 the cash conversion cycle was a *negative* thirty-six days.[1] (It was much higher—make that lower, in the negative forties and fifties—before Dell started in 2007 selling some of its goods at retail because of industry dynamics.) This means that it has negative working capital, with its growth funded by customers who pay in advance of receiving their products and suppliers that get paid long after they deliver.

Now consider Dell in light of the classic distinctions between goods and services. Goods are standardized for anonymous customers, while services are customized for a particular individual—check. Goods are inventoried, while services are delivered on demand—check again. Finally, goods are tangible, while services are intangible—and part and parcel of Dell's interaction with customers is the intangible service of helping each one determine exactly what product permutation he, she, or it needs. Checkmate. So even though at the core of the sale lies the physical hardware, selling the personal computers and other products themselves, customized and on demand, means delivering a service. As with all services, its offerings are inherently customizable, so Dell's capabilities put it in a better position to stage experiences for individual customers—something Michael Dell stressed as a priority when he returned to the CEO seat in 2007.[2]

Both goods and services, then, automatically shift up the Progression of Economic Value when they are customized, as shown in figure 4-1. (This shift does not occur for true commodities, which, being fungible, cannot be materially changed, much less customized.) As a result, companies create offerings more relevant to the wants and needs of individual buyers, differentiate their goods and services from the sea of look-alike competitors, and thereby increase the value provided, and thus the price charged, to users and clients. Businesses that wish to forestall commoditization by

FIGURE 4-1

Shifting up the Progression of Economic Value

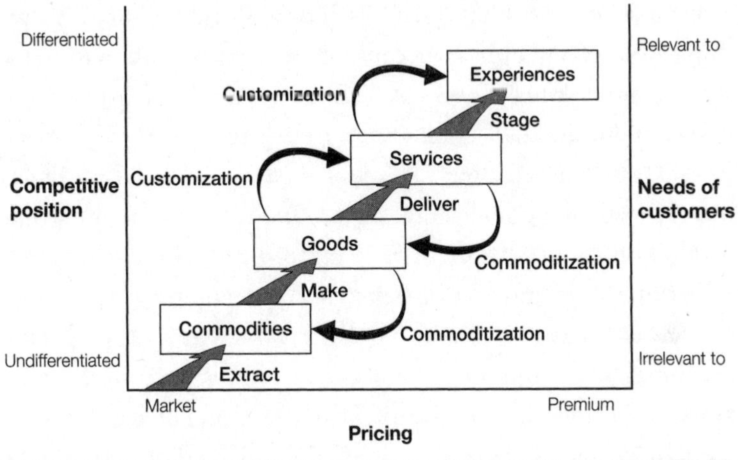

entering the Experience Economy should first get their act together by customizing their goods and services.

Mass Customization

Companies like Dell and Progressive *mass customize* their offerings. Mass Customization means efficiently serving customers uniquely, combining the coequal imperatives for both low costs and individual customization present in today's highly turbulent, competitive environment.[3] Of course, ad hoc or craft customization, in which a company must determine what to do differently every time it changes operations, achieves the same benefits, but at a higher cost. Companies that hope to gain the best of both worlds—the "mass" and the "customization"—must modularize their goods and services. This practice lets companies efficiently produce standardized modules but combine them in different ways for different buyers, just as Dell does with the hardware and software components that go into its offerings.

To understand modularity, think of LEGO building bricks. What can you build with LEGOs? The answer, of course, is anything you want. This is because of the many different sizes, shapes, and colors of bricks as well as the simple, elegant system of tabs and holes that enables them to be easily snapped together. These two basic elements—a *set of modules* and a *linkage system* that dynamically connects them—define the *modular architecture* that equips a company to mass customize.[4] This architecture determines the universe of benefits that a company intends to provide for customers and, within that universe, the specific combinations of modules it will deliver at this time, to this particular customer. In the case of Dell, the modules are the individual electronics components—CPU and memory chips, disk drives, USB ports, software, and so forth—and the linkage system is the computer motherboard to which everything connects; the composition of each computer can differ greatly from customer to customer.

Companies like Progressive Insurance that mass customize services build their modular architectures not out of tangible components but with process modules. Think also of FedEx. Every package it picks up and delivers is unavoidably unique, having different contents that must start at a different point A and end up at a different point B. FedEx accomplishes the task—overnight, at unbelievably low costs—because of its modular route system. A van picks up a package at point A and brings it and all the other ones it picked up to a local depot; that depot places all of its packages on big trucks to head to a larger depot at the airport; all those packages head out on airplanes to FedEx hubs such as Nashville, and then, with the proper sorting and dispensing all along the way, the package heads back out on the modular routes that get it to point B.

Or, because that's really the only way FedEx could supply its service (there is no mass produced alternative), consider CEMEX, of Monterrey, Mexico, one of the largest concrete companies in the world. Concrete may be more or less treated like a commodity, but CEMEX specializes in mass customizing the *service delivery* of its ready-mix concrete to its customers. Individual building sites often have tight deadlines for pouring the concrete to fit the weather and their construction schedules, with traffic conditions often a significant impediment to on-time delivery (think Mexico City). So CEMEX developed an operational system called GINCO (an acronym standing for "integral management of concrete" in Spanish) to handle all of its logistics, including GPS locators on each of its trucks. Because the company loads trucks with concrete mixture (in slurry form) and then tracks their every move, customers can now order the product with as little as two hours' notice. GINCO finds the trucks with the proper mixtures in the correct amounts and then *dispatches* (rather than schedules, the favored tool of mass producers) trucks to the right place at the right time. CEMEX creates customer-unique value from its customized delivery process more so than its standardized concrete.

In addition to a modular architecture, Mass Customization requires an *environmental architecture*, again composed of two elements: a *design tool* that matches buyer need with company capabilities, and a *designed interaction* within which the company stages a design experience that helps customers decide exactly what they want. Without this environmental architecture, companies often overwhelm potential buyers with so many combinations of modules that they can't figure out which one makes sense.

Design tools such as Progressive's laptop claims adjustment system, Dell's website configurator, and even CEMEX's GINCO software help manage the complexity that, on the one hand, allows companies to tailor their offerings to individuals' needs but, on the other hand, often gets in the way of customers' determining exactly what they want.

When in the 1990s its business began to turn from make-to-stock to make-to-order, window manufacturer Andersen Corp. of Bayport, Minnesota, developed a multimedia design tool called the Window of Knowledge to help its distributors collaborate with consumers on the latter's own window designs. The computer software featured an icon framework representing more than fifty thousand possible window components that allowed consumers and distributors to create and see exactly what potential designs would look like. (It also displayed videos of beautiful, cloud-swept vistas in the background, making more than one customer respond, "Wow.")

Providing the design tool alone was not enough, however. Andersen found that success depended on training its distributors to use the tool itself and, just as important, to use it to interact with customers on a personal basis. Over several years, those distributors that were properly trained on the tool increased their sales of Andersen windows by more than 20 percent; those distributors that either did not accept the tool or did not accept the training actually decreased their sales of Andersen goods. The beauty of Andersen's approach—since supplanted by software for its distributors called iQ, for Intelligent Quote, and a web-based tool for its consumers—lay in its ease of use: people could easily sift through a seemingly limitless number of possibilities. Had distributors instead presented all of them, consumers certainly would have found the interaction an overwhelming experience.

In situations with more limited possibilities, companies may *fully disclose* all possible combinations and let customers sort through them all. Such a "giant menu" approach need not be unpleasant. In fact, companies can make this interaction a unique experience by enriching the ways in which someone sorts through its menu or catalog, as when, for example, Land's End affixes Post-it Tape Flags in its catalogs to allow customers to easily mark pages before ordering, or when Amazon.com displays "most recently viewed" books for customers browsing online.

A second approach to designed interaction *progressively reveals* the possibilities in segmented catalogs, fill-in-the-blank menus, selection matrices, configuration or design tools such as Andersen's, even the proverbial blank sheet of paper. With its website configurator, Dell lets customers begin the customization process by selecting a starting point from among a set of fairly standard packages with varying features. Once they've decided on something close to what they need, then they can customize it further by selecting various components, including monitor, speakers, operating system, support services, and so on, with only ever a few choices on each web page. Design tools such as these give customers an opportunity to adjust selections until they eventually determine exactly what they want.

The third approach to designed interaction *deliberately conceals* the design tool from customers. Why would a mass customizer do such a thing? It's because sometimes customers desire customer-unique value but do not want to be too involved in the decision-making process. Such is the case with the environmental architecture surrounding CEMEX's GINCO system. Construction companies have little interest in participating in moment-to-moment dispatching decisions. CEMEX uses its design tool to respond with exactly the right combination of trucks for each site need without intruding on their customer's businesses. Progressive also keeps to itself the proprietary Progressive Automated Claims Management System (dubbed PAC-MAN), which includes a design tool for claims adjusting. By not bothering their often agitated, dazed, or just plain embarrassed members with the details, claims adjusters turn the normally loathsome interaction into an appreciated experience. And no one needs to get involved in specifying how FedEx gets a package from point A to point B—although FedEx nicely lets them track it online; shippers just need to know it gets there on time, every time.

For these companies, Mass Customization presents a new stage on which to introduce experiential value to their customers. They identified the inadequacies of existing mass produced goods and services, distinguished the individual characteristics of their customer bases, developed a modular architecture to efficiently serve their customers uniquely, and, finally, created an environmental architecture that used customization as the means to shift up the Progression of Economic Value. As a result, they now go beyond goods and services to offer what customers truly want.

And make no mistake: individuals more and more want their offerings individualized to them. Think of how we all customize our personal technologies—MP3 players, mobile phones, tablets, computers—to our personal taste. Apple, especially, excels at enabling people to customize each one of these devices to an extraordinary extent. After people create their own playlists, address lists, apps, software, and so forth, every device becomes its own unique artifact (and treasured possession). Particularly those now growing up, for whom such technology is almost second nature, would never give up this ability to make their devices their own—and increasingly will come to demand exactly what they want, across offerings, companies, and industries.

What *Do* Customers Want?

Most companies still resist mass customizing their offerings. Instead, they "manage the supply chain" by placing increasing variety into their distribution channels and leaving it to buyers to fend for themselves. Manufacturers maintain large inventories of finished goods, and service providers maintain excess personnel and provisions to meet an increasingly unwieldy number of potential demands. These practices offer a surefire way to add costs and complexity to operations.

Worse, customers must sort through numerous alternatives to find one that even approximates what they want. Increased variety may enable a few additional buyers to find a good or service that very closely matches their desires, but only at the expense of increased time sorting through alternatives—not an insignificant consideration given, for instance, the fifty thousand or more stock-keeping units, or SKUs, in the typical supermarket. The vast majority of buyers, however, still fail to find an exact match. It all amounts to one bad experience after another.

Producing more and more variety in anticipation of potential, yet uncertain, demand often represents a last-ditch attempt to preserve the Mass Production mindset in the face of rapidly fragmenting markets. *But variety is not the same as customization.*[5] *Variety* means producing and distributing product choices to outlets in the hope that some customer will come along and buy them. *Customization*, on the other hand, means producing in response to a particular customer's desires. As a result, businesses often overwhelm customers with so much product proliferation that they throw up their hands and walk away rather than go through a lengthy decision-making process with little or no support. Fundamentally, customers do not want choice; they just want exactly what they want. A mass customizer's designed interaction with each individual provides the means for efficient, effective, and (as much as possible) effortless determination of customer needs. To shift up the Progression of Economic Value, whether from goods to services or services to experiences, companies should use such interactions to figure out exactly what their customers want.

They must then bring that information about a customer's desires directly into operations for efficient, on-demand production or provisioning, effectively turning the old supply chain into a *demand chain*. Remember that mass customizing doesn't mean being everything to everybody; rather, it is doing *only and exactly* what each customer wants, when he wants it. Although a significant up-front investment may be required to develop the products, processes, people, and technologies required, mass customized offerings may ultimately cost nearly the same as mass produced ones, and sometimes less.

Take The Hertz Corporation's #1 Club Gold Program as a case in point. The Gold customer, who is told the program costs $60 a year, with the fee often waived, receives the same basic vehicle as everyone else but bypasses the line at the counter and need only give his name to the shuttle bus driver. He's then dropped off at the canopied Gold area, where he sees his name in lights on a large screen that directs him to the exact location of his car. When the customer arrives at his car, he finds his name in lights above it and again noticeably printed on the personal agreement hanging from the mirror, and, when the weather demands it (and local laws permit it), the car's engine running with the heater or air conditioner turned on. By not doing anything until the customer steps on the bus and gives his name, and then doing only and exactly what each customer requires on demand, Hertz discovered that its Gold experience actually costs *less* to provide than its standard service. That's why it often waives the $60-a-year membership fee, a practice that in our view is a mistake. Companies should charge for the value they add and not the costs they incur. Moreover, that money could be used to make Hertz Gold a still richer rental car experience.

Of course, determining what sort of customization would be worth a premium price is no easy task. Which features or benefits of the offering should be customized, and which left standard (such as the car, in Hertz's case)? Where in the value chain would buyers most prize customization? What key leverage points would provide the biggest bang for the buck? And what modular and environmental architectures would be most effective in creating memorable events?

To answer such questions, many companies turn to customer satisfaction, or "voice of the customer," surveys that use market research techniques to gather data. Such information provides a great foundation for understanding the *general* needs of one's customer base. However, these techniques do not go far enough to determine what and where a company should mass customize. After all, customer satisfaction really measures *market*, and not individual customer, satisfaction. Few managers bother to scrutinize the individual results. They just view a few "CustSat" numbers that supposedly represent various market segments. They design surveys to ease tabulation, and not to gain true insight into customer-specific wants and needs, and all the customers who bother to fill one out know that they will gain no direct benefit.

Further, rarely do customer satisfaction surveys even ask for information about the particular needs and wants of individual customers. Rather, they invariably ask buyers to rate how well the company or its personnel performed on a series of predefined categories. Managers gain precious little insight into what buyers truly want and need, as evidenced by what seems to be the most common theme of such surveys: how are we doing? What we are doing is inundating customers with incessant surveys that have little impact on what customers truly need. One airline questionnaire of this ilk even had a headline, incredibly, asking travelers to "Help Us Reinvent Our Airline"—an act that either overstates the impact of such generic customer input or underestimates the nature of corporate reinvention.

A More Memorable Measure

As Dave Power III of J. D. Power & Associates says, "When we measure satisfaction what we're really measuring is the difference between what a customer *expects* and what the customer *perceives* he gets."[6] In other words,

Customer satisfaction = What customer expects to get
− What customer perceives he gets

Customer satisfaction measurements essentially focus on understanding and managing customer expectations of what companies already do rather than truly ascertaining what customers really want. While such measurements have their place, companies must do more than merely measure against perception to mass customize effectively. They must understand the nature of *customer sacrifice*—the gap between what a customer *settles for* and what he *wants exactly*:

Customer sacrifice = What customer wants exactly
− What customer settles for

When we understand customer sacrifice, we discern the difference between what a customer *accepts* and what he *really needs*, even if the customer doesn't know what that is or can't articulate it.

While companies employ total quality management (TQM) techniques to drive up customer satisfaction, they must employ Mass Customization techniques to drive down customer sacrifice.

And while TQM programs help reduce the waste associated with mass produced goods and services—by eliminating redundancies, bottlenecks, and other inefficiencies—focusing on customer sacrifice eliminates the waste that occurs whenever a business performs an activity or expends a resource that a particular customer does not want. Indeed, because TQM programs often result in new features (of a good) or dimensions (of a service) geared to improving the satisfaction of the averred "average" customer, the solution to effect increased satisfaction becomes the source of additional sacrifice. No matter how many improvements are made, the offering remains uniform for all customers.

But individual customers differ in the exact combination of features or benefits they desire. They constantly face trade-offs, trying to decide if enough beneficial components exist to tolerate the marginal and offset the detrimental. Rarely do wants and needs match *exactly* the one bundle that constitutes a company's product, so whenever a customer buys *any* mass produced offering, he accepts the undesired components along with the desired, and this means that the company wasted resources in production or delivery. With products such as consumer electronics, for example, manufacturers constantly add incremental features in the hope that a new one may prove desirably novel. The same oversupply dynamic occurs when a hotel furnishes every room with an iron and ironing board that go unused ninety-nine out of one hundred nights, or when many of the bags of pretzels and cans of soda an airline worker piles on a beverage cart end up right back in the galley.

Designing for the average is the root cause of customer sacrifice; every mass produced product comprises a bundle of take-it-or-leave-it features or dimensions offered to all customers. The more features bundled, the greater the likelihood of introducing an element that disqualifies the product with a particular buyer (either because the buyer flat doesn't want the element or doesn't want to incur the perceived higher price for a marginal element). Similarly, talk about "designing for the customer" in many organizations really means designing for "the *average* customer"—who doesn't really exist. Unless people keep particular customers—real, specific, and known individuals—in view, such efforts only trigger initiatives to perform activities and expend resources without knowing the individual levels actually required.

Consider the airline industry. Customer sacrifice fills every flight across hundreds of service dimensions.[7] Let's examine, for simplicity's sake, a single dimension among many: the aforementioned beverage cart. Once a plane reaches a safe and comfortable cruising altitude, the beverage cart comes down the aisle, and the flight attendant asks, "Would you like something to drink?" A die-hard Pepsi drinker would naturally request one, only to be asked (on most airlines), "Is Coke OK?" Backing off from his true desire, the customer generally accepts the Coke. He sacrifices. On the next two, three, or maybe four flights with the same airline, the same question, request, and answer arises. Finally catching on, the customer begins asking for—what?—Coca-Cola! Learning that the airline does not carry his favorite beverage, the airline finally trains him to *expect* an unwanted alternative. Only then can the airline meet expectations. (And, of course, for those airlines that offer Pepsi, the Coke drinkers sacrifice.)

To the airline, that individual represents another satisfied customer because he always receives what he expects. But underneath this faux satisfaction lies a source of innovation that can turn an ordinary airline service into a memorable event: the opportunity to help customers experience less sacrifice. Every time a provider of a good or service interacts with a customer, both parties have an opportunity to learn. Eventually, one party changes his behavior as a result of that learning. Unfortunately, all too often that's the customer. He starts asking for something other than what he really wants—or perhaps he simply goes away.

CHAPTER 5

Experiencing Less Sacrifice

SOME BUSINESS COMMENTATORS SAY THAT conditioning customers (that is, coercing them to lower their expectations) to accept less than exactly what they want breeds good business practice, especially if a business reduces its costs without overly dissatisfying the customer. But herein lies another sure route to commoditization, for it unduly focuses the company on internal costs at the expense of customer needs. An attitude of "They won't mind" leads inevitably to operational practices replete with customer sacrifice. It may lead to *higher* costs if the company sidesteps an opportunity to ascertain individual needs and eliminate wasteful practices stemming from expending resources and effort that some customers simply do not want. More importantly, embracing this mindset makes you miss the opportunity to innovate and create customer-unique value that sets new expectations for the experience.

Consider cable and satellite television. Every provider in the industry requires customers to select from various bundled packages of channels. These cable companies force individual customers to receive some channels they do not want in order to get the one channel they do want. Offering "on demand" programs and movies only masks the fact that customers do not get to determine the specific mix of channels they want *in supply* to their homes, let alone determine the particular channel numbers assigned to each network (so that when channel-surfing, the stations would scroll through in an order determined by the customer). Such customization is possible technologically, given that the programming exists in digital form. In fact, there is no reason viewers could not treat individual programs (and not only networks) as modules, pulling favorite shows off the shelf from various networks to create a kind of "MyChannel" that would place hour-by-hour preferences on a single channel, eliminating the sacrifice of having to sort through hundreds of channels to find favorites each time the TV set is turned on. (Such functionality would bring to TV viewing the kind of playlists now available for music listening via an iPod or other MP3 players.)

Viewers can use digital video recorders (DVRs) to customize their TV viewing, but only on a delayed basis—and usually skipping through the commercials. If cable providers were to proactively provide the means for customized *live* viewing, people might watch more commercials, benefiting the network providers (and cable companies might be able to charge these networks to have shows placed on a "Serendipity Channel" for individual customers, with the lineup of seemingly random shows determined from actual viewing preferences). Just as the advent of TiVo led such providers to supply DVRs to customers, companies like Roku may put enough competitive pressure on them to finally lead to greater customization capabilities. As Daniel Roth put it in *Wired* magazine, the future should not require viewers to "still watch television the old-fashioned way, piped over cable or beamed in by satellite and available only in bloated packages of channels programmed by network executives."[1] Exactly.

Searching for Uniqueness

No longer should customers settle for standardized goods and services when companies can efficiently deliver, through Mass Customization techniques, only and exactly what each customer desires. If your company (like cable and satellite TV operators) resists doing so, some competitor surely will do so soon, forever disrupting the dynamics of your industry. But early entrants often find that ascertaining customer needs that lie buried beneath the surface of countless "how did we do" surveys isn't easy. Indeed, customers have sacrificed for so long that they often have difficulty discussing their exact preferences. Even after the concept of sacrifice has been explained to them, most customers remain unable to articulate the gaps between what they settle for and what it is, exactly, that they want.

Some skeptics cite this difficulty as evidence that customers cannot be counted on as sources for new ideas and innovation. The problem with customer input, however, doesn't derive from the inability of customers to identify and articulate their wants and needs; it stems from the context in which companies solicit that input. People tend to answer the questions posed to them. Often, their answers are as much a function of the Mass Production mindset that framed the questions as they are an accurate expression of customer needs. Harvard Business School professors Dorothy Leonard and Jeffrey F. Rayport, proponents of what they call "empathic design" (which is derived from watching customers in their own environments), say it this way: "Sometimes, customers are so accustomed to current conditions using company offerings that they don't think to ask for a new solution—even if they have real needs that could be addressed."[2]

Traditional research techniques—such as focus groups, "futures" scenarios, conjoint analysis, and, yes, surveys—can still be leveraged to detect customer sacrifice. Just dust off your most recent research studies (which were likely searches for a *commonality* that would point only to shared—and preconditioned—expectations among customers), and examine them anew through a different lens: search for the *uniqueness* within the responses that suggests dimensions of sacrifice previously unnoticed or mistakenly thought insignificant. Even a single customer interaction can provide clues about an otherwise unarticulated sacrifice dimension across which all customers settle for less (or more) than what they want. Those thought to be outliers may in particular point to dimensions of sacrifice that "average" customers simply could not articulate.

Companies must also craft a new set of probes into customer behavior— "What do you really want?"—that displaces inquiries about satisfaction that ask merely, "How did we do?" For example, pneumatic valve producer Ross Controls of Troy, Michigan, innovated its ROSS/FLEX process to get its best customers (automakers, material-handling machine manufacturers, etc.) to work with its engineers (who are called "integrators" because they effectively combine the normally distinct functions of development, manufacturing, and marketing) to design the exact valve system that would create dramatic improvements in the customers' assembly-line performance. By focusing on the sacrifices customers currently face in their production lines, the integrator designs a prototype valve system starting from a library of modules. If the first prototype doesn't meet fully the customer's needs, the integrator makes adjustments and tries another one, and often a third or fourth, until a customized valve system eliminates all the known sacrifice.[3]

Because of its inherent interactivity, the Internet provides a great place for understanding sacrifice. Think of how relentlessly Amazon.com learns about each of its individual customers to create a unique purchasing experience for each one. It learns your name to welcome you back personally. It learns your address and credit card details to eliminate the need for you to type such mundane information. It even learns more than one credit card should you want to, say, differentiate between business and personal purchases, and it remembers the names and addresses of everyone to whom you've ever had Amazon.com ship a gift directly; each of these details can be reselected with a click of the mouse. It remembers every purchase you've ever made, even asking you whether you really want to proceed should you click to buy something you've purchased before. And of course Amazon.com uses that purchase history, via its collaborative filtering engine, to recommend other items that you very well might like based on the similar purchase histories of your fellow Amazon.com lovers. It even lets you deselect particular purchases so as not to include them in its recommendations, whether because they are one-time gifts or because of some other anomaly.

Cultivating Learning Relationships

A continually expanding array of interactive technologies—including electronic kiosks, the World Wide Web, personal digital assistants, and smartphones—enables companies to better learn the particular wants, needs, and preferences of not just thousands but millions of individual customers. The combination of Mass Customization in operations with what marketing gurus Don Peppers and Martha Rogers call *one-to-one marketing* forms the basis of a *learning relationship* that grows, deepens, and becomes

FIGURE 5-1

New learning curve

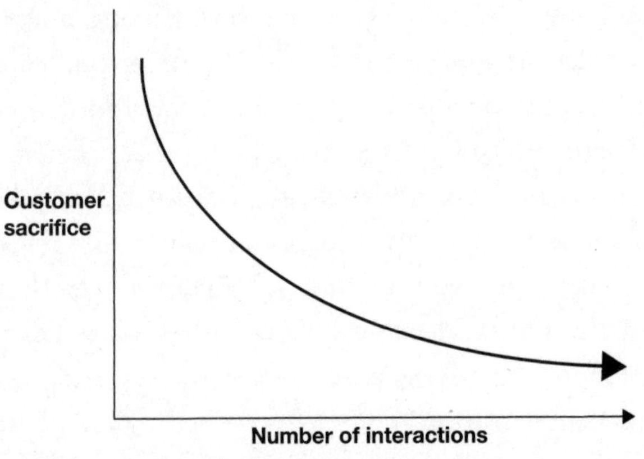

smarter over time.[4] The more customers teach the company, the better it can provide exactly what they want—and the more difficult it will be for competitors to lure them away. Even if a competitor were to build exactly the same capabilities, a customer already involved in a learning relationship with a firm would have to spend a considerable amount of time and energy teaching the competitor what the current firm already knows. That's why customers of Ross Controls remain loyal to ROSS/FLEX. A $20 billion division of General Motors (the company that seems to have patented supplier squeezing) won't buy pneumatic valves from anyone else and won't let its suppliers go elsewhere. James Zaguroli, Jr., CEO of Knight Industries, related that when a competitor tried to win his business away from Ross, he told them, "Why would I switch to you? You're already five product generations behind where I am with Ross."

In effect, mass customizers that cultivate such learning relationships drive down a new learning curve, as seen in figure 5-1.

Everyone's familiar with the old learning curve, in which costs come down with volume—the very basis of Mass Production. Here, customer sacrifice comes down over time as the company interacts with customers.[5] Think again about Amazon.com. Every time it learns something about you, it lowers the sacrifice you encounter the next time you shop with it. Every time you make a purchase, it incorporates that information into its collaborative filtering algorithm to better recommend something else you might want.

Now imagine that you are a diehard Amazon.com customer and one of its competitors—say, Walmart—develops exactly the same capabilities as Amazon.com. It can provide the same selection of goods (the modules of the customized Amazon.com architecture), learn your address, credit cards, and gift recipient information, even make the very same recommendations over time in the same way that Amazon.com does. Would you switch? No way! It would take you months to teach this new company what Amazon.com already knows. In the meantime, you would miss out on many custom recommendations that the new company would neglect to make while it was still learning your needs.

In this way, firms can keep their customers forever—with two provisos. One, the company doesn't excessively hike up its prices or cut back on service once in a learning relationship, and two, it doesn't miss the next technology wave. (Amazon.com, for example, developed its own e-book reader, the Kindle, to ensure it does not lose out should book purchases move rapidly from physical to electronic.) The advantages of this approach improve a company's fundamentals in significant ways:

- *Premium prices:* Because your offerings are tailored precisely to customer needs, your customers receive greater value and, as a result, willingly pay a premium price.

- *Reduced discounts:* Every time you sell an offering at a discounted price, you in effect pay customers to experience greater sacrifice. The less they sacrifice, the less you must push the product at promotional prices or discard it outright.
- *Greater revenue per customer:* Because you know more about each customer than does any competitor, customers keep coming back to you every time they enter the market for what you offer.
- *Higher number of customers* (at lower acquisition costs): Because your customers find the experience so pleasing, they tell their friends and associates, many of whom will also want to do business with you. These new customers will tell others, and so on, and so on.
- *Increased customer retention:* The more each customer teaches you about his individual wants, needs, and preferences, the more difficult it will be for him to obtain an equivalent level of value from a competitor.

Most important, those companies that systematically reduce customer sacrifice—eliminating the negative cues of the relationship—heighten the experience their customers have when using their goods or partaking of their services, thus fulfilling needs left unaddressed by their mass produced counterparts.

Responding to Various Kinds of Sacrifices

Mass Customization bids us to return to an axiom frequently ignored in the homogenized world of Mass Production: *every customer is unique*, and all deserve to have exactly what they want at a price they are willing to pay. Customers once were willing to subsume their uniqueness to benefit from the low prices of standardized offerings, but no longer. Companies must therefore efficiently and systematically reduce the customer sacrifice that occurs whenever a unique individual encounters standardized goods or services designed for some imaginary average. Surely no one-size-fits-all approach will serve to eliminate sacrifice; that would run contrary to the very notion of Mass Customization. Indeed, four different categories of sacrifice need attention. Each detracts from an individual's overall experience with a company's offering in a very specific way, and this requires a different customization approach if it is to be eliminated.

In response to individual customer sacrifice, mass customizers can change or not change the actual *product*—the functionalities of a good or the dimensions of a service. Similarly, they can change or not change the *representation* of the product—its description, packaging, marketing materials, placement, terms and conditions, name, stated use, or anything else outside the good or service itself. (Whereas a company's modular architecture lies in the domain of the product itself, the environmental architecture lies in the domain of its representation.) As seen in figure 5-2, these strategic choices yield four distinct approaches to customization: collaborative, adaptive, cosmetic, and transparent. Each is appropriate for reducing a different kind of sacrifice that, in turn, provides the basis for a particular type of experience.[6]

Collaborative Customization: The Exploring Experience

First, customers sacrifice when forced to make difficult and multidimensional *either-or* choices, such as length versus width, complexity versus functionality, or amount of information versus relevancy. The inability to resolve these trade-offs with

FIGURE 5-2

Approaches to customization (types of sacrifice)

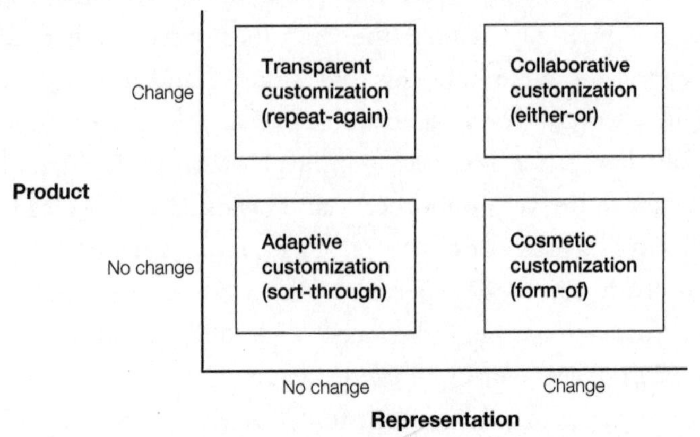

mass produced offerings propels many customers to work with such mass customizers as Dell, Andersen (windows), and Ross Controls, all of which employ *collaborative customization*, a process by which a company interacts directly with customers to determine what they need and then produces it for them. Collaborative customizers let customers explore ways to obtain what they desire in one dimension of the product without having to sacrifice in another dimension.

Dell's customers need not buy standard computers off the shelf of the nearest big box retailer but instead can go online to order only and exactly the system they want. Ross Controls customers no longer must wait months for a new product to come off the line. Instead, they explore with their ROSS/FLEX integrator potential improvements in their processes through successive, rapidly manufactured prototypes. And Andersen customers no longer have to wait for their homes to be built to see what the windows will look like. Instead they get to see the final outcome on a computer screen after exploring myriad possibilities with an Andersen distributor. A host of celebrated companies—adidas and Nike in athletic shoes, Tennant in floor-cleaning equipment, The Hartford in insurance support, Build-A-Bear Workshop in stuffed-animal toys, McGraw-Hill in textbooks, to name a few—embrace collaborative customization as a means of reducing the sacrifice prevalent when customers face too much choice and unnecessary trade-offs. The end result: a new kind of design experience.

Consider choosing a pair of eyeglasses. Few people can walk into a store and easily figure out exactly what frames they want by wading through the row upon row of empty frames placed in tray after tray on shelf after shelf. Yet Japanese company Paris Miki draws exact eyewear specifications from each interaction with consumers, thanks to collaborative customization.

The Tokyo-based company, one of the largest eyewear retailers in the world, spent five years developing the Mikissimes Design System. This design tool both eliminates the customer's need to review myriad choices when selecting a pair of rimless eyeglasses and turns the design interaction into an *exploring experience*. The optician first takes a digital picture of the consumer's face, which the Mikissimes Design System analyzes for distinctive attributes. The system also takes into account a set of adjectives selected by the consumer about the kind of look he desires (formal, traditional, natural, sporty, elegant, etc.). The system then recommends a distinctive lens size and shape and displays the lenses on the digital image of each consumer's face. But this only begins the exploration. The consumer and optician next collaborate to adjust the shape and size of the lenses (by rotating, enlarging, or even using a mouse to create a new curve) until both of them like the look. In similar fashion, they together select from a number of options for the nose bridge, hinges, and arms until the consumer discovers the pair of eyeglasses he desires—exactly. The final step: the optician presents a photo-quality picture of the customer wearing a pair of eyeglasses that have yet to be produced. (One more thing: the customer receives the actual glasses, mass customized, in as little as an hour.)

Collaborative customizers work with individual customers to change first the representation of the product and then, once the customer figures out his true needs, the product itself. Customer and customizer thus mutually determine the value to be created. The customizer relinquishes some control of the process, allowing the buyer to participate directly in decision making and even some of the setup work. Build-A-Bear Workshop, for example, is basically a retail factory, but one that cements a relationship not only between the company and its consumers but also between the guest and the stuffed animal. As Chief Executive Bear Maxine Clark told us, "When guests pick out exactly the right stuffed animal they want from our thirty-odd assortment, by the time they themselves stuff it to just the right amount, take a heart and then close their eyes to make a wish on it, and then choose clothing and accessories in concert with our associates, they are so connected to their stuffed animal that they become friends for life." The seemingly necessary trade-offs found in selecting and using most mass produced goods vanish when customers more richly explore their unique needs in this way. Ideally, in addition to getting exactly what they want, customers often uncover aspects of their own wants and needs that they never before knew existed.

Adaptive Customization: The Experimenting Experience

The second kind of customer sacrifice occurs when customers are presented with too many finished goods or too many component parts and must engage in an unwieldy *sort-through* process.

Here, companies should adopt the approach of *adaptive customization*. In this case, neither the product itself nor the representation of the product is changed for the individual customer; rather, the good or service itself changes as needed, with or without customer input, using *customizable* functionality embedded into the offering.

If the universe of customer demand spans an enormous set of possibilities, it's imperative to use some form of adaptive customization. For example, Lutron Electronics Co., Inc., of Coopersburg, Pennsylvania, makes lighting controls (switches, dimmers, etc.) that allow for an immense degree of customer-unique variation. With the exception of cookie-cutter buildings, such as franchise restaurants, every customer's environment is unremittingly unique.[7] The shape, decor, and window placement of each room vary. Additionally, weather conditions affecting external light change from day to day and hour to hour, as do the composition of people in the room and the way those people use it. So, while Lutron collaborates with customers on some issues (such as matching colors of switch plates), it makes use of adaptive customization by having customers experiment with the lighting system in their own office or home. The company's GRAFIK Eye System, for example, connects various lights in a room and lets users test and then program different effects for, say, lively parties, romantic moments, or quiet evenings of reading. Rather than having to adjust separate light switches for each use, customers spend time up front programming settings until they find the right combinations. They then achieve the desired effects merely by punching in the programmed settings each time they use the room.

Collaboration remains the right approach when each customer must choose from a vast number of elements or components to get the desired functionality or design. When alternative combinations can be built into the product, however, adaptive customization becomes a promising alternative for efficiently making many different options available to each customer. And the process of *experimenting* with the possibilities becomes an experience unto itself. For example, Select Comfort of Minneapolis, Minnesota, designs and manufactures the Sleep Number Firmness Control System: mattresses that contain air chambers that automatically adjust to the desired firmness level of anyone who lies on them. Using a handheld controller, people can play with various levels of firmness, and couples can even select different levels on each side of the bed. Similarly, Peapod, an online grocery-shopping and delivery service based in Skokie, Illinois, and owned by Royal Ahold of the Netherlands, eliminates the sort-through sacrifice inherent in going to a grocery store filled with aisle after aisle of items. Its PC software and online service enable customers first to create personal shopping lists to store only those items they want to peruse. These lists can be recalled at a moment's notice. For less frequent purchases, customers can search product information through various sorting methods (such as price, brand, or nutritional content).

With adaptive customization, customers independently derive their own value. Adjustable controls, as represented in Lutron's programmable settings, Select Comfort's handheld controller, and Peapod's software, allow customers to experiment time and again with different combinations and permutations. Once they have figured out what is right for them, they no longer have to sort through all the alternatives each time they want to use the good or access the service. As Joel Spira, chairman of Lutron Electronics and the inventor to first put a microprocessor in a lighting control, says, "Creating adaptive controls differentiates us from the competition, and the way we do it lets customers easily and even enjoyably figure out the settings right for them." This approach to Mass Customization, fundamentally different from collaborative customization, also creates customer-unique value.[8] The adjustable nature of the designed interaction with the product itself promotes the experimentation required to find that value.

Cosmetic Customization: The Gratifying Experience

When customers sacrifice not on the basis of a product's functionality but based on its form—how it is packaged or presented, where or when it is delivered—then companies exploit cosmetic customization. Based on what we call *form-of* sacrifice, this third approach presents a standard good or service differently to different customers. The product is not customized (as with collaborative) or made customizable (as with adaptive); instead, a standard offering is *packaged* specially for each customer. By wrapping the good in a customized representation—perhaps through custom printing or packaging, tailored marketing materials, personal placement on delivery, private labeling, or personalization of other stated terms and conditions—each customer obtains the ego-gratifying experience of seeing the item personalized "just for me."

Hertz does this with its #1 Club Gold program. Each customized element alters only the representation of its rental cars and not the base product itself. Yet it is enjoyed by customers because each instance of customized packaging clearly shows that the company values the customer. Similarly, Zazzle, of Redwood City, California, created a simple but exceedingly effective website for customizing illustrations on T-shirts, mugs, mouse pads, and just about anything else on which anyone would want to place text, a logo, graphics, or any other form of image. Consumers simply select the type of product they want to cosmetically customize, often choosing size, color, and so on, and then upload the text or image they want to place on the item. The site's design tool lets consumers orient the design and otherwise modify it to fit their exact desires. Very quick, very simple, very "me."

In the business-to-business arena, Whirlpool Corporation successfully wrapped its next-day delivery program, called Quality Express, around its standard Whirlpool, KitchenAid, Maytag, and Roper appliance lines to create customer-unique value. Originally, dealers could order any quantity of appliances they wanted—as long as it was a full truckload. This meant that dealers couldn't always tell consumers when their appliances would arrive, because it depended on what and when others would order. Now the company schedules each distributor for a set number of deliveries per week—five, four, three, two, or one—based on annual volume, and efficiently delivers exactly the right set of appliances each dealer ordered (thanks to a sophisticated logistics system that integrates manufacturing plants, regional warehouses, local distribution centers, and contract trucks via real-time information). Furthermore, because Quality Express can deliver every day, Whirlpool uses the service to accommodate retail customers that have an unusual need outside the normal delivery schedule, with a focus on making each dealer feel special. Quality Express also adds other tailored services to personalize each delivery. At home-builder sites, for instance, uniformed drivers uncrate boxes, rearrange door swings, and install ice makers immediately before mortgage closings. The drivers even call from cell phones en route to make sure the dealers prepare for the delivery.

For many companies, cosmetic customization provides a starting point from which to offer customers a personalized experience. While the basic functionality of their product remains the same, cosmetic customizers signal an acknowledgment of the diverse form-of requirements found among their customers. They postpone many activities in order to perform them before the watching eyes of the customers, who feel that the performance is being staged just for them. As former Whirlpool executive Ralph Hake said about Quality Express, "The value we provide to our distributors is visibly demonstrated whenever they see our truck coming down the road, and in every added service we perform for them, with them, or in front of them." Whether delivering appliances to distributors, images on T-shirts, or people to rental cars, this approach admittedly appeals to the desire for personal gratification inherent in each one of us. By customizing the representation of a standardized offering, the customizer gives its customers personalized attention.

Transparent Customization: The Discovering Experience

Finally, when customers must repeatedly perform the same task or provide the same information, they encounter *repeat-again* sacrifice. Such impositions serve only to bother customers and detract from their overall experience. In such cases, transparent customization does the trick, providing individual customers with a tailored offering without letting them know explicitly (through representational changes) that it is customized for them. Customers see the value of the offering only *through* its standard representation.

ChemStation, a manufacturer and distributor of industrial cleaning goods in Dayton, Ohio, transparently customizes the formulation of individual cleaning products for a wide variety of commercial uses—from car washes and truck depots to restaurant kitchens and paper mills. It doesn't bother sharing the details regarding the particular compounds used to address a customer's cleaning needs. Instead, it tacitly formulates exactly the right combination for each customer and then represents everyone's customized good as being the same "ChemStation Solution."

Every customer even gets the same company logo emblazoned on the side of every storage tank. As a result, customers focus more on how nice and clean their facility is and less on the specific attributes of the supporting product, the exact nature of which remains elusive.

Transparent customizers fulfill the needs of individual customers in an indiscernible way. Instead of requiring customers to take the time to describe their needs, transparent customizers observe behaviors over time to determine predictable preferences and then presciently fulfill those preferences. Of course, a business must have the luxury of time to deepen its knowledge of customers and to move progressively closer to meeting individual preferences. To become a transparent customizer, a business also must have a standard *package*—like a ChemStation tank—into which it places the product's customized features or components. In this way, transparent customization is the exact opposite of cosmetic customization, which has standard content but a customized package.

Businesses ripe for transparent customization include those whose customers don't want to be bothered with direct collaboration, often because the company asks them to repeat information they've already provided. For example, to avoid annoying customers by asking the same standard questions every time they check in to a Ritz-Carlton hotel ("King size or two doubles? Low floor or high floor?"), the chain established a less intrusive means of learning about individual needs. Its associates *observe* the preferences that individual guests manifest or state during each stay, whether it be for hypoallergenic pillows, contemporary jazz radio stations, or perhaps even Pepsi over Coke. The company then stores that information in a database and uses it to form a learning relationship with individual guests, thus eliminating unnecessary service intrusions on subsequent visits. The more frequently someone stays in Ritz-Carlton hotels, the more the company learns, and the more customized goods and services it fits into the standard Ritz-Carlton room, thereby increasing the guest's preference for that hotel over others.

Ritz-Carlton, a unit of Marriott, chose transparent customization specifically because its management wants to create a mystique around the fulfilling of guests' individual preferences. How the hotel does it may elude them, but guests discover they've had a particularly pleasant experience whenever they stay at a Ritz-Carlton. Similarly, ChemStation founder George Homan hit on this form of customization because he realized that his potential customers all wanted to run their business and not manage their industrial soap: "We want them to discover the value we provide as they're using the soap, not think about what it is or how it gets there. We don't want our customers to ever think about how our product gets there, only that it always is there." Every order for soap, as with every request at a hotel, is a routine sacrifice. In any industry, those companies that practice transparent customization eliminate unwanted intrusions, simplifying interactions to let customers discover the offering's essential nature.

Choosing the Right Approach

Which approach should you choose? There's no simple answer to that question. As summarized in table 5-1, not only does each of the four types of customization address a different kind of sacrifice, but also each acts as the basis for a distinct kind of experience. Manufacturers and service providers must discern the uniqueness of their offerings, ascertain the sacrifices their customers currently experience, and then identify which form of customization will yield the best results. Often a combination of approaches is needed to address complex sacrifice issues.

TABLE 5-1

Customization distinctions

	Customization approach			
Characteristic	**Collaborative**	**Adaptive**	**Cosmetic**	**Transparent**
Sacrifice addressed	Either-or	Sort-through	Form-of	Repeat-again
Nature of offering	Customized	Customizable	Packaged	Packable
Nature of value	Mutually determined	Independently derived	Visibly demonstrated	Indiscernibly fulfilled
Process characteristics	Sharable	Adjustable	Postponable	Predictable
Nature of interaction	Direct	Indirect	Overt	Covert
Method of learning	Conversation	Solicitation	Recognition	Observation
Basis of experience	Exploring	Experimenting	Gratifying	Discovering

More important, why choose to customize at all? It's very simple: customizers stage fundamentally different experiences for customers. They *ing* the thing. Collaborative customizers Andersen and Paris Miki create new window- and eyeglass-*designing* experiences. Adaptive customization yields unique Lutron *lighting*, Select Comfort *sleeping*, and Peapod grocery-*shopping* experiences. Hertz offers a distinctive car-*renting* experience through cosmetic customization, while Whirlpool uses this approach to stage a one-of-a-kind appliance-*delivering* experience for retail dealers and home builders. ChemStation, on the other hand, uses transparent customization to enhance the soap-*dispensing* experience, and Ritz-Carlton uses the same approach to turn a room into a truly memorable *lodging* experience.

All mass customizers create new value in the Experience Economy. Rival mass producers, lacking any distinctive approach to eliminating customer sacrifice, will quickly find their offerings commoditized. We heard it best expressed some years ago by a Pennzoil Products Company executive who feared the day when people would say, "Motor oil is motor oil is motor oil." Such a fate awaits any company that doesn't get its act together by helping customers experience less sacrifice.

★ INTERMISSION ★

A Refreshing Experience

When Sir Colin Marshall first realized that British Airways was really in the business of orchestrating experiences, he thought that the "wear-out factor" for the BA brand was "somewhere in the five-year range. Now I am pretty convinced that five years is about the maximum that you can go without refreshing the brand."[1] Actually, experience stagers must constantly refresh their experiences—change or add elements that keep the offering new, exciting, and worth paying money to experience all over again. Failing to do so devalues the offering. Rather than an experience that remains the same between visits, people would rather try a new one where they don't know quite what to expect and are sure to be pleasantly surprised.

That's why the repeat business at many eatertainment restaurants is poor: guests know exactly what to expect each time, both in the restaurants and in the retail stores. Restaurateur T. Scott Gross, who wrote a series of insightful books on what he calls "positively outrageous service," describes a strikingly simple way to surprise diners. He tells of Philip Romano opening an out-of-the-way Italian restaurant named Macaroni's (now Romano's Macaroni Grill, a chain of hundreds of restaurants).[2] Rather than issue discount coupons to encourage new patronage (a ubiquitous, expectation-setting practice among many restaurant chains these days), Romano gave away free meals to every diner in the restaurant once each month on a Monday or Tuesday. The random practice was announced by a letter that arrived at each table in place of the check, saying how awkward it seemed to charge guests for a meal, so this one was free. Whereas most restaurants might extend such generosity only when customers have experienced poor service or a bad meal (when some recompense is expected), Romano's restaurant did so only after guests had been very well served with very good food (and guests expected nothing more than to pay their check). The surprise of the free meal created both a desire and a sense of obligation in guests to return again . . . and again . . . and again. Gross figured that surprising customers in this way cost Romano perhaps 3.3 percent of his monthly gross, but it had a much greater impact on customers than an ad budget of that size or a 3.3 percent discount across the board. It turned an already good dinner service into a memorable dining experience.

Staging Customer Surprise

Reducing customer sacrifice through Mass Customization requires an awareness of individual customer needs and the behavior they influence. This awareness lets companies deliberately and systematically take the next step toward more experiential offerings by instigating *customer surprise*, which is perhaps the single most important ingredient needed by any manufacturer or service provider to begin staging memorable experiences.

Contrasted with both customer satisfaction and sacrifice, when companies stage customer surprise they exploit the difference between what the customer *gets to perceive* and what the customer *expects to get*.

Customer Surprise = What customer gets to perceive
− What customer expects to get

Rather than merely meet expectations (by providing satisfaction) or set new ones (by reducing sacrifice), companies deliberately attempt to *transcend* expectations, to go off in new (and unexpected) directions entirely. This doesn't mean trying to "exceed" expectations, for that would suggest an improvement along a known axis of competition, nor does it mean uncovering new dimensions on which to compete; those are the domains of satisfaction and sacrifice, respectively. Rather, it means *staging the unexpected*.

Creating such events still requires a platform of satisfaction and sacrifice. As indicated in figure I-1, without concerted and fruitful efforts to drive up customer satisfaction and drive down customer sacrifice, there will be no foundation on which to instigate customer surprise. Companies embracing the 3-S Model shown in this figure must go beyond "how we did" and even "what you want" to "what you *remember*."

The most memorable flight experiences, for example, have nothing to do with the expectations of normal—good or bad—airline service but with events that occur outside the domain of expectations. These may include times you have read a particularly

FIGURE I-1

3-S Model

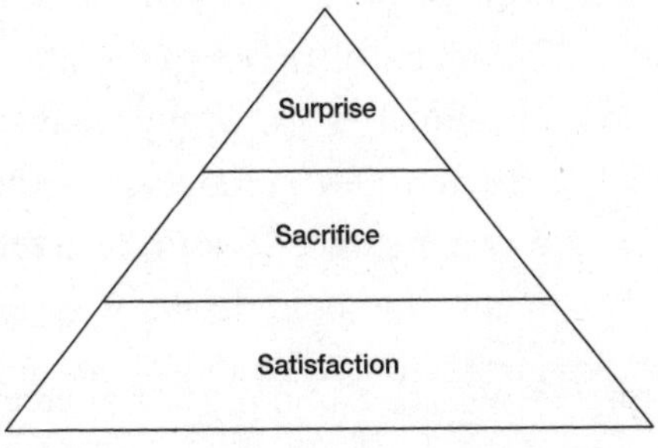

eye-opening book, have met a celebrity, or have become totally engaged in conversation with a seatmate.

The Reverend Jim Ignatowski. Recognize the name? On one episode of the old TV show *Taxi*, this usually atrocious (but fun-loving) cabbie decided to become the best taxi driver in the world. He did it by surprising his patrons with totally unexpected events: he served sandwiches and drinks, engaged them in sparkling repartee, conducted tours of the city, and even sang Frank Sinatra tunes over a jury-rigged intercom. So engaging was Iggy's use of customer surprise that the experience of being *in* his cab yielded greater value to his customers than the service of being transported by the cab from point A to point B. And in the TV show, at least, Iggy's customers happily responded with bigger tips. By asking to go around the block again just to prolong his enjoyment, one patron even paid *more* for demonstrably *poorer* service; after all, it took longer to get to his destination. The service Iggy provided—taxi transportation—was simply the stage for the experience that he was really selling that week.

Real-world entrepreneurs also employ surprise to turn mundane services into truly memorable events. Consider one of the most basic of businesses, the shoe shine stand. Based in the airport of Kalamazoo, Michigan, Aaron Davis—not only a great shoe shine man but a showman as well—uses customer surprise in many ways. In addition to his meticulous touch when applying polish and the syncopated snaps of his cloth—sensations rare but not unique to Davis—he introduces elements to the shoe shine experience that have little or nothing to do with polishing shoes. If he finds a loose thread on a stitch, Davis produces a pocket lighter to burn it off. And at the conclusion of the shine, he not only ties each shoe's laces but then gently pulls up the guest's socks. Davis also offers proverbs to guests in need of a pick-me-up. And should a hurried traveler who regularly gets a shine fail to stop by one week, the very next shine is, as Davis says, "on me." From then on, such travelers make sure they leave enough time to take in a shine.

Unfortunately, larger enterprises often lack the surprise savvy of smaller businesses. But bigness is no excuse. Managers must stop setting routine expectations and start thinking creatively about how to leverage some service dimension to stage memorable surprises. Why do airlines upgrade only their most frequent current flyers to first class? That well-dressed college kid flying to New York for an interview with a consulting firm, for which he will fly every week in his imminent career, may be the best person to surprise with a seat in front of the curtain. A hotel could occasionally place a storage canister, the kind resembling a can of soda, in minibars so that a surprised guest may discover, say, a roll of fifty one-dollar bills inside with a note confirming that the guest may keep the money, compliments of the host. Wouldn't that create greater loyalty, more repeat business, and more guest referrals than issuing discount certificates via direct-mail campaigns?

Companies should also rethink rebates. Automobile manufacturers, for instance, further commoditize their own products via constant rebate promotions—buy this or that model, get this much money back—setting expectations that focus prospects purely on price. Some 90 percent of car owners claim to be satisfied, according to an Arthur D. Little survey, and yet car buyers defect by the millions each year. Only 40 percent buy their next car from the same manufacturer (let alone get the same model) that supposedly "satisfied" them the last time. Surprise payments sent unexpectedly to car buyers—after the purchase—rewarding them for their selections would do more to generate repeat sales. Rebates assume a one-period model in a multi-period world; surprise programs always help the company influence the buyer's next decision.

Consider, too, the many "frequent purchase" programs sponsored across a wide spectrum of businesses, from airlines to parking garages, from credit card companies to coffee bars. Designed to foster customer loyalty, these programs in fact have a fatal flaw: they encourage customers to expect free goods and services. While some increased purchasing frequency may be stimulated by giving away merchandise (in what's essentially a retailing equivalent of the old manufacturing line, "What we lose on each customer we'll make up in volume"), many customers join multiple programs within a given product category, and they all know that other customers can participate in the same programs. Customers are simply not engaged on a personal level, and over time, they take the benefits for granted; after all, they "earned" their free stuff. As with rebates, this serves merely to commoditize a company's offerings.

Instead of leading customers to expect free goods, companies could use the same money to create a memorable experience. Like Romano, these companies could give away the same percentage of items at random on certain days. Every fifteenth or twentieth item sold at the store could be free, for instance, or every fifteenth or twentieth customer could receive all his items for free. Alternatively, a store's register system could transparently inform the sales associate that this particular customer is highly valued and should be surprised with a purchase on the house.

Wait Until You Hear This One . . .

To truly differentiate themselves, businesses must focus first on increasing customer satisfaction, then on eliminating customer sacrifice, and finally on creating customer surprise. Taking these three steps will help shift any company up the Progression of Economic Value. But—surprise!—there's actually a fourth *S* in the 3-S Model. Once a company successfully stages customer surprise, customers start *expecting* to be surprised. There's nothing wrong with that, as long as the company then stages customer suspense as well. Built on a platform of surprise, *customer suspense* is the gap between what the customer *remembers* from past surprises and what he *does not yet know* about upcoming events:

Customer Suspense = What customer does not yet know
– What customer remembers from past

One example should suffice to demonstrate customer suspense. Before Continental Airlines united with United Airlines, premier Continental flyers (those who traveled fifty thousand miles or sixty segments per year) received an elaborately packaged kit containing priority baggage check tags, upgrade coupons, a frequent flyer program guide, and other incidental reference material. The first year customers received this unadvertised package, they were indeed pleasantly surprised. In year two, Continental may have managed to surprise a few customers (those who forgot the previous package). But for Continental's consistently high-traveling customers, after three, four, or five years of receiving the same old kit . . . well, they not only came to expect it, they considered it a ho-hum occasion. Now suppose that Continental had cleverly changed the contents each year, one year adding a humorous letter from the CEO (à la Warren Buffet's annual stockholder letters), the next, a gift gleaned from knowledge about the past year's travel (for instance, a subscription to some magazine, a free dinner at a restaurant in the frequent destination city, a fine cigar or bottle of wine), and the next, maybe even a new piece of luggage to replace the one worn out by such frequent travel. Then Continental's very best customers would happily look forward to the next package rather than be bored by its inevitable arrival. This suspense, built on top of "how we did," "what you want," and "what you remember," creates a sense of anticipation that encourages customers to actively look forward to doing more business with the airline—"what will happen"—just to make darn sure they maintain that premier status and get next year's package.[3] (Time will tell whether the merger of Continental into United will focus the company solely on reducing internal operating costs or whether the new United will become a platform to respond anew to unique customer needs.)

Together, the four *S*'s in the 3-S Model form a framework for enhancing customer relationships. When managed in unison, satisfaction, sacrifice, surprise, and suspense help companies encourage buyers to purchase goods and services for fundamentally new and different reasons. No longer do customers purchase goods merely for their functional use but also for the experiences created during purchase and use. Similarly, clients do not buy services merely for the sake of having a benefit delivered by another party but for the memorable events surrounding those services.

In the Experience Economy, companies should realize that they must make *memories* (and not goods) and create the stage for generating greater economic value (and not deliver services). It is time to get your act together, for goods and services are no longer enough. Customers now want experiences, and they're willing to pay admission for them. There's new work to do, and only those who perform that work so as to truly engage their guests will succeed in this new economy.

CHAPTER 6

Work Is Theatre

BARBRA STREISAND HAD NOT YET gotten her act together as an aspiring actress and singer when she tried out for Harold Rowe's musical *I Can Get It for You Wholesale.* In his book *Audition,* casting director Michael Shurtleff relates how he thought the then-unknown actress was ideal for the role of Miss Marmelstein.[1] He was concerned, however, that Streisand's prominent nose would not get past producer David Merrick, who had told him, "I don't want any ugly girls in my show." Despite the admonition, or perhaps because of it, Shurtleff scheduled Streisand for the last audition slot.

Streisand, draped in a gaudy raccoon coat and wearing mismatched shoes, walked in late, chewing gum. (She had found the "fabulous" shoes at a thrift shop on the way to the audition, Streisand explained to Shurtleff, Merrick, and director Arthur Laurents, but only one of each pair fit.) Curtly, she ordered a stool brought on stage. Once settled on the stool, she began to sing, but stopped unexpectedly after only a few notes. She started and stopped again, this time to remove her gum and stick it beneath the seat of the commandeered stool. Finally, she sang the full number and, as Shurtleff put it, "She mesmerized 'em." She then sang two more tunes and left. After a heated argument, Merrick succumbed to the wishes of Shurtleff and Laurents: Streisand got the part. As the three prepared to leave, Laurents, who had taken a seat on the stool, ran his hand underneath it, because he had noticed that Streisand had failed to retrieve her gum. To his surprise, there was no gum! Chomping so visibly—during the audition—*had been an act of pure theatre*. She wasn't chewing gum in order to calm her nerves but to create a specific impression on the potential buyers of her theatre skills.

One can only speculate as to why Streisand chose this particular set of behaviors to portray her character on stage. Perhaps she wanted to make the impression "I can *sing* it for you wholesale," or "Appearances don't matter—it's the vocal cords that count," perhaps even "It ain't over 'til the ugly lady sings." Her tactics launched what became, by any measure, a remarkable career. Whatever her motivation, even during her humble beginnings, she understood the secret to her later success: recognizing that each and every action contributes to the total experience being staged, no matter what the venue. Businesses entering the Experience Economy must be no less deliberate.

Consider the business of baseball. The past twenty-five years have seen an unprecedented level of new ballpark construction; more than twenty of the thirty Major League Baseball franchises have built new stadia, and still others have undergone major renovations to enhance the fan experience. Yet the remarkable turnaround of one its franchises, the Cleveland Indians, attests to the benefit of also considering the value of theatre in deliberately staging events in these new venues. On April 4, 1994, the Indians played the Seattle Mariners in their first official game in Jacobs Field (since renamed Progressive Field), a new $175 million stadium built specifically to showcase professional baseball. Prior to 1994, fewer than five thousand season ticket packages were purchased annually by Cleveland fans. In the new ballpark, the team went on to sell out all 43,368 seats for 455 consecutive games. Of course, the new stadium did not by itself account for the entire jump in sales; other teams have built new facilities and have not met with nearly the same early success. The difference? The Cleveland Indians management recognized that the new venue represented a new stage for enacting deliberate non-baseball performances of its own.

That crisp day in April 1994 was not, in fact, the first time the Indians played a game in the new ballpark. It had happened two days earlier when the team contested the Pittsburgh Pirates in an exhibition game. A full house, made up of many of the same individuals who would later attend Opening Day, poured into the stadium on a Saturday afternoon to get their first taste of the new Indians and their first view of the new facility. The event did not threaten to spoil the thrill of attending the first official game because this was a dress rehearsal, a chance for fans to preview the new Indians extravaganza.

Just outside the park, a uniformed man busied himself with a broom and dustpan-on-a-stick, sweeping the sidewalk immediately adjacent to the East Ninth Street entrance. His blue pants and red-and-white striped shirt stood out among the passing crowd, clearly demonstrating that this street sweeper worked as an employee of the ballpark. Many people witnessed the seemingly small act, but few paused to examine the extraordinary nature of his gestures: his whisks gathered no debris, for the place *already* sparkled! After all, the grounds couldn't very well get dirty when no one had yet visited. So why did the man perform this work? For the same reason Streisand chewed her nonexistent gum: his was an act of pure theatre. He did not sweep in order to clean the pavement but to create a specific impression on the passing parade of first-time customers. After playing for sixty-two years in Cleveland Municipal Stadium, the ball club had directed this individual to don his costume and sweep in order to support the Indians' new theme: "There Is No Place Like Home"—that is, to show ticket holders that the new ballpark was clean, safe, comfortable, and eager to come to life.[2]

The Act of Acting

Political commentator and avid baseball fan George Will has helped many casual observers of baseball to see the game differently in his punctilious book *Men at Work*. His single-minded point: "Professional baseball is work," demanding mental as well as physical exertion of those who take the field.[3] Will strove to encourage a greater appreciation of the game by persuading readers of one fact: the players are working. Major League Baseball, the business, furnishes the workplace. Players practice, analyze past performances, and constantly adjust the way they go about their duties. These star performers share the stage with extras, who, like the sweeper at Jacobs Field, labor in more minor roles.

All business, as well as the work that defines it, from executive suites to factory floors, demands the same kind of performance as that featured on Broadway and in ballparks. In the Experience Economy, performers of all sorts—executives, managers, and other laborers—must take a different view of their occupations. Work is theatre. Think about it. Pause. Reflect. And now say it aloud: Work *is* theatre.

In acknowledging this truth, we strive not to detail every nuance of theatre, nor to provide a comprehensive list of theatre how-tos. Neither can we resolve any number of alternative or conflicting views of how theatre is best conducted. Rather, we simply aim to share enough about theatre to persuade you to think differently about your work and to embrace some principles of theatre as your model for work in the Experience Economy.[4]

Let us be very clear: we do not mean to present work *as* theatre. It is not a metaphor but a model. We do not apply the principles of theatre to work merely to force new comparisons. Too many metaphors already litter the contemporary business landscape. We have no interest in dancing with elephants, swimming with sharks, toppling the pyramids, jumping the curve, finding blue oceans, or pursuing any other kind of mismanagement-by-metaphor that all too often distracts executives and managers from the real issues they face. Rather, we seek to focus attention on the quintessentially dramatic nature of an enterprise. Thus, we literally mean, Work *is* theatre.

The word *drama* derives from the Greek *drao*, meaning simply "to do." In all companies, whether or not managers recognize it, the workers are playing, not in some game but in what should be a well-conceived, correctly cast, and convincingly portrayed real-life drama of *doing*. Indeed, understanding this crucial point brings whole new meaning to often-used business terms borrowed from or shared with the performing arts, such as *production, performance, method, role, scenario*, and a host of others.

Studies of theatre often begin with Aristotle's profound *Poetics*.[5] It serves as the foundation of our Western understanding of theatre, even with its emphasis on literary forms. Aristotle's notion of plot—what he called "the arrangement of the incidents"—forms the basis of any staged experience and the sequencing of cues required to create a desired impression. And his components of plot—surprising reversals, progressive revelation, unity and balance of events, and the emotional effect of tragedy—explain much about what makes an experience memorable. Likewise, his prerequisites for a compelling portrayal—good choices, befitting the role played, and consistency within character—delineate suitable job qualifications for anyone cast in the staging of an experience. Indeed, in defining theatre, Aristotle differentiated it from all other daily activities. Consider some of the following theatre concepts advanced by Aristotle and their implications for work.[6]

First and foremost is the issue of *choice*. Acts of theatre demand that boundaries be drawn; actors must formulate and pose tough questions that no one else can ask or answer for them; and they must discern the significant from the insignificant elements in any play performed. Even those businesses that do not yet stage experiences must understand that whenever employees work in front of customers, an act of theatre occurs. What should occur on that stage, and what should be relegated to offstage activities? One grocery clerk talking over a customer's head to the clerk in the next aisle about what they're going to do after work may seem to them insignificant, but for the customer it is an act of indifference. So what acts make for compelling theatre? The grocery clerk should ask himself how he might scan the canned goods with flair, what dramatic voice and entertaining words he might use when asking for a credit card, and especially how to perform the personal touches that come with exchanging cash, credit card, or receipt. The most important questions are often those for which no answer appears readily available, but you know an answer would prove invaluable to your performance.

Second, consider the *sequence, progression*, and *duration* of events. How are work activities arranged? What continuums exist in the organization of events? Where does work begin, reach a dramatic climax, and have its dénouement? Consider an office sales call. When does it begin? When the sales representative makes an appointment with a secretary, the moment he arrives on-site, as he waits outside the door, or only on making eye contact with the prospect? Different answers yield decidedly different contexts within which to craft the performance. Once the rep is face-to-face with the prospect, how should the event proceed? With small talk? Or should the rep dispense with that and get right down to business? What sequence of discussion points—call them sales scenes—should be painted in the mind of the prospect over the course of the call? What's the best way to move toward the intended climax of the call, known as clinching the sale? The old saw in sales circles—that you should stop talking once you make the sale—should not be taken literally, but it does serve to signal that the culmination of the sales event has occurred and that now the task shifts to dealing with outcomes and bringing about an effective dénouement. Only after you thoughtfully answer questions such as these can any experience be captivatingly staged.

Finally, consider the *rhythm* and *tempo* of work, for these define the relationships between dramatic elements. What transitions present themselves and need to be managed? What building, diminution, contrast, and release enrich the scene's energy level? How many incidents of what intensity occur over specific periods of time? FedEx employees deliberately rush about to convey the impression of speed as the essence of the company, but so should the burger flippers in a fast-food joint, even when they aren't busy. (Visit Pike Place Fish Market in Seattle and specifically observe all the action that occurs when fish are *not* selling—action that induces customers to start buying!) Or think of a waitress in a fine restaurant, where every course presents a dramatic scene in the dining experience. How long should she make each last? How should the end of one course flow into the next? Should she unobtrusively remove the salad plates while making a show of refilling the water glasses, or perhaps the reverse? And at what precise right moment should she deliver the check? Answers to questions such as these distinguish engaging performances from the monotonous on the one hand and the overly intrusive on the other.

Think back to your last encounter with a cab driver, sales rep, or checkout clerk, and you will quickly come to the conclusion that these Aristotelian design elements, although known for thousands of years, remain regrettably absent from much work today.

Renowned stage director Peter Brook declared, "I can take any empty space and call it a bare stage. A man walks across this empty space whilst someone else is watching him, and this is all that is needed for an act of theatre to be engaged."[7] Business enterprises would gain an invaluable perspective by similarly declaring their work to be theatre. For when a business calls its workplace a bare stage, it opens up opportunities to distinguish itself from the myriad humdrum makers of goods and providers of services that perform work without recognizing the true nature of their acts. With theatre furnishing the operating model, even the most mundane of tasks can engage customers in a memorable way. Furthermore, new work elements, previously unimaginable within a goods and services mindset—such as sweeping clean sidewalks—can be introduced to this new stage solely to enhance the experience.

Technology-mediated interactions also present a bare stage for business theatre. Brenda Laurel provides a detailed application of Aristotle's philosophy to computer-based performances in her book *Computers as Theatre*. Laurel, believing human–computer interaction should be a "designed experience," defines principles and techniques using computers as a *medium* rather than an *interface*.[8] Describing this technological stage, she writes, "Thinking about interfaces is thinking too small. Designing human-computer experience isn't about building a better desktop. It's about creating imaginary worlds that have a special relationship to reality—worlds in which we can extend, amplify, and enrich our own capabilities to think, feel, and act."[9] Exactly. It is clear from Laurel's book (despite her unfortunate use of the word *as* in its title) that she truly believes that working with computers is—or at least should be—theatre.

Laurel also analyzes the model of dramatic structure advanced by nineteenth-century performance theorist Gustav Freytag in explaining the structure of compelling performances. Plotting complication over time, Laurel presents the "Freytag Triangle" in not three but seven stages, as seen in figure 6-1. These are exposition (introducing the context), inciting incident (setting the action in motion), rising action (rapidly increasing possibilities and intensity), crisis (heightened activities and obstacles), climax (of the many things that could happen, only one does), falling action (resulting consequences), and finally the dénouement (tying together plot threads; a return to normalcy).[10] A too-flat structure, or one that climaxes too early or too late, results in a much less engaging experience than the ideal that Freytag identified. That explains why making instant coffee lacks the appeal of brewing one's own cup (even if in a single-serve maker), as well as why the morning frenzy of finding one's own cup on the round delivery shelf at Starbucks actually enhances the experience by

FIGURE 6-1

Dramatic structure

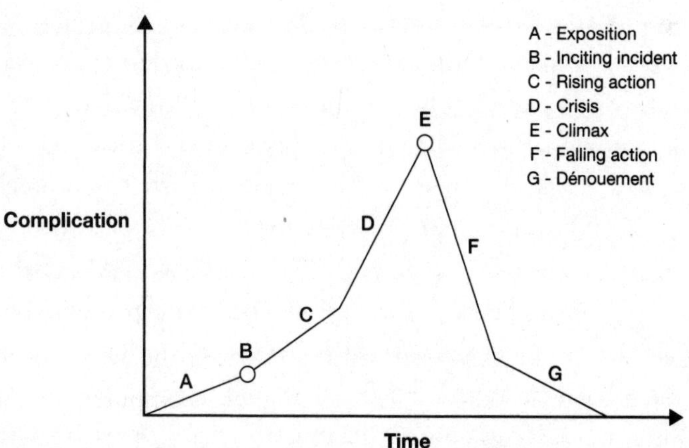

Source: Brenda Laurel, *Computers as Theatre* (Reading, MA: Addison-Wesley Publishing Company, 1993), p. 86; derived from Gustav Freytag, *Technique of the Drama*, 2d ed. (Chicago: Scott, Foresman, 1898).

making the coffee more cherished once secured from the hovering masses. (It's indeed worse service, but it stages a more compelling experience!)

In the emerging Experience Economy, any work observed directly by a customer must be recognized within the dramatic structure of the performance as an act of theatre. Indeed, flight attendants and hotel staff routinely perform acts of theatre when they direct patrons to the nearest exit or hotel room. The work of retail store associates is theatre when they straighten merchandise on a shelf. Bank tellers, insurance agents, and real estate brokers engage in theatre when they explain terms and conditions. So do cabbies when they converse with taxi riders. Your costumed UPS route driver performs an act of theatre with every package he delivers, and FedEx's overnighting is absolutely, positively theatre. Watch your food server the next time you dine out: the taking of orders, the placing of dishes, the busing of tables—it's all theatre. Selling, whether the salesperson pitches automobiles or bottles of perfume, is theatre. A presentation by an ad agency to a client's marketing manager, after all, is an act of theatre. Doctors who perform surgical operations in an amphitheater also perform theatrical operations by the side of every patient's bed. But how differently (and more memorably) would all these activities be performed if those executing them understood that their work is theatre and acted accordingly?

We've all heard the phrase, "Walk the talk." This platitude takes on meaning when we recognize that work is theatre. That's because it not only means practicing in person what one espouses in public but also declares that *someone else is watching*.[11] The very notion of aligning behavior with stated values presupposes an audience. While customers certainly are the primary audience for the onstage work of business, sometimes the only audience is a vendor, a peer, or a supervisor. This internal viewing, without the presence of a customer, is no less theatre and no less important. Indeed, "offstage" work affects the connections formed with customers because internal performance influences external relationships.

Thus a stevedore unloading cargo engages in theatre. Two guys tossing pizza dough back in the kitchen are performing. A floor full of claims adjusters shuffling papers for an insurance company is choreographed. A foreman overseeing workers on an assembly line observes the way they act. A proposal to the boss entails theatre; likewise, a presentation to the board of directors. All this work is theatre, even when the audience isn't made up of paying customers, because internal acts make impressions on customers who do pay. In the Experience Economy, businesses must figure out how to make work, whether performed onstage or off, more engaging.

Sociologist Erving Goffman perhaps first recognized that theatrical performances offer a model for work. In *The Presentation of Self in Everyday Life*, published in 1959, Goffman examines the dramaturgical principles evident in a number of ordinary social and work situations. Studying personal expressions, he recognized that people exhibit differing degrees of awareness of how they appear to others from one moment to the next. Some are oblivious to everything, while others simply don't care what others think of them. Yet others, as a means to other ends, manipulate their expressions in order to create certain impressions in other people. Goffman called such people "cynical performers" who "are interested in deluding the audience." But he called "sincere" those "individuals who believe in the impression fostered by their performance."[12]

For Goffman, all human activity is acted, whether rehearsed or not. "The incapability of the ordinary individual to formulate in advance the movements of his eyes and body," Goffman writes, "does not mean that he will not express himself through these devices in a way that is dramatized and pre-formed in his repertoire of actions. In short, we all act better than we know how."[13] This point alone should encourage workers to gain a better understanding of the impact their behaviors have on customers and to exert what Goffman calls "expressive control" over actions in order to create sincere impressions. Calling one's work theatre, treating it accordingly, and developing the capability to influence perceptions through performance separate the magical from the mundane. It is the *act of acting* that, in the end, differentiates memorable experiences from ordinary human activity.[14]

Staging Business Performances

Richard Schechner, a prominent expert in the field of performance theory, provides an invaluable perspective for thinking about the basic components of performance. Echoing Peter Brook, Schechner defines performance as "an activity done by an individual or group in the presence of and for another individual or group."[15] This definition embraces not only the staging of plays but also the bare stage of business. Within that construct, Schechner developed a valuable framework for understanding different kinds of staged "enactments," as he calls them, centered on four key concepts: drama, script, theatre, and performance.

For Schechner, *drama* is central to the whole structure of performance. It consists of "a written text, score, scenario, instruction, plan, or map. The drama can be taken from place to place or time to time independent of the person or people who carry it."[16] Residing at the core of the performance, drama may be expressed in different media in different situations and cultures, business included. Drama depicts the theme of the experience for internal consumption, telling the actors what they should do. On the bare stage of business, *strategy is drama*, central to what an enterprise does but expressing itself through a wide variety of means, such as strategic visions, mission statements, business plans, competitive imperatives (such as Komatsu's single-minded focus from the

1960s on to "Beat Caterpillar!"), or elaborate lists of programs (as in the objectives generated in a GE Workout session). No matter what form the strategy takes, the owners of the enterprise reveal the drama over a duration of time (the strategic horizon). Even as employees come and go, drama remains the enduring crux of all commercial activity for those who play a part in the enterprise. Drama provides the substance of actions hoped for, regardless of the workplace in which the business stages its performance.

Similarly, a *script* is "all that can be transmitted from time to time and place to place; the basic code of events" that "pre-exists any given enactment."[17] The script, then, transmits the drama in ways that transcend specific moments, instances, or conventions. In business, *processes are the script*, the (usually) codified approaches that an enterprise uses to enact its strategy. Employees must learn the script, identify its subtext (ideas not explicitly stated in the strategy), and refine it for production, modifying it as required to ensure the best possible performance. The script must interpret the drama, remaining true to the drama's original meaning, exploiting the expectations of the audience in a surprising way.

Within this context, *theatre* is "the event enacted by a specific group of performers; what the performers actually do during production . . . the manifestation or representation of the drama and/or script."[18] In other words, theatre embodies both the internal work of those who perform the production and the outward representation of that work to the audience—both the *function* and the *form* that bring the drama and its script to life.[19] Theatre connects the drama and script to customers by staging a performance that engages them as an audience. Once again, we must recognize that in the Experience Economy *work is theatre*.

Last, according to Schechner, *performance* is "the whole constellation of events, most of them passing unnoticed, that take place in/among both performers and audience from the time the first spectator enters the field of performance—to the time the last spectator leaves."[20] It is the broadest category, the fullness of events enacted at a specific place and time. As seen in figure 6-2, performance subsumes each of the other dimensions of enactment: theatre, script, and drama. Clearly, *the offering is the performance*, the economic value businesses create for customers. In equating theatrical performance with business performance, we then have the following result:

[drama = strategy]
[script = processes]
[theatre = work]
[performance = offering]

All economic offerings—not only experiences but also commodities, goods, and services—are the result of an enterprise's progression from drama through script to the theatre that stages performance.

FIGURE 6-2

Enactment Model

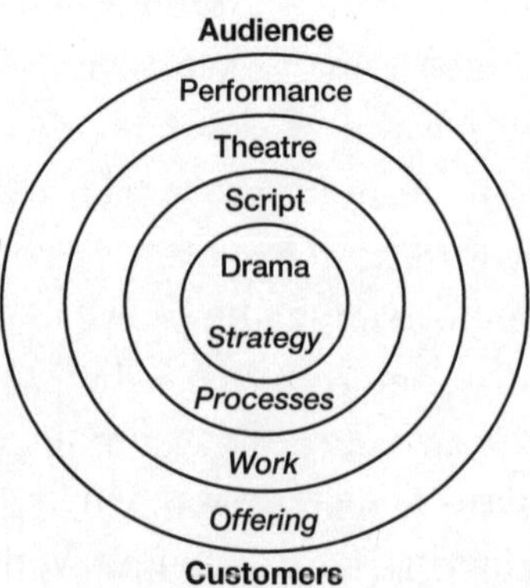

Source: Adapted from Richard Schechner, *Performance Theory* (New York: Routledge, 1988), 72.

Returning to Schechner: "The drama is the domain of the author, the composer, scenarist, shaman [to which we add strategist and line executive]; the script is the domain of the teacher, guru, master [as well as the manager, supervisor, and team leader]; the theater is the domain of the performers [whether acting in plays or business]; the performance is the domain of the audience [which includes customers who now want experiences]."[21]

Whether or not your company fully enters the Experience Economy by charging for staged events, no matter what position you have in the company or what your coworkers do, *you are a performer.* Your work is theatre. Now you must act accordingly.

Did You Say "Act"?

Some people misunderstand acting. They regard movie celebrities as egotistical, flighty, or fake, and Broadway stars as pretentious or worse. Outside the realm of show business, many people associate acting with a showy real estate agent, an irritating infomercial emcee, or a conniving car salesman. Are we really suggesting, then, that you, too, should act? Absolutely. For such misconceptions confuse awful actors and bad acts with acting itself. Acting is the taking of deliberate steps to connect with an audience. To dismiss acting as dishonest or fake relegates you and your employees to bland roles, with little prospect for engaging customers in new and exciting ways.

Aversions to acting may stem from a belief that only that which is completely revealed is completely genuine. But would Barbra Streisand have been more genuine if she had chewed real gum? No. In business terms, Streisand was simply "doing more with less," efficiently achieving the same output with fewer inputs. The decision to use or not use gum does not raise issues of authentic or inauthentic, fake or real. Rather, such decisions center on whether or not to use a particular prop to effect a particular impression. Nor was Streisand's act less genuine because it occurred before the audience expected her performance to begin. Drawing artificial (dare we say, fake?) boundaries around when work begins, or ends, often kills innovation. If servicing a car, for example, begins only when customers bring in their vehicles, Lexus never would have thought to send employees to customers' homes to retrieve them.

A reluctance to act may also arise from the view that acting means misrepresenting oneself. But acting does not mean pretending to be someone or something else. Think again of those world-famous workers at Pike Place Fish Market. They genuinely are fishmongers, and they absolutely act on their fish market stage. ChartHouse Learning of Burnsville, Minnesota, immortalized these workers in the *Fish!* video, which illuminates four principles they use to create the Pike Place Fish Market experience—including the signature moment of tossing fish from worker to worker.[22] Each of the four principles is an acting technique:

- *Play:* Although it's a serious business, it's also about having fun, with workers as well as customers put on stage for the enjoyment of everyone.

- *Make their day:* The focus is on customers—the audience of the show—and doing everything possible to create wonderful memories within them.

- *Be there:* A variation on famed director and acting teacher Konstantin Stanislavski's dictum to "be present," this means forgetting about everything else that is going on to be there in the moment.

- *Choose your attitude:* As Aristotle first pointed out, acting is fundamentally about making choices. We all act differently in front of colleagues than with customers; when with our

> children than with our parents; before friends than with strangers. It is not that we are fake or phony in any of these circumstances; we are simply choosing that part of ourselves to reveal to those we are with

Acting entails making discoveries within, drawing from a personal reservoir of life experiences and using those experiences to create a new and believable character for the role one has accepted, whether in the performing arts or in business theatre. An actor must behave in a manner thoroughly consistent with that character or run the risk that the audience will disbelieve the act and lose interest in the offering.

The hallmark of bad acting is for actors to constantly remind the audience that they, ahem, are acting. Only when performers are poorly prepared to act do audiences perceive their behavior as pretending. The great Russian actor Michael Chekhov put it this way:

> *The talented actor reads the play. The nonactor, or spoiled actor, reads the same play. What is the difference between the two kinds of reading? The nonactor reads the play absolutely objectively. The events, happenings, and characters in the play do not stir up his inner life. He understands the plot and follows it as an observer, an outsider. The actor reads the play subjectively. He reads through the play and by doing so he inevitably enjoys his own reaction to the happenings of the play, his own Will, Feelings, and Images. The play and the plot are only pretext for him to display, to experience the riches of his own talent, his own desire to act.*[23]

Chekhov was renowned for his ability to transform himself so as to bring *any* role alive. He performed "character work" so well that people didn't realize he was acting.

The most thoroughly engaging people also have a sense of their role so keen, an ability to stay in character so perfected, and an effect so pronounced that observers seldom realize that they are constantly onstage. We see such actors in all walks of life: Warren Buffett in industry, Warren Bennis in academia, the late Ronald Reagan in politics, and Bono in charity, to name a few. Everyone, even workers in business, should strive to engage others in this way. Too many workers fail to act, behaving no differently onstage from the way they do in their private lives. They execute their day-to-day responsibilities as mere happenings; their work is lifeless. To engage customers in the Experience Economy, act as if your work depended on it!

Only when you stage work explicitly for [audience = customers] will experiences flourish as the basis for new economic activity. You can begin this staging by examining the activities performed within your enterprise and then designating the workplace as a special place: the performance stage. Deliberately staging an engaging experience requires much more than simply designating such a place, but doing so is an indispensable (and not too difficult) step in that direction. So don't delay. Do it. And then proclaim, This is my stage.

Getting into Character

Now that you have your stage, you are truly an actor. And how well you act depends on how well you prepare to act. In fact, the vast majority of an actor's job is done before he or she ever goes onstage. Preparation takes on many forms, but perhaps the most important is the way you *characterize* your role, a practice that determines the impressions people will form as a result of your work. Proper characterization makes any drama seem natural, believable, spontaneous, and real.

Eric Morris specializes in helping such actors as Jack Nicholson develop their characterizations. Listen to his advice: "For generations, the popular concept and the belief in the theater has been that 'the actor becomes the character.' This is taken to mean that the actor assumes or acquires the behavior, idiosyncrasies, thoughts, and impulses of a particular character in a play. But I believe that the reverse is true: *the character becomes you!*"[24] Exactly. Successful acting, as opposed to pretending, never creates a noticeable gap between the characterization of the role and the actual person playing the role. That is, the character conforms with self—who the worker really is—drawing on the emotional, physical, intellectual, and spiritual uniqueness of the individual playing the role. Morris further explains that "when you absorb the character into your person, all that you are in terms of your unique way of relating to the world, your impulses, thoughts, and responses, will be included in everything he does. It is thus that an actor makes a unique and personal statement through every part he plays."[25]

Building character into roles distinguishes the work of staging experiences from that of other business activity. In fact, the absence of such character explains why many service workers seem to operate like automatons. How many times do hotel receptionists greet you in the same, monotonous manner? How many car salespeople use identical pitches? How many fast-food lines put customers through the same old drill? Proper characterization can turn these mundane service activities into memorable performances. Thus a bellhop at a Ritz-Carlton warmly welcoming guests back by name—by reviewing a daily printout of expected new guests and their distinguishing traits (much like a soap opera actor learns new scripts on a daily basis)—makes a remarkable impression. Similarly, a visit to a Lexus dealership offers a refreshingly different experience from the norm, in which salespeople corral customers into a cubicle to haggle over price. Even a soda jerk can create memorable events by characterizing the role. Consider the character we encountered at the refreshment stand at

Cedar-Lee Cinema in Cleveland Heights, Ohio, who spun lines like, "Who's next to be refreshed?" His acting was better than that of some of the movie stars on the screen. Guests *wanted* to wait in his queue.

Actors may deploy a number of theatre techniques to develop ideas on how to fill an onstage role with character. These include *journaling* (documenting daily events in a diary and then decomposing each event into potential choices for future work), *charting* (creating a map of the actor's chosen behaviors that overlay the script, line by line, scene by scene), or *relationship mapping* (creating diagrams that assess the relationship between each onstage character). In each instance, acting flows from role to character; the latter absorbs the former, becoming the basis on which the actor engages the audience.

Turning a role into a character requires careful management of the *subtext*—that is, everything not in the formal script. Agreed on by the actors in collaboration with the director, who together translate the [script = processes] into real [theatre = work], subtext renders a fullness beyond the surface-level script. The onstage actor completes the performance by using inflections, gestures, and other elements. This includes *body language*—such as posture, gestures, eye contact, and other expressions (a sales representative's smile sends a powerfully positive message)—*props* (a cell phone conveys accessibility, while one conspicuously turned off and thrown into a briefcase calls for attention), and *costumes*—clothing and accessories (a CEO's speech delivered in sandals and khakis conveys a dramatically different message from the same speech delivered in a three-piece suit, but either might be appropriate, depending on the characterization the CEO wants to convey).[26]

No element proves too small to contribute to the creation of character. Consider the lowly business card. It is one of the most basic props of workplace interactions with customers, and yet it is often treated in a pedestrian fashion, with little consideration as to how it contributes to the development of character. In most cases the only differences in the cards of different individuals working for the same organization are name, title, and telephone number. Certainly the basic design of a card can communicate a general message, but most cards present one standard look for every worker, as if all actors were merely extras in the performance. This approach reflects a Mass Production mindset, placing each person in one and only one box on an organizational chart.

But people play multiple roles in today's changing productions, so they need multiple ways to characterize their performance. We know of a few individuals in large corporations who now carry multiple cards, each representing a different character they play. And we know entrepreneurs who use their PCs to desktop-publish unique cards for each business meeting they conduct. And they do this not to deceive others (as did James Garner's title character in the old TV show *The Rockford Files*) but to represent the legitimately different roles they play in different situations. (We withhold their identity and that of their companies to preserve the transparent customization approach they use across customers and meetings.)

Names also characterize a role. Actors in most businesses today "play themselves" (not so in show business, where most actors take on the assumed names of their characters). But here, too, change dawns. At the call centers for a major manufacturer of computing equipment, each representative must use a different name. Only the first "Caitlin" or "Chad" hired gets to keep that name. Anyone cast afterward takes on an assumed name. This characterization element allows callers, should they desire, to request the same representative when placing multiple calls into the call center, whether during a single series of ordering or servicing interactions or across multiple, episodic interactions.

Customers value the policy in and of itself, and that allows the same one-to-one relationship to become the basis of service. The most intriguing point, however, lies in how the policy could become a stage for further characterization of the role. No longer cast as interchangeable parts, these phone reps are freed to use the assumed names to express themselves as engaging performers through a unique style of personally selected expressions, routines, and other telephone mannerisms that shape and focus conversation in memorable ways. Great call center actors would find themselves in great demand, from customers and from companies.

Getting into character gives all the workers in an organization a sense of purpose, uniting them in the overall theme of the experience offered to guests. Without such character development, the work yields little opportunity to connect with customers. Perhaps no other company understands this as well as Disney. Each day, cast members—whether portraying cartoon figures, ride attendants, or street sweepers—don their costumes, grab their props, and enter various staged experiences. Each contributes to the portrayal of the place as a haven for family, fun, and fantasy. Cast members keep offstage work offstage and conduct onstage work onstage. Period.

The Project on Disney, a group of observers that takes a dim view of working conditions at Walt Disney World (it titles a chapter on the subject "Working at the Rat"), shares this insight: the paid employees, like the paying guests, "say they know it's not real, that it's not what it appears to be, and then proceed to talk about it *as though* it were."[27] Bravo. This disposition goes to the very heart of characterizing a role. Stanislavski labeled it the "Magic If."[28] Many acting teachers since have parlayed the notion into a formal acting technique called "as if." Says one such instructor, Michael Kearns, "Acting *as if* is a great technique to apply to real life. As obnoxious as it sounds, it's a bit like positive thinking. You're at a party, feeling glum and determined to have a lousy time. Sometimes an adjustment—acting as if you're having the time of your life—will actually alter your mood, allowing you to look at the occasion through a different filter."[29] Onstage service personnel who let it show when they're feeling blue, lacking any "as if" resources to characterize their role, suggest realness only in one sense—real rudeness. There is no room for such behavior in pleasant business experiences. When having a rough day (and we all have them), workers must act as if they are cheerful. When confronted with an ornery buyer (and some truly present difficult challenges), actors should act as if they don't mind. A funny thing then happens on the way to the performance: cheerful service presents the stage for memorable experiences, and insufferable customers often regret their behavior and lighten up.

Trained actors—and any audience—know the difference between roles performed mechanically and those masterfully expressed through characterization. The former exemplifies most service positions today, with customers eager to end their transactions as quickly as possible. (As mentioned previously, managers in service industries know this and expend tremendous energy to reduce the time it takes to serve each customer, thereby promoting a world of poor-service, self-service, and no-service outlets.) But when workers choose appropriate roles and then characterize those roles well, they stage experiences with which guests willingly spend more time. And what induces this willingness? Simple: the way one acts.

Acting with Intention

Stanislavski constantly admonished actors to "cut ninety-five per cent."[30] With this simple slogan, he addressed the frequent tendency among actors to do too much. Stanislavski not only meant that actors performed too many actions but also that they incorporated too much commotion into any given action. (In business, too, many workers, from doctors to auto mechanics, go through excess explanations and histrionics when customers want the simple facts.) Stanislavski wanted to rid theatre of unnecessary gestures, movements, words, and other energies that detract from the main purpose of the activity. He reduced acting to its essential core, so that it clearly communicated the theme (what he called the "super-objective") of the play. Legend has it that Stanislavski once asked Sergei Rachmaninov the secret of his mastery of the piano, to which the great pianist and composer replied, "Not touching the neighboring key."[31] Stanislavski must have liked the answer, because he held it as a standard for theatre.

Thanks to the widespread influence of total quality management (TQM) and business process reengineering (BPR), most organizations now understand the idea of redesigning and improving work processes. These business improvement programs usually involve process mapping as a tool to redesign operational activity. In most instances, however, such exercises only delineate *what* activity organizations perform, and not *how* the work should be performed. Simply put, the resulting work processes still lack a sense of *intention*. Merely completing an activity is not enough: some underlying motivation must invigorate the performance so that it ultimately affects the buyer of the final offering. Everyone can, for example, detect the difference between a receptionist who merely takes names and calls for parties, and one who graciously greets each visitor and performs otherwise identical tasks with intentional style and color. The encounter in the lobby, however brief, affects the guest and sets a particular tone for the entire meeting that follows—and on occasion perhaps even alters the outcome.

Focusing not only on the *what* but also on the *how* serves as the core distinction between mundane service interactions and memorable experience encounters. Economic activity truly engages customers when each worker fills activities consciously and thoroughly with intention. Every movement becomes a meaningful action when richly designed with intention in mind. Without it, work is dull, monotonous, a cliché. (How many processes are as thoroughly unimpressive from start to finish as those that end with "Have a nice day"?) Because many people perform acts without deliberate intention, Stanislavski could comfortably and universally demand that actors cut 95 percent of what they do. The same admonition applies to business acts. Process excellence—at least in the sense of truly engaging customers—surfaces only when workers decide to enrich *how* they perform each activity. As acting instructor Kearns relates, "Deciding what you want is critical to your success . . . If you haven't decided what it is you want, you're likely to be un-focused . . . and the result will be a vague, meaningless encounter. When you've conscientiously spelled out your intent beforehand, you are more likely to be specific and clear, and the result will be an energized connection."[32] Any offering increases in value when every worker on stage—in farmyards, on shop floors, at service counters, within themed attractions—fills work with intention.

Kearns supplies a most useful tool for doing so. For every piece of work, one must describe his intention using the phrase "in order to."[33] Barbra Streisand chewed gum *in order to* demonstrate that appearances don't matter; it's the vocal cords that count. The Jacobs Field performer swept the street *in order to* show that the new ballpark was clean, safe, comfortable, and eager to come to life. The inspired receptionist greets visitors *in order to* welcome them to a place where great things happen.

Imagine that you're standing outside the closed door of your boss's office. Your very next task is to knock on that door. How would you do it differently if you were to knock *in order to* announce you had just arrived? *In order to* apologize for being late? *In order to* let him know you were there, but without disturbing his work? *In order to* state that the time for a meeting was at hand? Each intention calls for a decidedly different knock.

Or consider the very real world of doctor–patient relationships. Medical research shows that women with breast cancer who choose lumpectomies (simple tumor removals) live just as long as those who select mastectomies (total breast removal). Despite laws requiring doctors to explain lumpectomy as an option, the rates of breast-conserving surgery in some parts of the United States remain unchanged. According to the *Wall Street Journal*, "Part of the reason for the lack of impact is that it's not just what the doctor says, but *how* it's said."[34] Doctors must therefore provide patients with options *in order to* ensure that each properly considers the alternatives.[35]

Lawyers addressing a court also must fill their work with intention. "You want to plan every detail, the way you dress [and] the way your table looks," says Fred Bartlit, who practices in Chicago.[36] Bartlit is one of a growing number of trial lawyers who closely scrutinize every single thing they do, from how they walk across the floor to where they stand to how and when they make eye contact to what gestures they make when handling files and using a laptop computer to how they deliver ad-libs and prepared quips.[37] Their intention in performing each activity determines how it contributes to the overall performance. If no intention exists other than to be done with the work (that is, performing *in order to* be finished), then the work inevitably lacks the potential to engage.

It's not surprising that doctors and lawyers, whose decisions intimately affect the lives of their customers, must apply intention to their work. Yet any activity proves more valuable, worthwhile, and meaningful when performed with intention. Consider this simple example. In the Hill House dormitory at the University of Pennsylvania, a woman everyone just called Barb provided a daily demonstration of intention. Until a few years ago Barb worked in the dorm's cafeteria. For many, she was the most memorable person encountered in their entire educational experience. Her job consisted of only one activity. For three meals a day, Barb sat at a table at the entrance of the dining hall and swiped students' prepaid meal cards—one after another—through a machine that registered a green light if meals remained for the week and a red light if not. That was it. To the casual observer, this surely constituted the most mind-numbing job imaginable. Yet Barb richly filled this simple task with intention. First, she took a student's card *in order to* learn his name. Then she took the card *in order to* greet him back by name. If someone missed a meal, she took the card *in order to* inquire about his earlier absence. She would even take a card *in order to* inform its holder where a friend sat in the cafeteria. In every instance, by word or merely with gesture, her intentions fulfilled her theme of warmly welcoming students to the school's dining experience. She may have been one of the greatest welcomers ever to grace the globe. No wonder Barb's position was not automated and eliminated immediately upon her retirement.[38]

One meets such individuals in all lines of work. For every Barb the card taker in Philadelphia, there's a Fred the lawyer in Chicago and an Aaron the shoe shine man in Kalamazoo. You remember them when you encounter them. Their intention-filled work spills over into passion for their character, caring for the company, and empathy for the customer. They are the world's true actors, and we all should follow their lead.

CHAPTER 7

Performing to Form

LINDA LEADS THE NEW OFFERING development team for a U.S. automobile manufacturer.[1] She arrives at her office and reviews her schedule for the day: "Let's see. There's my usual talk at the Executive Briefing Center for a group of supply partners at 10 a.m., a 1:30 on the fall strategy cycle, and then the 4 p.m. call at that local dealership. Not a bad day, but I'm going to have to get right at finishing my prep. It'll take some work . . ."

Linda boots up her laptop and opens the PowerPoint file for her morning presentation. Scanning through the slides, she realizes that the graph on one slide is out of date. She texts her assistant, who is working from home today, to get the new data and revises the slide. She then goes over in her mind what she'll say to reflect the latest information, jotting a few notes on a pad. Soon, another slide causes her to pause, as she remembers a snag in her performance last time. Linda stands up, faces the closed door, and explores what she will say—and do—at that point in the presentation. After a few dry runs she figures out the problem: there's too much going on. The slide's so busy that she has to keep looking back at the screen, she talks too fast to get through it, and her mannerisms are all over the place.

To rectify the problem, Linda sits down and removes all unessential information from the slide. She makes some more notes on what she'll say to cover the streamlined points and then stands up again and talks from the notes. Going over them again and again, she finally hits on the cadence and gestures that will bring home her crucial points. Satisfied with her performance, Linda takes one more run at it—this time without notes. Then she opens up her Word file and updates her script, including descriptions of the mannerisms to use.

Just then she hears a knock on the door. It's Paul, one of her managers—again. Linda closes her notebook and flips down her laptop screen to show Paul that he has her undivided attention. She doesn't really want to hear about the latest problems with the market research study, but she acts as if she's hearing his woes for the very first time. The details of their discussion remain confidential, but suffice it to say that Linda thinks fast on her feet to defuse the latest installment of the saga. As Paul and Linda shake hands to close their session, she briefly holds his right arm with her left in order to show that she appreciates him and his sincere desire to bring the problem to a resolution.

Linda then turns her attention back to the final preparations for her presentation to the group of suppliers, and finally she heads down to the Executive Briefing Center. Shortly before arriving, she stops at the restroom to ensure that her outfit is neat, her hair just so, and nothing from breakfast remains in her teeth. Oh, and she remembers to take out that PartnershipPlus pin from her purse and puts it on her jacket. As she takes one last glance in the mirror, a look of reserved assurance comes over her face, whereupon she strides confidently out. "To the Briefing Center," she says to herself, as she begins reciting lines to an imaginary audience to help her get in the moment. In a few short minutes she's introduced by the host. Reaching the podium, just before launching into her speech, Linda pauses, eyeing the audience, beginning in the back, scanning down the middle, and finally making eye contact with a supplier sitting up in the first row. They both smile.[2] Then she delivers her four-word opening, "Partnerships demand learning relationships." A pause. And she's on . . .

Linda performs flawlessly and finishes her thirty-minute talk with a spirited, "So no more guerilla warfare!" to great applause. She immediately exits with a last glance and a smile to that person in the front row. One of the purchasing managers in the back comments to the host's assistant, "Wow—I can't believe how spontaneous and informal she seemed, yet she just walked right through every pothole out there." "Yes," the assistant replies, "but I've seen her give this same presentation a half-dozen times before. Except for some minor changes here and there, virtually every word is identical each time." To which the manager can only respond again, "Wow."

Meanwhile, back at her office, Linda's already preparing for the 1:30 p.m. strategy meeting. This will not be like her morning performance: no PowerPoint slides, no prepared remarks, no applause. The key to success, in fact, is to ensure that everyone across the line functions gets involved and provides input to the company's first-ever strategic exhibition, where the automaker's top management will experience what it's like to work in a business system where faultless development plans are flawlessly executed. No longer the Confident Executive, her role at this meeting event will be Inclusive Guide.

To that end, Linda reviews her notes from past meetings and interim telephone calls, a memo or two, and e-mails that various participants have sent back and forth commenting on how the desired results can be better achieved. She focuses her preparation primarily on ensuring that this meeting picks up on the outcomes from the last session, matches the tone of concerns expressed since, and moves toward delivering the set of impressions everyone has agreed the company should make on the exhibition participants. This will keep the meeting focused and on track, avoiding costly diversions (and as a side benefit, prevent her from being late for her 4 p.m. sales call). Linda takes out her list of "runplan" techniques, storyboards her plan for facilitating the session, and outlines the flip charts she'll use.

Once again her preparation pays off. While having to respond to a hiccup or two, as Inclusive Guide Linda not only keeps the meeting on track but also pushes forward the greater agenda of planning the orchestration of the event. Now, she's off to the sales call—after first changing her clothes to a more casual look, befitting the culture of the company she's visiting—and meets up with Steve, the vice president of leasing.

This won't be a "normal" sales call, like one she would make with a fleet manager. She and Steve are meeting with the owner of a large local dealership to enlist him in the automaker's prototype offering: the Pre-Lease Executive Automobile Sampling Experience (code-named PLEASE, which rhymes with "lease"). With PLEASE the company aims to stage an event at its test track in which potential high-end lease clients will pay more than $15,000 to test drive a number of high-end cars—from the luxurious to the exotic—under various exhilarating circumstances, whether racing others (including local celebrities) or sliding on rain-slicked surfaces. At the end of the day the guests will take home the cars of their choice, receiving a year's free lease and a customized video of their driving experience. With the experience priced at two to three times the cost of an annual lease, Linda, Steve, and their cohorts know it will be very profitable. And now top management, finally warming to the fact that the company makes more profits from leasing than from manufacturing, has agreed to include cars from other manufacturers in the event.

As Linda and Steve drive to the dealership together, they map out their plan to sell the owner on participating in the pilot program for his area. From their past experience in selling the concept up the ladder, each has become quite adept at promoting certain aspects of the proposal, with Linda focusing on the nature of the PLEASE experience itself and Steve on the financial justification. Linda suggests she open with the panoramic "B" version of what they're going to accomplish. Steve will then show what it could mean to the owner's bottom line, and then, after dragging out the formalities a bit to increase the anticipation, for the finale Linda will reveal the scripts and colored drawings their design firm created to demonstrate what a great experience PLEASE will be. Throughout, Steve will play the role of Straight Man to Linda's Affable Enthusiast. Just as they arrive, he reminds her of the line about the winter tires that works every time with the version "B" opening.

Once settled in the dealership owner's office, Linda and Steve masterfully play off each other, making their points in swift succession, even finishing each other's sentences on occasion. Everything goes perfectly, except, that is, for the twenty-minute late start, the constant interruptions by dealership personnel, and the frequent objections by the owner. But throughout, since Linda and Steve know each other's role and their own lines of explanation so well, they turn every interruption into a joke or an enjoyable respite and turn every objection into a positive segue to another point. To overcome the dealer's final objection—that including other nameplates would cannibalize his own inventory of cars—Linda subtly motions to Steve, they rise in unison, go to the owner's bookshelf, and simultaneously point to the replica of a DeLorean sports car they had spotted earlier. Anticipating their question, the owner blurts out, "Well, that was my dream, my first sports car . . ." to which Linda responds, "And you loved the experience of driving it, didn't you? We're going to give your customers the experience of driving their dream cars, and you'll make more money off that than you would selling five of our average models. Who cares who makes the car? That's just a prop for the driving experience that'll line all of our pockets because it creates such value for your customers." Soon all three walk toward the door, with Linda slapping the owner on the back as they shake.

The Four Forms of Theatre

This vignette illustrates many of the elements of theatre discussed in chapter 6—and a few new ones. Linda truly understands what it means to be an actor and how becoming one turns every interaction—no matter what the offering being produced, no matter where the workplace stage may be—into an experience. But notice how differently she approaches each of the four onstage roles she filled this day. While preparing for her speech, she's confronted with a problem by her subordinate, Paul, and must extemporaneously handle the situation. Here, Linda performs *improv theatre.* As much onstage as when she's with people outside the company, Linda quickly decides how to respond to Paul by relying on the reservoir of managerial techniques she has stored up from past experience.

When speaking to the supply partners, Linda performs *platform theatre.* She scripts in advance every line and every gesture, practicing each over and over again until she can confidently give a performance so accomplished that it comes off as fresh and spontaneous. In planning her performance for the afternoon strategy meeting, she is careful to review each and every prior interaction with those attending the meeting—telephone, e-mail, correspondence, and face-to-face meeting. She then engages in *matching theatre* by piecing all these disparate facts and events together in a unified whole, much as a film editor or director does.

Finally, when working with Steve to sell the dealership owner on the preleasing experience, Linda finds herself in a setting that she cannot control. Rather than rely on improvisational techniques—too risky for this venue—the two of them perform *street theatre*, in which small, atomic units of activity are called on demand to construct a performance (and to handle whatever interruptions or objections arise). Although nearly every move they make is part of a practiced routine, the order of the routine isn't planned but occurs in the moment.

Now consider the various roles you must take on at work. Like Linda, before you can act, you must determine which form of theatre it makes sense to perform given a certain time, situation, and audience. Figure 7-1 diagrams each of the four forms of theatre—improv, platform, matching, and street—drawing from the point made by Richard Schechner in his model of enactment (figure 6-2) that theatre is bound on the inside by *script* and on the outside by *performance*. The extent to which the performance and

FIGURE 7-1

Four forms of theatre

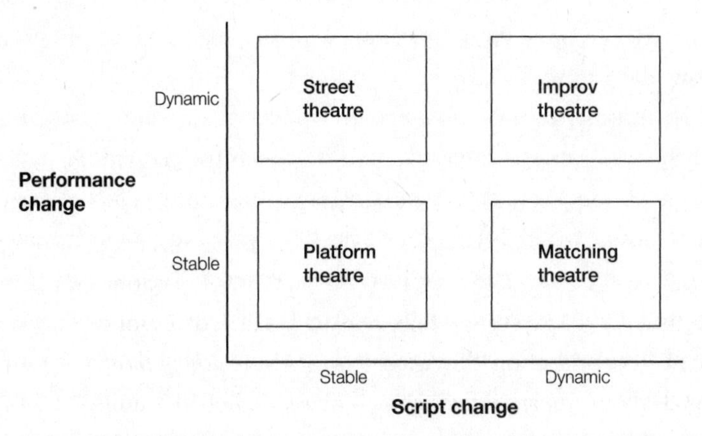

the script each change—whether they are dynamic (constantly changing) or stable (changing little)—for each audience determines how the actor must act. Each of these four forms of theatre thus represents a different way of performing work, a different approach to plotting a sequence of events to generate economic output. It is the nature of the offering and the circumstances in which a company engages its customers—or any actor engages his fellow workers—that determine which of the four to use.

Improv Theatre

Improvisation involves imagination, creativity, and new-to-the-world performances. Improv theatre provides a spontaneous, liberating, and unpredictable mode of work based on finding value from something new: creating, inventing, moving laterally or even impulsively from one idea to another, or simply ad-libbing. The dynamic movement of improv theatre, however, does not entail only simple acts of free association or aimless mental wandering, void of any structure or routine. Quite the opposite: improv requires systematic and deliberate methods of originating creative ideas, fresh expressions, and new ways of addressing old problems. The script, while rarely written down (or codified) except in very broad terms, emerges from the improvisation.

In improv, those who stage the performance anticipate mistakes, even going so far as to cause situations to "go wrong" just to see what happens. This occurs even in the course of the actors' performing other forms of work, by responding to mistakes—improvising—as errors surface unexpectedly. In any situation, improv involves a certain set of learned skills (meaning they can be taught), as well as various tools and techniques that take seemingly unrelated notions and combine them in unusual ways to make previously unarticulated discoveries. The methods of improv theatre fill courses and handbooks and include speaking in gibberish, gesturing in pantomime, interacting with random props, and wearing masks. Each technique relies on deliberate stimuli to force a changed perspective, a different set of possibilities, or an alternative approach, all aimed at facilitating the improvisational flow of new ideas for taking action.

These techniques date at least as far back as the sixteenth-century Italian *commedia dell'arte*. This outdoor theatre drew on stock characters who employed broad physical gestures and who always wore distinctive masks and simple but instantly recognizable costumes. The names of these four-hundred-year-old characters remain familiar even today: Pantalone, Columbina, Il Capitano, Scaramouche, Arlecchino (from which we get the English Harlequin), Pulcinella (who became the puppet Punch), Zanni (from whom we derive the word *zany*), and so forth. Each play would be staged not from written dialog but from a *scenario*, which means, as John Rudin writes, "literally 'that which is on the scenery,' i.e. pinned up backstage. All it consists of is a plot summary, the bare bones of who does what when."[3] All of the dialog and much of the action would then be improvised, given the nature of each called-upon character, from this base scenario in the wings.

If you're "winging it," you're doing improv. And whenever anyone assumes the role of a particular stock character with no preparation or rehearsal, such as that of car salesman and sales manager taking on "good cop/bad cop" roles with a prospect, that person draws from the tradition of the commedia dell'arte. Performers may also draw upon such improvisational characters in more complex selling situations. Suppose a four-person, cross-functional team from a travel agency—we'll call them Bob, Carol, Ted, and Alice—gets together to sell a company on outsourcing its travel operations. With little time to prepare, they quickly settle on the three distinguishing characteristics of the offer they believe will win the business: cost containment, quality service, and improvement in employee morale. In addition to their functional roles of, say, sales, agency operations, finance, and human resources (respectively), each team member chooses a particular stock character to create an impromptu cast for the sales call, and they quickly work out the proper scenario. Bob plays Glad-Hander, throwing smiles, filling coffee cups, and freely complimenting everyone's remarks. Ted unreservedly assumes the role of Penny-Pincher. He economizes his words, cuts off tangential conversations, and constantly pushes to keep the meeting on track. Meanwhile, Carol and Alice play Sports Analyst 1 and Sports Analyst 2 in a routine not unlike that of *Mike and Mike in the Morning* (two sports analysts who host a show broadcast on radio, TV, and the Internet), in which the two women debate various alternatives that will make the outsourcing proposal work. This improvisational selling performance expresses the company's proposed economic value in an engaging manner.

Companies can also use improv theatre whenever they must create wholly new offerings for customers, as do research and development groups, architects, and graphic designers, or when they must handle the new, unforeseen situations that come up in all lines of work. This form of theatre applies not only to what people do but also to how they think. The techniques of creative-thinking guru Edward de Bono, for example, provide improvisational exercises for the mind to stimulate new ideas.[4] A definite structure lies behind de Bono's methods to focus, provoke, move to, shape, and harvest ideas. His techniques provoke active mental operations that structure one's cognitive improv work by setting up provocations and then stone-stepping from one notion to another. In one exercise, de Bono recommends the use of *random words* to stimulate new ideas about predefined areas in need of new thinking. Do you need new ideas for refreshing a marketing program? Then draw words at random from whatever source is handy: a dictionary, a newspaper, even a children's book. Let's see: what principle can we extract from . . . a turtle? ("Well, a turtle's head pops out of its shell. Maybe our ad campaign is a shell—only in the final ad in a series does the message 'pop out.'") Or how can we compare it to a . . . tricycle? ("An adult riding a tricycle would look contorted. The sacrifices customers endure with our competition make them look similarly contorted, whereas our mass customized product provides a 'perfect fit.' Now sell that!")

The emergence of the Experience Economy coincides with, albeit not coincidentally, heightened interest in creative thinking. It also introduces a real need for greater improvisational skills in the workplace, especially for work performed in new venues.[5] One example: Home Shopping Network, where sales associates employ a host of techniques drawn from improv theatre. They make sharp, sure entrances and exits. They emphasize visual props. And they play off other members of the selling team (or, in improv terms, what might be better described as a retail selling *troupe*). Note, too, the important use of voice training: learning to select pitch, adjust volume, alternate tempo, change emphasis, and establish rhythm, all often taught in improv classes. Why is it that HSN sales reps give such good performances? It's because they know there's an audience out there. Workers in all sorts of other situations demanding greater improv skills must come to the same realization.

Today these skills are often required from workers who interact over the phone. Here we can learn much from radio, which once was prominent in the theatrical landscape. Prior to the popularity of television in the years following World War II, the countless audience members huddled around radio receivers only *heard* actors performing in their favorite shows, and yet the performances captivated their imaginations. Even today, at the peak of television viewing, radio provides a stage for performing. Witness the popular shows hosted by Jim Rome, Rush Limbaugh, Howard Stern, and the many local "zoo crews" who create and cast engrossing characters for their listening audience. In these radio performances, the performers must rely on improv skills to do their work, at no time more so than when hosts field calls from listeners. One may question the politics or caliber of these performances or simply dislike the shock jock mentality, but one cannot dispute the fact that these broadcasters perform acts of improv theatre. In fact, improv is their job!

So it is for those who use the telephone for a living: a phone line is empty space waiting to become a bare stage. How much more engaging might call center representatives be if they conducted their phone conversations as if they were performing improv? Take the worst type of live phone call—not the 900 numbers or even the psychic hot lines advertised on late night infomercials (these hired "psychics" surely understand that their work is theatre), but the telemarketing call. Does any other type of phone call come off more poorly? Could any other call benefit more from improv techniques? A telemarketer's script is intended to help the worker make more calls, but how often does a call truly engage the potential customer? Prospects tire of the telemarketer's prepared remarks and often hang up—an understandable response, since the prospect's answers have little or no impact on what question comes next. A telemarketing paradigm based on improv theatre would stand a real chance of drawing potential customers into stimulating conversations, because the customer's remarks would prompt innovative responses to unique needs. Requests for repeat performances would replace abrupt hang-ups.

Platform Theatre

The form of theatre that immediately comes to mind when most people think of the term is platform theatre. Its name harks back to the classical stage, where actors performed on a platform raised above the audience. The performance was further separated from the audience by a proscenium arch (a picture-frame opening, often covered by a drawn curtain between acts).[6] The actors in platform theatre work from a formal script of lines known as a *playscript.*[7] In business, playscripts exist in the form of drafted speeches, lines of programming code, or standard procedural instructions—anything, including a factory's production processes, that codifies work to generate value from something done. Platform work, linear and fixed, flows sequentially and so allows for little variation from the planned steps or prepared script. Platform performers seek to stabilize everything, through rehearsals, and then duplicate that one best way of working over and over again. No matter which performance one sees—be it a musical or product assembly—the lines delivered will be the same.

This stability is often a good thing, whether found in hard-coded routines set by cubicles of computer programmers or set talks to board members, investors, vendors, and employees meticulously developed and delivered by senior executives. For this reason, methodologies abound to help businesses develop information technology solutions and stabilize processes, and swarms of trainers (many with performing arts backgrounds) exist to coach presenters on their speeches. This assistance primarily addresses the delivery of lines. A mechanical reading of written words does not constitute good platform theatre; in fact, it can't even pass for bad acting! The *Wall Street Journal* reports that many chief financial officers take acting lessons to prepare for quarterly discussions with financial analysts, a situation in which improvising could land the company in financial hot water.[8]

In platform theatre, the actors must rehearse their lines, whether they intend to memorize them or read from cue cards or a teleprompter. They must internalize the lines until the script becomes second nature. When an actor knows his lines—really knows them—he doesn't merely recite them but brings them to life through intention.

There is a danger in relying too much on platform theatre. Too many companies, particularly mass producers, command their workers to follow standard scripts, having them do and say the same things repeatedly, in a vain attempt to gain efficiencies. (That's why telemarketers give the term *scripting* a bad name—they use platform scripts in an arena calling for improv or street theatre scripts.) The most bureaucratic organizations—think of the Department of Motor Vehicles or, to only a slightly lesser extent, airline service counters—create rules that workers must always follow, no matter what response the customer truly requires. But platform theatre can be the right form when workers perform standard activities in front of customers but do not directly interact with them. It may be the theatre of choice, for example, for the fast-food workers at the counter, for the technicians behind the glass at a one-hour eyeglass retailer, the maintenance workers fixing a bare stage, the flight attendants reciting FAA-scripted safety warnings, and anyone giving a keynote presentation.

Platform skills also befit people who follow a set script on audio or visual recordings, such as the pronouncements of every voice response unit or voice mail system. Consider the billion-dollar audiobook industry. While the audio book format as we know it is only a few decades old, major publishing houses and dozens of smaller firms now release hundreds of titles per year. Book publishers now call the William Morris Agency to schedule labor from a pool of trained voices! The industry often employs actors from Broadway and Hollywood to record audio versions of best sellers and specialty books. Rick Harris, executive producer of Harper Audio, relates, "Musical comedy actors do well at this because they know how to inflect, to color, to phrase." The better reader, says Jenny Frost, president and publisher of Bantam Doubleday Dell's audio division, "really works hard on the scripts before going into the studio."[9] Other recordings in need of good speaking voices and great script reading include talking toys, hosted chat rooms on the Internet, video games, and training materials.

Annual meetings, investor relations get-togethers, and trade shows provide other venues for platform theatre, which is often staged by such outside companies as Populous, George P. Johnson, The Jack Morton Company, or dick clark productions. The latter, founded by Dick Clark of *American Bandstand* fame, charges $150,000 to $10 million to stage such platform events. "All these shows had the same format: a speech, a financial presentation with some graphics, then you'd end up with the chairman," Clark relates. "I figured I could use what I knew from television: Get the audience in, entertain them, then get the corporate message across."[10] The work involves adapting a standard script and then producing the platform event according to that set script.

Matching Theatre

Matching theatre, exemplified by film and television, requires the integration of work outcomes from one disconnected time frame to another. The end product results from piecing together distinct portions of work, performed at different times and often in different places, into a unified whole. The producers of matching theatre must concern themselves not only with the quantity of material lying on the cutting room floor but also with the alignment of all those pieces, the way they should be linked to complete the entire performance. People in show business rarely use the term *matching* to describe their work, generally referring to it simply as "film" or as "jump-cut" theatre, in recognition of the need to jump between various takes and scenes and then cut and splice them together.[11] As V. I. Pudovkin, the great Russian director of silent films in the 1920s and 1930s, put it, "the foundation of film art is editing."[12] Whenever companies integrate the outcomes of work across many disparate business performances, they, too, perform matching theatre.

Have you ever seen a movie or TV show in which (1) a character appears on screen, (2) the picture jump-cuts to another character, and then (3) the picture returns to the first character, whose position, pose, expression, temperament, or even outfit doesn't match that of the first shot? Then you've seen a poor performance of matching theatre. Not only does this fail to engage an audience, it all too often disengages them by focusing on how (poorly) the work was performed. The same potential for mismatching exists in many business processes, particularly when mass producers partition work into functional silos—vertical slices of activities that often do not quite fit together. Companies that embrace Continuous Improvement (or Lean Production) business models solve this problem by focusing horizontally, via matching theatre, on linking work activities into one seamless process.

While directors of matching theatre, as in platform theatre, generally start with a fully written script, it is the rare production in which the process of filming does not change the script, often significantly. Actually, such changes *always* occur. Why? It's because the actual filming reveals the flaws in a script, just as the actual production of any economic offering—commodity, good, service, or experience—reveals flaws in the codified processes followed to create it. So scripts in matching theatre are always dynamic, sometimes via wholesale corrections and revisions and at other times *through real-time adjustments*. (Script changes occur in platform theatre as well, but only during the development process, before production begins. As in Mass Production, workers are not allowed to make script changes on the fly.) And as in Continuous Improvement, all parties involved focus on the highest-quality outcome by getting better and better at their work activities, generating value from something improved.

Workers should thus employ matching theatre whenever they strive to improve the quality of the same basic outcomes. "Workers" includes marketing managers (as opposed to the advertising agencies they hire, who should use improv techniques to generate new campaigns), counter personnel at fast-food restaurants (as opposed to those in the kitchen, where platform theatre may be most appropriate), and retail shelf stockers (as opposed to sales associates, who should use street performance skills). Not to mention flight attendants greeting and sending off passengers and repeating the same salutations over and over, without conviction.

At a higher level, companies should embrace the techniques of matching theatre whenever the same customers interact with that company—often with the same workers—over and over again. Here, work must be *matched across time*. Consider a sales representative calling on the same customer on a periodic basis. What occurs during a visit should match the impressions left during the previous visit as well as match episodes to be performed in future visits. If, for example, sales reps want to give prospects the impression that they are professional, qualified, knowledgeable, and helpful, then *every* visit must reinforce at least one—preferably all—of these impressions, while *no* visit should contradict them.

And the communication between visits, whether via phone, text, e-mail, or paper letters, must leave the customer with the impression of a harmonized and consistent performance. If a company wishes to achieve the desired effect, then it can perform no event without first considering all others in the sequence of visits and communication. As Arthur Shaw, senior vice president of electronic brokerage at Charles Schwab, told *BusinessWeek*, "The challenge is to make the branch and the Web a seamless experience."[13] Exactly. Each episode with customers, across whatever media, should be scripted so as to progressively build toward a climax that accomplishes the particular objectives of the communication.

Poor salespeople execute these tasks without regard to how they come off over time, while polished salespeople carefully match every detail. As a result, the work ultimately requires fewer takes and has a greater likelihood of creating the right impressions.

Matching multiple people from the same organization who must interact with the same customer over time must also be done with care. Situations requiring such matching include all retail operations, salespeople from different divisions or business units all calling on the same customer, and various order-processing, technical support, and customer service personnel who communicate directly with end users. Not only do such circumstances point to the need for someone to direct the overall performance, but also each individual representative must be aware of how his or her work aligns with that of fellow actors. Employee uniforms, whether the skimpy outfits at a Hooters restaurant or the blue suits and white shirts of old-time IBM, represent management's desire to present a consistent appearance matched across all those who represent the company. The same attention should be given to sets, props, gestures, and a host of other details that together enhance the experience of interacting with the company.

The importance of matching people also exists in team selling, when everyone meets a customer at the same time and place. Even those people who have no lines must match their performance with those in speaking roles. Not only must the physical reactions of the non-speakers reinforce what a colleague (perhaps the "star") says and does, but also they must be chosen with a scrutiny equal to that with which they would select or emphasize a spoken word. One shouldn't just sit there behaving any which way, but act in a deliberate manner that enhances the credibility of the overall performance: a nodding head, an attentive look, a seemingly not-to-be-noticed gesture to be noticed by a key decision maker—all contribute to the performance. As in the closing scene of the classic movie *Casablanca,* in which a glance and a tear impart volumes, the final success of a sales call can be as much a function of what is seen but not heard as of the few spoken words that really matter.

Matching theatre isn't easy; it requires deliberation and thought. Yet the everyday pace of business often precludes spending much time rehearsing a performance scene by scene across the full spectrum of possible activity. In the performing arts, the amount of time devoted to rehearsing (and the tolerance for multiple takes) varies depending on the medium. Major motion pictures, indies, thirty-second commercials, television sitcoms, soap operas, and webisodes all have different thresholds. In business as well, preparation time for meetings varies, and the need to succeed with only "one shot" often dominates the performance scene. Still, matching remains the key to success. Just as improv and platform techniques can be learned, so too can matching—even in such unfavorable circumstances. Thomas W. Babson instructs aspiring actors in the matching skills required within various film venues. His book *The Actor's Choice: The Transition from Stage to Screen* describes how to move from platform to matching theatre. Babson's "three-level system"—which encompasses physical, motivational, and emotional behaviors across "six choices" (character, relationships, objective, opening emotion, transitions, and what he calls "speak-out": what the character thinks when he's not speaking)—applies as much to any business venue as it does to any film set.[14]

Street Theatre

The fourth and perhaps most engaging form of theatre is street theatre. Historically, it is the domain of jugglers, magicians, storytellers, puppeteers, acrobats, clowns, mimes—all those actors who must first draw people to their performance and then amaze this found audience with their skills and abilities, and, finally—often the most difficult part—ask them for money. While a doctoral student in performance studies at New York University, Sally Harrison-Pepper analyzed the street performers of Washington Square in lower Manhattan. She describes the essence of this form of theatre in her book, *Drawing a Circle in the Square*:

> *Forgoing the sanctity of a walled theater space, with darkened auditorium, fixed seating, prepaid audiences, and reassuring reviews, the street performer instead engages and manipulates the urban environment, using its traffic, noise, and passersby as props for his shows. Buses rumble by; helicopters hover overhead; hecklers interrupt the rhythm of the performance; rain, cold, or police can defeat the performer entirely. The audience surrounds the street performer, restless, waiting, impatient. Yet the street performer succeeds in transforming urban* space *into a theater* place, *turning visitors resting on steps into an audience seated on bleachers.*[15]

What a perfect description of successful selling. When going into a prospect's office, factory, or home, sales reps have no control over what they find there. They must instead "engage and manipulate" foreign space and thereby turn it into a stage on which to enact their selling performance. Rather than rely on the settings of a permanent stage, the best sales reps use whatever they find at hand as props by dynamically applying what worked in the past to the new situation. Neither bothered nor flustered by interruptions, they use the well-timed remark or expression to draw disruptions into the flow of the overall performance. Whether juggling, doing magic tricks, clowning around, or selling, street performers demonstrate a high degree of skill and ability.[16] How do they do it? Practice, practice, practice.

Seemingly improvisational, street performers in fact studiously rehearse—just as much as those in platform theatre, if not more so. In street theatre, though, every performance differs, depending on the composition and conduct of the audience as well as the specific outside elements that occur (an ambulance rushing by, for instance), not to mention the mood of the performer on that day. Street performers must gauge the audience, identify those who will go along with their gags and those unlikely to (sometimes even delaying or postponing performances when the audience doesn't seem "right"), and then turn every disruption into part of the act itself, lest they lose the audience completely and have to start all over again. While following a general outline based on past successes, every street performer determines on the fly which bits from the repertoire to include and which to forgo. The end result: an audience-unique performance that creates value by reusing something known.

In other words, rather than improvise their show, *street performers actually mass customize their performances*. Their bits—whether a clever remark, a particular routine, a sales trick, or a seemingly extemporaneous response to a naysayer—are standardized modules dynamically linked together on demand to create one seamless performance, or "gig." Each [bit = module] flows from a stable script, while the final street performance text emerges from the choices made along the way, as depicted in figure 7-2, just as mass

FIGURE 7-2

Street performance script

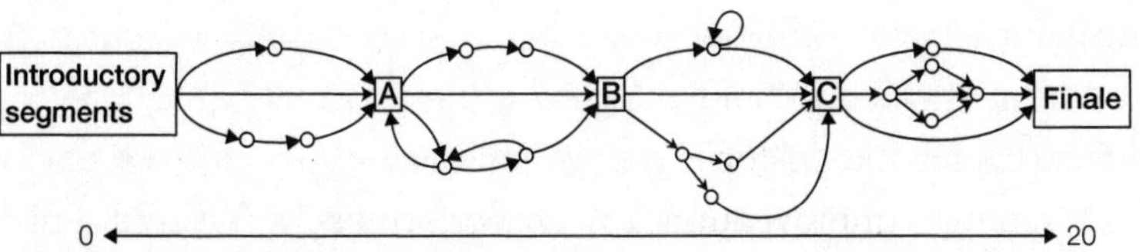

Source: Sally Harrison-Pepper, *Drawing a Circle in the Square* (Jackson, Mississippi: University Press of Mississippi, 1990), 117.

customized offerings emerge from the choices made during the designed interaction.

The finale of all street performances remains the same, however. As Harrison-Pepper relates, "Often, the timing of the entire street performance is built around the crucial final phase—the pitch . . . Street performers learn that the pitch must be precisely timed to transform [an] audience's greatest emotional energy into the greatest number of dollar bills." Consider again personal selling: whenever a sales rep draws from a portfolio of internalized selling routines, he performs street theatre. The timing of the entire performance flows into the final pitch, asking for the sale.[17] The sales rep determines in advance the basic script—just like the introductory segments, main points A, B, C, and finale of figure 7-2—but adjusts it in real time based on the needs of the audience. He may lengthen one routine if a prospect gets excited, shorten another when the energy in the room declines, or throw in an unforeseen routine when he discovers a particular interest. All the while, he reacts to objections and interruptions (like heckles and disruptions on the street) as they occur by pulling the proper bit from his repertoire of practiced routines.

Interestingly, this aspect of street theatre, like improv, also draws on techniques first used in commedia dell'arte, which, after all, was first performed "in the market place where a crowd has to be attracted, interested, and then held if a living is to be made."[18] Over time, commedia players became adept at various standard bits and set gimmicks, called *lazzi*, many of which remain immediately recognizable even today: Arlecchino making a loud noise by sitting on a pig bladder; Zanni counting money in a "one for you, two for me" fashion; Pierrot pulling a chair out from under Il Capitano as he sits down; Arlecchino miming the catching of a fly buzzing around his head. And whenever a performance falters, a character might pull out a long stick and beat a fellow player (from which we get the term *slapstick*).[19] These were not improvisations but dependable, repeatable routines, known to be effective from past performances, introduced at will whenever the situation seemed to warrant it.

Harrison-Pepper reports that fire-spitting Tony Vera, in the 1980s the acknowledged "King of Washington Square," always began his performances with the lazzo of drawing a large chalk circle on the sidewalk south of the square's prominent arch and then writing his name around its perimeter. Thus would he turn an empty space into a bare stage: "All I have to do is step into that circle and my crowd starts to develop," he said. "It happens by itself. It's magic."[20] To engage the growing audience, Vera would ignore them while focusing intently on the proper placement of his various props at strategic locations within the circle (again, a time-honored lazzo dating at least to the medicine man shows of the nineteenth-century Old West). Finally, before beginning, Vera would "inspect" the area for debris and start whisking with a small broom (a lazzo shared with the Jacobs Field sweeper).

Each of Vera's shows emerged as he selected on the fly the routines he felt would yield the most money from a particular audience. He would always include the best of his bits and, after first dragging out the finale to heighten its anticipation—not unlike Barbra Streisand and her gum-chewing routine—would conclude with his stock, yet utterly amazing, routine of spitting ten-foot fireballs from his mouth. Throughout, he masterfully responded to the disruptions that inevitably occurred. Vera actually hoped a fire alarm would go off sometime during his performance, for it enabled him to employ one of his best bits, as related by a fellow street performer: "One thing Tony did that I thought was one of the greatest things I'd ever seen was when he lit one of his fire torches and a fire alarm went off somewhere. He looked up, gave the torch to somebody in the audience, and left! Just stood in the audience, going 'La dee da, I don't know what's going on.' And it appeared to the audience that it was phenomenally spontaneous. I'm sure that it had happened before but, you know, it was just perfectly timed. It's a very flowing thing."[21] Now *that's* how to handle what would otherwise be a very distracting disturbance. How much more should we be ready and able, no matter what our job responsibilities, to handle the questions, objections, disturbances, and interruptions that inevitably occur during any interaction with a customer?

While executives' presentations to financial analysts must remain pure platform theatre, if they follow with a Q&A period, then they absolutely must *not* rely on improv skills. Rather, they should use street performance to anticipate possible lines of questioning, work out the perfect answers in advance, and then practice, practice, practice until they come off as great extemporaneous responses to each question that arises. Every performer, no matter what the circumstances, should be prepared with practiced bits to seize the spontaneous opportunities that arise in the course of doing business.

For example, customer service reps at inbound call center operations need exceptional street theatre skills to connect and empathize with customers seeking information, initiating orders, or simply asking for help with a problem. Some corporations retain coaches to help train their reps on how to handle calls. One of the best is the "Telephone Doctor," a stock character created by Nancy Friedman of St. Louis, Missouri (founder of a company named Telephone Doctor Customer Service Training). The good doctor appears in more than a hundred routines in an eighteen-tape DVD training library. Topic titles include "Selling Skills A to Z," "How to Handle the Irate Caller," and "That's Just Rude!" Each routine provides a bit that any rep can pick up, rehearse, and deliver on demand.

The Hartford uses street theatre in its Personal Lines Insurance Center, realizing that no one representative could adequately handle all possible calls from members.[22] Hugh Martin, the center's former head, modularized the organization into an ensemble of specific roles: generalists, who answer all calls and handle those they can, and a variety of specialists, who handle more difficult questions related to particular issues, such as widowhood or the regulations of certain states. Each generalist keeps a stock set of routines that can be brought to bear at a moment's notice once he realizes a caller's needs exceed his knowledge. In essence, the generalist has access to a raft of bits waiting to be called into action, even though they'll be performed by someone else. Martin says the center forms an "instant team" for every call, although "on-demand cast" would be just as accurate. He further relates, "No two phone calls are exactly alike because no two members placing them have the exact same needs. But we couldn't afford to look up answers all the time, so we designed a system where each response, while seemingly spontaneous, is really a pre-engineered routine performed by someone who knows the right answer."

Indeed, street theatre characterizes the work performed by all mass customizers, including Andersen Corp., Ross Controls, Paris Miki, and others introduced earlier in the book. Their work consists of gigs made up of bits or, if you prefer, activities made up of modular capabilities that stage a direct encounter between performer and audience. Mass customizers "profile" individual audience members to initiate the encounter's interaction and, in the process, amaze the audience by making the apparently complex seem simple, revealing only and exactly those elements that need to be made known. And then, before the performance is completed in the finale, the audience first must wait so as to heighten the anticipation for the end of street performance work: the mass customized offering.

Such [street theatre = mass customization] cannot be faked. The street performers must develop a high degree of expertise before even attempting to amaze an [audience = customers]. He must focus on the management of his repertoire of [bits = modules], on how he will dynamically link them in new and exciting ways, and, most important, on his ability to sense and respond to the unique characteristics of the individuals walking across his otherwise bare stage.[23]

One Bit at a Time

A street performer's bits cannot be picked fully formed out of a hat (even by a magician). Rather, they appear one bit at a time as the performer methodically advances his techniques—by determining which old bits no longer work well, responding spontaneously to new kinds of disruptions, or creating a new idea for a routine. Because just-invented routines have never before been performed, this first-time showing is no longer the province of street theatre; rather, it is improv theatre. All new bits must first be improvised, whether in front of an audience or in rehearsal. But rarely, if ever, does improvisation yield a perfectly formed bit. Perhaps a rejoinder falls short of the mark but provides the basis for developing a great routine. Or an idea for a new bit turns out wrong, even though it leads down an unforeseen but fruitful path. However he arrives at the bit, once he's figured out its steps and nuances, he still isn't ready to use the bit in front of an audience. First, he must practice, practice, practice; the performer must repeat it over and over again until he has it down and can effectively replicate it at will, and this means he's now performing platform theatre. He then must refine the bit via matching theatre, making sure that it gets the right reaction every time, tweaking it as necessary until it works consistently and, as a final step, ensuring that it fits in with whatever bits might precede or follow it. Only then can the performer recall the new bit on demand to provide the audience-unique value he deems appropriate. Only then can he renew his repertoire of street theatre routines, refreshing his performances with the new bit.[24]

This cycle of activities, from street theatre to improv to platform to matching and finally back to street theatre, enables accomplished street performers to work new bits into their acts.[25] This is exactly how the great Tony Vera created bits for his seamless, on-demand performances, as he explained to Harrison-Pepper:

> *"You work every day in the streets and find out what you're doing wrong, okay? And you're doing something wrong, you don't do that. Try something else. It works, keep it in the act. Keep doing it 'til your act is polished." What did he mean when he said something "works"? He replied: "People laugh, they have a good time, and mostly you can tell by what's in your hat at the end of the show. If it didn't work, that means not as much money—and vice versa."*
>
> *Essentially, then, the street performer constructs his performance text through a process of trial and error, adding, removing, or revising segments of his individual routines in a process of constant, often moment-to-moment revision. Each adjustment is prompted by ideas about what "works" in the show, that is, what entertains an audience and results in the greatest profits. But Vera is not selecting parts at random; rather he is dealing with the performance text as a whole, in which each choice affects the subsequent choices of his act.*[26]

So it is for all street performers *cum* mass customizers, whether their bare stage be the literal streets of a city or the figurative streets of business theatre.

CHAPTER 8

Now Act Your Part

THE PROSPECT OF ACTING MAY UNDERSTANDABLY bring stage fright to many a worker: improvise? Learn my lines? Match my peer? *Lazzi?* Oh my! You may feel like James Stockdale, Ross Perot's running mate way back in the 1992 elections, who was qualified to run, perhaps, but certainly unprepared for the vice-presidential debate against Al Gore and Dan Quayle, as he pondered, "Who am I, and why am I here?" Discomfort with the notion of acting, however, does not justify the dismissal of theatre as a useful operating model. This uneasiness only points to how individuals and groups must *learn to act differently* when staging experiences versus merely providing goods and services.

Sole practitioners—solo acts—know what it means to perform all the roles required in a business. Most enterprises, however, need a multitude of people to perform all the work necessary to generate output. The greater the number of people working for a business, the more likely it is that some organizational model—that is, a set of assumptions, both explicit and implicit, about organizing people's work—influences the way things get done.[1] These sets of assumptions, varying with company culture, have existed for years, many of them evolving from a Mass Production mindset that seeks to classify all aspects of work into a single standard of behavior. Some examples come to mind: everyone has a title; bosses conduct performance appraisals, men wear ties to work. Many businesses today challenge these practices, seeking new means to attract, motivate, and retain a high-quality workforce. More and more we now see titleless organizations, 360-degree performance evaluations, and casual attire, all in an effort to rethink the most effective employment of human resources.

Theatre provides a new framework of particular value when one seeks to stage experiences. Embracing the theatre model prevents the misappropriation of old economic paradigms, such as data "mining" and service "factories," which run the risk of perpetuating work practices out of sync with the competitive demands of today's Experience Economy.[2] Performing work as merely the delivery of services (or worse, as the manufacture of goods or the extraction of commodities) simply won't engage [audience = customers] in uniquely memorable ways. There are times when workers, from corporate executives to frontline reps, need a new vocabulary to see and respond to a changing world. Now is such a time.

Taking Stage in the Workplace

Richard Schechner's Enactment Model (shown in figure 6-2) can be amplified for use in our Performance Model shown in figure 8-1, where people move to center stage in any performance of business theatre. They are the *cast*. Fully applying theatre principles to a business, therefore, begins with *casting*, the process of selecting actors to play specific roles. The success of any business obviously relies on picking the right people to play various parts. The notion that employee turnover stems from hiring under- or overqualified candidates for jobs often obscures a more fundamental source of

FIGURE 8-1

Performance Model

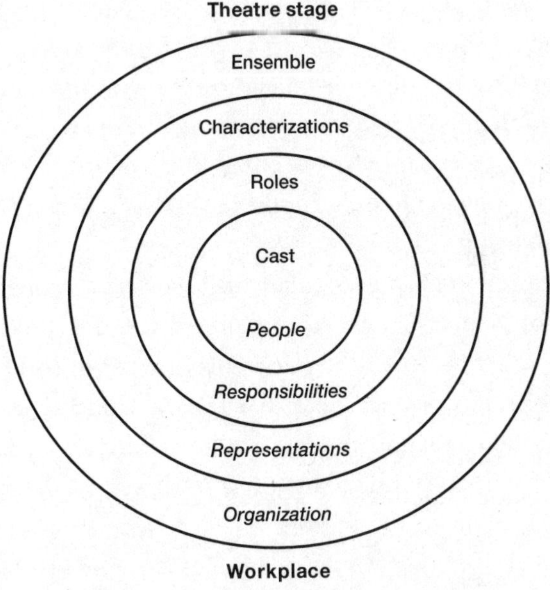

employee dissatisfaction and defection: casting *mis*qualified people in roles ill suited to their capabilities in the name of getting the best and the brightest (arguably what Ross Perot did in selecting Stockdale as his running mate). To get the best talent for the role being cast, casting should match individual skills to appropriate roles. To effectively stage its [drama = strategy] a company must have the right [cast = people] to implement that strategy.

Formally, a *role* is the part one or more workers play. It is divided into functional *responsibilities* to support the acting out of the [script = processes]. Contributing as much to the success of the enterprise's onstage performance are many backstage activities, some of which the cast completes before the performance (designers setting the stage) and some during the live performance (stage managers and crew getting the act together). Although usually associated only with those onstage, the terms *actor* and *role* apply equally to all workers and their responsibilities. For this reason, Disney refers to *all* employees as cast members. When a business views the responsibilities of all those individuals working in it as playing roles, those roles become the means to engage customers in more captivating ways. Without defined [roles = responsibilities], work becomes only another thankless job, done only for the sake of being done.

As discussed in chapter 6, acting well requires thorough *characterization* of each role. A character represents all the choices made by each worker to depict the role in his [theatre = work]. People take on roles, but they act out characters. As Gillian Drake, part-time theatre director and coach of platform skills for lawyers, says, "In the theater, every single thing that is viewed by the audience is a choice, down to the buttons on a character's costume, how they roll their hair, the props, the lighting; the same is very true in law."[3] The same choices inherent in [characterizations = representations] engage audiences in accounting, banking, catering, dry cleaning, engineering—indeed, in any business.

When players perform their roles with character, the [performance = offering] transcends ordinary services. The individual characterizations, however, must fit within the entire *ensemble*, which, according to the National Textbook Company's comprehensive *Dictionary of Theatre and Drama Terms*, is "the type of acting in which a cast works as a team to create a total effect rather than a group of individual performances."[4] The power of characterization lies in the integration of every worker's role into an organized whole. Whether a troupe, a more formal acting company, a production company, or a collection of street performers, this [ensemble = organization] gives individual performers freedom to create their own characters, with the proviso that their characterizations contribute positively to the total effect. In the performing arts, a *star turn* happens when a member of the cast promotes his or her own interests over those of the overall performance, upstaging a peer. In business, we call it playing politics. Great actors become true stars by gleaning diverse skills, bit by bit, from the many individuals they've worked with (not against) over the years. They observe, listen, and respect their fellow ensemble members and truly seek to promote the performances of each. In the process, they advance their own capabilities and reputation. Consider what everyone asks of those who have brushed with greatness—namely, "What's it like to work with Jack?"

Great character work should exist in all industries, and not only show business. As more and more Service Economy jobs become automated, the focus of human-to-human interaction in business shifts to staging experiences.[5] Each role, therefore, must contribute to a unique audience–actor relationship represented in the company's experience offerings. In the end, a company's

[cast = people]
must take on
[roles = responsibilities]
by each making choices to develop a compelling
[characterizations = representations]
that form a cohesive
[ensemble = organization]
to engage guests in memorable ways

This structure constitutes the essence of Experience Economy businesses, with profound implications for both the on- and off-stage actors within them. While the full effects of this economic shift on businesses and their workers cannot yet be fully known (the tremendous impact of the Industrial Revolution on people from all walks of life was not fully understood for more than a hundred years), we can discuss the nature of work in the new Experience Economy. In chapter 6 we explain what it means to become an actor; here we describe what it means to be a producer, a director, or one of the various players who supports them (dramaturg, script-writer, technician, and stage manager and crews). We also discuss the role of the casting director, who helps producers and directors find the right people to fill all these roles, whether onstage or off.

A Big Role to Fill

In any business, the *producers* financially back the enterprise, whether it be closely held by private investors, financed by venture capitalists, or managed by executives representing millions of shareholders. Producers determine what the business will produce. Will it be extracted commodities? Commoditized goods and services? Or new experiences? No one else in the organization can answer these questions, for they point to the most basic consideration: *what productions do we want to stage*? There are no easy answers or cookie-cutter approaches to this question. Producers originate change, because crafting any strategy always entails desiring and envisioning the future. They choose which [audience = customers] they wish to serve and the nature of the [theatre stage = workplace] in which the drama will unfold before a buying public.

Producers inadequately fulfill their roles when they do not define what change their businesses seek to affect through their performance offerings. Unfortunately, we find today countless mission statements riddled with nebulous notions about just what a particular business seeks to accomplish. These are generic visions that could apply to any business; they make a poor substitute for rigorous thinking. Mission statements, strategic plans, and action steps must be grounded in the uniqueness of a business. This isn't a simple question of differentiating the business from its competitors but of discovering the *unexamined* dimensions of one's corporate self. This self-examination, like that conducted by any individual actor, supplies an organization with a source of renewal (just as examining the uniqueness of customers is the means to uncovering their unarticulated needs). A producer's vision is meaningful only if the actors called on to execute it understand—viscerally—how the company plans to alter the very nature of the world through its industry. Every activity of the [ensemble = organization] must be performed to advance external change.

Too many companies seem to passively observe their futures, failing to understand that it is their behavior that may be the strongest influence on developments in their industries and the rise and fall of economic eddies that follow. The choices made by real people within a business—and not some law of nature—determine its fate. Good producers make their own future by doing one thing: *exploring what leverage points in the economy they can exploit for their own strategic advantage.*

The emerging Experience Economy opens up possibilities for new strategies of moving beyond goods and services as the primary source of profits. In the face of rapidly commoditizing goods and services and an increasing number of customers who want experiences, producers must demand that their executives and managers be accountable for answering some key questions:

- *Recognizing* how new experiential elements can be added to increase demand or charge higher prices (or both) for existing goods and services. How can you enhance your present offerings by appealing to the senses? What negative cues can be eliminated, and positive cues added, to better integrate customer impressions into an engaging theme? What could you mass customize and thereby shift up the Progression of Economic Value?

- *Identifying* which goods and services will command higher prices and therefore serve as critical resources for true experience stagers, repositioning one's goods as props and one's services as the stage to support new experience offerings of potential customers. How can the company help other businesses shift up the Progression of Economic Value? Can your things be *inged* to enhance a customer's experiences? Can services be restaged as platforms for such economic experiences?
- *Eradicating* current practices of providing experiential elements for free merely as a means to sell more goods and services, redefining these elements as explicit experiences that can command a distinct price. What would you have to do differently to charge admission? How would you move current experiences into the sweet spot of the entertainment, educational, escapist, and esthetic realms?
- *Commoditizing* the competition by staging wholly new experience offerings: how would you set the stage via THEME-ing: theming the experience, harmonizing impressions with positive cues, eliminating negative cues, mixing in memorabilia, and engaging all five senses? Which forms of theatre would best portray the experience you wish to create?

These strategic probes point to the mere beginnings of exploration. The bottom line: good producers insist that these questions be convincingly answered before financially backing the full production. That is because the answers define the [drama = strategy] to be staged by the [ensemble = organization].

Leaving a Mark

The role of *director* involves making the conceptual material of [drama = strategy] become operational reality.[6] Those people who fill this position face pressures unparalleled in other roles, because directors have accountability for everything, literally everything, that takes place on this new stage of business theatre. Directing requires coordination of all the players—actors, dramaturgs, scriptwriters, technicians, and stage crews—while securing the producers' approval of decisions at key junctures leading up to the performance. And yet it involves much more.

The directing role demands *organizational* skills: scheduling and conducting auditions (with the help of casting directors), ensuring that technicians meet timelines in the design and construction of sets, selecting appropriate costumes and props, and determining the day-to-day movements, or *blocking*, of the cast. Directors must help actors prepare through formal rehearsals as well as coaching on the side. They must spend time alone with the [script = processes], developing their own point of view about how best to orchestrate all the activity. And time must be spent with the producers, keeping them apprised of the progress toward fulfillment of the [drama = strategy]. It falls to the director to create a harmonized whole.

To meet all these demands, the role of director has necessarily evolved into an authoritative position. At times, directors must tell people what to do. Enlightened directors, however, do not blindly impose their whims on the rest of the ensemble. Rather, they perfect a rare fusion of collaboration and command. This blend of collaborator and commander *is* directing. To successfully blend the two into one, directors require certain motivational skills. The resulting mix dictates to actors without having them lose their own sense of discovery in their roles. Characterization emerges through collaboration, while both director and actor maintain distinct, even dogmatic, points of view about the performance.

The director must also exhibit *interpretive* skills.[7] What stage should be set? What actors should be cast? The answers to both questions require interpretation of the strategy into an appropriate set of actions. As the actual offering progresses from idea to implementation, this interpretation manifests itself in a constant stream of decision making during the preparations and rehearsals leading to performance: what to include and exclude from each performance, what to keep in and take out as the drama unfolds, and what work should be done offstage versus onstage. The basis for making these decisions, all along the way, resides in discerning which actions best fit the strategy. Such discernment necessarily puts the director in the world of concepts and principles, the stuff of interpretive action. To leave his mark, the director must learn to fly at thirty thousand feet while managing the details of the performance transpiring on the ground.

Finally, directing requires *storytelling* skills. Indeed, every director ultimately aims to enact a performance that completely engages the audience in its story. Former Hollywood and now IBM scriptwriter Peter Orton makes the case to the IBM directors he teaches that "stories enhance attention, create anticipation, increase retention. They provide a familiar set of 'hooks' that allow us to process the information that we hang on them."[8] As the title of the article in *Fast Company* quoting Orton puts it, "Every Leader Tells a Story."

Turning Drama into Performance, Strategy into Offering

To meet their primary obligations—turning drama into performance, strategy into offering—directors look primarily to four roles for support. Each corresponds to one of the four elements (as presented in figure 6-2) that contribute to the staging of an experience for the [audience = customers]:

- *Dramaturgs* assist in creating the [drama = strategy].
- *Scriptwriters* help with developing the [script = processes].
- *Technicians* aid the production of [theatre = work].
- *Stage crews* coordinate the operational elements of the [performance = offering].

Each role, as discussed next, helps the director create a unified performance.

Dramaturgs

The *dramaturg* advises the director in matters of [drama = strategy]. Theatre arts professors David Kahn and Donna Breed explain: "The dramaturg may act as a sounding board for the director's analysis, pointing out patterns, issues, images, character functions, and other elements that contribute to the play's meaning. Dramaturgs should be skilled in the mechanics of dramatic structure and can be helpful in identifying how the play is constructed and what models might be useful for analysis."[9] In business theatre, internal *planning personnel* or external *strategic consultants* may play this role. In either case, the dramaturg researches and analyzes the economic and competitive environment in which the company plans to release its production and then synthesizes the findings for the director. Of critical importance to the dramaturg role is the ability to distinguish which customer phenomena should influence decision making, especially any industry discontinuities—such as the advent of social media or the increasing digitization of experiences—that might be exploited to the company's advantage.

In the arts, dramaturgs help interpret previously written plays for ensembles performing them here and now. Similarly, previously existing strategies must be interpreted for frontline performance. Of course, all strategies are old the moment they're written. Dramaturgs must not alter the existing strategy to *fit* contemporary circumstances but rather alter everything else to enact that strategy *given* contemporary circumstances. In fulfilling this role, dramaturgs must remember three important rules. One, the dramaturg must make the offering compelling for the audience of customers. Two, the dramaturg must bring clarity of thought to parts difficult to interpret or characterize. And, finally, the dramaturg must describe, and not prescribe, scenarios and options for the director and cast. Whether inside or outside the organization, the dramaturg must not act like the producer or director; that's not his job.

Directors may differ in how participatory a style they wish the dramaturg to possess and will choose dramaturgs accordingly, but they should not tolerate any who usurp their directing powers. Directors who allow the dramaturg to migrate into their role, from providing input to dictating output, have weakened their authority to direct. And all the actors in the ensemble will know it. To help prevent this situation, dramaturgs should not try to have all the answers but to apply their expertise to crafting provocatively useful questions.

In the end, directors rely on the dramaturg to help tell the story they envision. At 3M Corporation, for example, the company's internal dramaturgs—its planners and strategists—have pushed its directors—line management for each business unit—to completely overhaul their strategic dramas, moving from bulleted lists of stuff to what retired company executive Gordon Shaw called *strategic narratives*: "Planning by narrative is a lot like traditional storytelling. Like a good storyteller, the strategic planner needs to *set the stage*—define the current situation in an insightful, coherent manner . . . Next, the strategic planner must *introduce the dramatic conflict* . . . Finally, the story must *reach resolution* in a satisfying, convincing manner."[10] It's imperative for company dramaturgs to tell the internal strategic stories that help fulfill the director's vision of the external performance.

Scriptwriters

Directors ask *scriptwriters* to define the set of processes that will generate the end performance.[11] They must therefore concern themselves with the four different forms of theatre and the unique combinations of [script = processes] and [performance = offering] highlighted in figure 7-1. Improv requires systematic techniques to help the actor find imaginative responses to audience input and feedback. Platform theatre calls for formal lines. Matching benefits from highly refined and scrutinized schedules that define who does what when. Street theatre depends on a rich portfolio of bits dynamically used to create unique performances. In each form, the [script = processes] supplied by scriptwriters contributes a crucial component to the performance.

Scriptwriting in business has gained prominence as a result of the total quality management and business process reengineering movements. Much has been written about both TQM and BPR, so only a few highlights need mentioning here. TQM seeks to script processes through a series of small, continuous improvements, while BPR pursues dramatic, discontinuous improvements via large-scale redesign of processes. Reengineering proponents rightly point out that TQM efforts are susceptible to generating high-quality processes for work that is not really needed. "Don't automate, obliterate" such processes, urged the late Michael Hammer.[12] The message resonated with executive producers impatient with the results of TQM. And the BPR scriptwriters were right in one important aspect: for too many years, companies used information technologies merely to automate existing business processes, when every new technology possesses characteristics with which companies can script entirely new means of performing work.[13] While powerfully articulated and clearly different, BPR mirrors TQM in assuming business strategy as a given. Reengineering proponents urged organizations to simultaneously rethink technology and processes, but the real need lies in simultaneously rethinking processes and strategy, as rightly pointed out by professors Gary Hamel and the late C.K. Prahalad, who urged the reinvention of entire industries through imaginative scriptwriting.[14]

Today, because of TQM and BPR, a plethora of process management techniques are available to business scriptwriters. And thanks in no small part to Hamel and Prahalad, most businesses understand the importance of innovative processes not only in designing efficient production but also in crafting imaginative strategies. Too often directors (and meddling producers) look only to dramaturgs for advice in crafting their [dramas = strategies]—often to the point of relinquishing control of the drama altogether—when scriptwriters contribute equally, if not more so, to envisioning creative strategies.

Consider a few examples in which new processes enabled wholly new strategies, which in turn revolutionized entire industries. Prior to the 1980s, consumers looking for new eyeglasses went to a local optometrist working out of a small office, where after an eye exam they could choose from a few dozen frames. The office sent the order to a centralized factory, where it would sit for weeks before technicians finally produced a pair of glasses, which were then sent back to the optometrist for pickup and fitting. Dean Butler, founder of LensCrafters—being an entrepreneur, he was producer, director, and scriptwriter all—figured out how to bring the lens-manufacturing process to the very point of sale and scale it up, refining it periodically over time. LensCrafters' new [script = processes] gave the company such a competitive advantage that the very nature of the industry changed. Today, retail stores employ or provide space for optometrists, who give exams and then mass customize lenses in about an hour while consumers shop.

As discussed in chapter 4, Dell represents another mass customizer that grew spectacularly via scriptwriting, going from zero to $60 billion in twenty-five years. But after successfully scripting the Mass Customization of computer goods, Dell failed to develop a sequel for mass customizing its supporting services (much less retail experiences). As Best Buy acquired the Geek Squad in 2002 as the means to create a new script for in-home encounters, and as Apple revolutionized the script for computer retail experiences with its revolutionary store format in 2001, Dell found itself more and more commoditized and desperately resorted to selling via the retail channels it once avoided.

Scriptwriting enabled new strategies in other industries, including the steel business, in which minimill producers like Nucor, Gerdau Ameristeel, and Gallatin Steel, which dramatically lowered costs and increased flexibility over the old mainline mass producers. Consider how the scripts of Prodigy and CompuServe were bettered by America Online, only to be eclipsed by those of Facebook, YouTube, and Twitter. Or witness how U.K.-based Pilkington Brothers changed the script when it instituted a series of process innovations that enabled large sheets of plate glass to be produced in one integrated process.[15] The scripting of processes is an inherently creative act that ought to be inexorably bound to strategy development. In the arts, who could imagine a drama without a script? Why, then, do many businesses devise strategies without considering how processes affect what they want to offer?

Technicians

Various *technicians* also contribute to defining the nature of company offerings. The technical presentation of the performance defines the *context*, or operating environment, for the [theatre = work].

This presentation generally includes a designed set, supporting props, and costumes. The exact combination and presentation of these technical elements vary according to the form of theatre being employed and even to the offering employing each form. Sales representatives exert little design control over the set of the customers they call on. As a result, their improv or street performances become highly dependent on a collection of portable props and on their ability to take advantage of whatever props they find lying around (or happening by). Platform and matching theatre usually afford greater opportunities to design the desired set on which the ensemble stages the experience.

SET DESIGNERS In cases where the [theatre stage = workplace] remains under the company's control, as in platform theatre, set designers focus on the six areas that together constitute the set: backstage, stage, auditorium, proscenium, entrance, and exit. Only the backstage areas, unseen by the audience of customers, can be designed solely for functionality, for the *what*. All others must consider *how* the set design supports the [theatre = work]. Entrances and exits cannot be overlooked, for they introduce and reinforce the experience in the minds and memories of guests. Set designers must pay particular attention to the stage, of course, but also to the auditorium that guests occupy and the proscenium through which guests view the stage. Recall that at the Forum Shops in Las Vegas every store creates an inviting proscenium-like façade that fits in with the place's overarching theme of an ancient Roman marketplace.

Clearly, set design abides within the domain of architecture, and experience stagers must employ architectural expertise—for both internal and external purposes—to design new experience settings. In this technical work, only three rules apply. First, traditional architectural considerations must be supplemented with explicit consideration of the impressions the set will make on paying customers. This extends to everything guests may encounter. One of the simple, but indispensable, cues Walt Disney used at Disneyland was trees; their utter normality and everyday reality helped ground the fantasy he wanted to create. As explained by biographer Bob Thomas, Disney "wanted trees to be part of the beauty and the drama of Disneyland, and to play their roles, they needed to be big . . . Walt wanted each tree to fit its location—maples, sycamores and birches for the Rivers of America; pines and oaks for Frontierland, etc. He sometimes rejected a tree with the comment: 'It's out of character.'"[16] It falls to set designers to ensure that *no thing* is out of character; it would ruin the integrity of the performance.

Second, design around all five senses: sightlines, comfort level, acoustics, aromas, even food options. Think of all the sensory design innovations that have occurred in the hotel industry over the past two decades, from the attention given to the sheets' thread counts, pillows, and bed linens, to the use of scent machines to emit smells into lobby spaces (such as the white-tea signature scent at Westin Hotels) and offers of signature food items (such as the chocolate-chip cookies at DoubleTree Hotels). In some cases, set designers must design from scratch the proper sensory environment, as the Rainforest Cafe did with its five-sense water mist, or as Virgin America did by installing mood lighting in the seating cabins of its aircraft. Such sensory design, like all other aspects of design, must have integrity in the sum of its component elements.

Third, don't be bound by convention, for you make your own rules! Declared Francis Reid, for years head of the department of theatre design at London's Central School of Art and Design (now Central Saint Martins College of Art and Design), "Theatre has reached a development point where virtually anything goes. A point where a production's style is no longer expected to be either derivative of the past or based upon the logic of a new philosophy. The only requirement is internal consistency . . . A production may take virtually any proposition as its starting point so long as the consequences of that starting point are followed through."[17] In business theatre, that starting point is the theme of the experience; everything flows from the manifestation of that theme in acting performances and, of course, in set design.

PROP MANAGERS In addition to set designers, a director often needs technicians to recommend the appropriate mix of props to use during the [theatre = work]. Used wisely, props play a significant part in engaging customers in positive ways. Props may be introduced simply for esthetic purposes (to create specific impressions) or for functional purposes (to help an actor perform some task), but esthetic considerations actually come into play for functional props as well.

Consider again the legal profession. Jury consultant Robert Hirschhorn, of Cathy E. Bennett & Associates in Lewisville, Texas, advises law firms to consider every physical good that appears in their performances, not only onstage but also in the entrance and exit areas of their sets. "You never know when a juror is going to see you getting in or out of your car in the parking lot," says Hirschhorn, who therefore counsels counselors to stay away from luxury cars in favor of minivans or no-frills utility vehicles.[18] Is this trickery, or an indication of thoroughness that extends into the courtroom as well? Before answering too fast, bear in mind that the importance of automotive props extends beyond lawyering to other industries (you may use such a prop yourself). One international business machines company headquartered in Armonk, New York, long directed sales representatives calling on Detroit automakers to drive only U.S.-made cars onto automakers' lots. More sweepingly, a consumer goods company headquartered in

Cincinnati, Ohio, insists on U.S. vehicles for reps calling on *all* companies based in the fifty states. Clearly, the car model a company selects for its sales force entails more than just what vehicle best transports reps from point A to point B. Some of the largest corporations in the world use five-figure goods as mere props for their matching theatre.

Sometimes onstage actors serve as their own prop managers. Briefcases, pads of paper, even choice of writing instruments all contribute to one's act. But whoever selects the props, remember to eliminate negative cues. A prop that is misused or poorly selected can lose business. When in a meeting with a prospective client, don't stop your pitch midsentence to check your phone. If you must respond to it, improvise to turn the interruption into an opportunity to score points. (And if it works, add it to your repertoire of bits à la Tony Vera.) Prospects may brand an entire selling team annoying because one person's phone proved bothersome to the performance.

Presentation materials offer another lesson: never use a prop as a crutch. Overhead slides crowded with words often make a poor substitute for learning one's lines. Lengthy presentations that exceed the boundaries of allotted meeting times are no replacement for meticulous scriptwriting. Don't expect props—even cleverly designed ones—to cover for failings elsewhere in the ensemble's act. Rather, prop managers should see to it that actors use props to enable and accentuate important features of an act that cannot be staged without their use. When in doubt, help them figure out how to do without, or at least with less.

COSTUME DESIGNERS Demand is also emerging for technicians skilled in the design and selection of wardrobes for the cast. The attire of workers has long been important in some businesses, especially those in certain service industries: airline pilots and crew, hotel staff, food servers and hosts in restaurants, delivery company drivers, security guards, and so forth. In most instances, costuming these workers consists of fitting them with uniforms, standard costumes worn by all the actors on stage. Uniforms send visible cues to customers to help them identify members of a company's ensemble. Who doesn't immediately recognize a UPS driver because of his familiar brown garb (not to mention the brown prop he's driving)?

A few costuming principles can help in almost any line of work.[19] First, *segment costume assignments by role*, as did the cast of characters in commedia dell'arte, each of whom could be immediately recognized by a distinctive costume and mask. The airline industry is good at incorporating this element of theatre into its act. Folks at the check-in counter and gate wear one type of uniform, for example, pilots another, and ground crews yet another (and at British Airways, queue managers don red coats to play their parts). If a baggage handler ventures from backstage to the proscenium jetway, his knee pads and earplugs make his role very clear.

Second, costume designers must *make sure each costume conveys a message consistent with the theme of the experience and characterization of the role* the director wants portrayed, as is the case with the Geek Squad's geeky attire.[20] This explains why airlines such as Southwest abandoned traditional airline garb in favor of more casual attire (while the Transportation Security Administration went the other way; conventional uniforms convey an aura of authority, especially if the costumes draw from military motifs in their design). And what do the polo-shirted and sneakered costumes of Southwest say? We're perky! And ready to jump up and down with you (in four connecting flights) to California, as if participating in an athletic event. Don't be misled by this example: the design of uniforms goes beyond assignment of formal versus casual costumes. Clothe workers in apparel that encourages the desired behavior by using costuming as a performance-inducing mask. The effect of such mask work proves readily apparent when companies employ mascots; but you can achieve the same influence without placing workers inside an enclosed suit.

The third costuming principle calls for directors and designers to *allow actors to personalize their costumes*, completing their characterizations, even if only in seemingly small details. For instance, restaurant chain T.G.I. Friday's, a business unit of the Carlson Companies, grants food servers license to supplement its standard-issue, red-and-white striped shirt with a hat of their choice and encourages them to adorn hat and shirt (and even suspenders, socks, and trousers) with buttons displaying slogans and symbols of the wildest variety imaginable (no profanity, though, thank God). The simple costuming feature contributes powerfully to the sights and sounds that connote a T.G.I. Friday's dining experience.

In many business roles, the only article of clothing traditionally available for males to personalize their costumes was the necktie. Over the past forty years, however, this limitation has been lifting, and we now see a wide variety of colored shirts and styled collars—not to mention socks, shoes, and belts—in the workplace. Even the buttoned-down halls of IBM and Procter & Gamble have loosened their ties. But something's often amiss when companies relax attire standards: who, then, coordinates the costuming, making sure the cast of characters matches from actor to actor and scene to scene? Without formal costuming roles—such as the team at East Jefferson General Hospital that put together its *EJ Look* book detailing the dos and don'ts of hospital costuming—these considerations usually go unattended.

Because costuming concerns more than formal/casual issues, the selection of clothing attire and accessories involves much more than a quick "dress-for-success" study. Costuming may involve any number of wardrobe decisions to help actors use attire to assume their roles. Consider the advisers of investment firm The Motley Fool, played by actor-directors David and Tom Gardner. The brothers' costumes consist of only one article of unusual clothing added to the traditional attire of trusted financiers: each wears a jester's hat. Older brother David explains the significance of the hat: "There's a war for your money out there. And the more I study it, the more I realize that the guys wearing the pinstripe suits—with all their complicated graphs and their numbers that don't have any context you can understand—aren't on my side, and they aren't on your side either. Indeed, if those guys are Wise—and that's what they call themselves, on TV and in all the glossy financial magazines—then we want to be Fools."[21] Consider, too, financial adviser Jim Cramer, host of the TV show *Mad Money*. Although he does not don any special article of clothing like the Gardner brothers' hats, Cramer forsakes a formal jacket and rolls up his shirtsleeves—no less an act of costuming. No one using as many props for sound effects and visual effects as he does thinks any less intentionally about the costuming he wears.

Image is everything, in costuming as with other technical facets of design. The trend toward casual attire in the workplace opens up opportunities to create unique [theatre stages = workplaces] for staging engaging experiences, such as with investment advice from The Motley Fool. But relaxed standards of attire must be actively directed toward intentionally staged cues, lest relaxation itself become the new standard and roles become confused.

Stage Crews

Stage crews have one simple responsibility: to "ensure that everybody and everything is in its right place at the right time. They document every on-stage move by anybody or anything during the production. They must be calm in a crisis, patient with frayed tempers, and infinitely understanding of everyone's problems."[22] The crew must get the right sets, props, costumes, and even actors where and when they are needed so that the [performance = offering] goes off without a hitch. Ultimately, the members of the crew are logisticians. Whether a warehouse worker dispatching inventory to a distribution center or a housekeeper making a hotel bed, members of the crew must procure, maintain, transport, and shuttle the resources prescribed by the director, within a process outlined by the scriptwriter, using devices designed by the technicians.

In fulfilling this role, the stage crew must be both effective and efficient. They must richly attend to details with an intention all their own—*in order to* enhance the quality of the output. Without such precise care, a crew may turn a wonderfully conceived drama and a well-scripted strategy into an embarrassing performance. But the crew must also be careful not to drive up the cost of production by wasting money, people, or time. Crew members must roll up their sleeves and perform the backstage work that, more often than not, goes unnoticed and unappreciated.

The *stage manager* is responsible for ensuring that all goes according to plan. Stage managers must also track the performance—from issuing periodic reports to monitoring and tracking moment-to-moment movements. For platform and matching theatre, stage managers and their crews must document, document, document—institutionalizing *how* the ensemble runs the production so that each performance is repeatable. They must measure, measure, measure, since, as we all now know, what you don't measure, you can't manage. And they must *stay out of the way* when onstage actors prepare to enter, perform on, and finally exit the stage. Yet they must always be accessible, immediately on the scene when something goes awry.

Their tasks may seem thankless, but crew members should understand how significant these roles are to the overall offering. Stage crews, after all, run all the operational elements of production, the vehicles through which technical design adds value. Set design, props, and costuming exist to help bring the actors' unwritten subtext to life. For onstage actors to manifest such subtext, stage crews must make sure everything's in its place.

Consider how stage crews enabled the late president Ronald Reagan to capitalize masterfully on subtext for his White House news conference performances. Open doors to the East Room allowed cameras to see the Gipper emerge in the distance from a faraway room. He then purposefully made his way down the long, red-carpeted hallway to the platform, where one last hop up brought him to the podium. Julius Fast, a leading expert on the use of body language, said of Reagan's performance, "The subtext was communicated before he spoke: vigor, authority, ease."[23] And when he spoke, Reagan's attitude and style provided a compelling context for his words. His appeal—like that of all good actors—manifested itself not in how he said his lines but in what he meant when he said them. President Reagan's performances would have been impossible without a stage crew working behind the scenes to position cameras, place carpet, open doors, and signal Reagan onstage at the appropriate time. Frontline personnel—the onstage actors of any performance—cannot by themselves make all the necessary preparations to act their part. No actor is an island.

A Casting Call for Companies

To fully realize the Performance Model presented earlier in figure 8-1—providing an appropriate ensemble of actors, technicians, and stage crew members for each production created by directors, dramaturgs, and scriptwriters—the human resources department must become the *casting director*. Hiring candidates for jobs essentially becomes casting actors to fill [roles = responsibilities]. And this means significant change for the HR department.

Any enterprise looking to stage experiences must discontinue its reliance on interviews as the dominant method of evaluation and must begin conducting auditions instead.

Words matter. Vocabulary affects behavior. Calling your offering an experience, your work theatre, and your interviews auditions will certainly bring about some movement in the right direction. But make no mistake: it will not be enough to sustain lasting improvement. HR departments, along with the producers and directors for whom they hire, must stage real auditions, for they present the principal means to gather information about how an actor will actually perform.

Most information gathered in traditional face-to-face interviews concerns actors as individuals; knowledge of their ability to perform (as well as their true desire to play a particular role) can be garnered only from auditions. Information gathering should be done, but only as a means to screen aspiring actors for participation in the auditioning process. Babson College president Leonard Schlesinger once described how the fast casual restaurant where he once worked as an executive effectively used auditions: "An integral part of the Au Bon Pain selection process is a paid two-day work experience in the stores prior to final selection interviews. This experience weeds out applicants both through self-selection and through management observation of behavior."[24]

Several principles, then, govern auditions.[25] First and foremost, companies must create places to conduct the simulations, role-playing, or live tests that constitute real auditions. With candidates no longer parading around interviewers' offices for a series of conversations, new venues need to be established—HR's internally staged experiences. Many consulting companies already put candidates in role-playing situations in real-world offices and team rooms; others should do the same. If you are staging auditions for a buyer role in the purchasing department, then have virtual vendors call on each prospective buyer, who is furnished with an office for the occasion. If you are auditioning for new bank tellers, set up a simulated counter or booth and have individuals process deposits, cut cashier's checks, and check balances. If you are in need of more call center representatives, set up a bank of phones to test how prospective reps field incoming calls. In every case, establish a place—perhaps even in the real customer place, as Au Bon Pain does—where you can observe the actor performing the intended role. The candidate need not act out the whole play before a full audience, only some important and revealing scenes for those doing the hiring.

Next, if you're creating a specific place for auditions, strip it down to its essentials. Minimize props, deliberately remove features normally present in the real setting for the everyday role, and position the auditors in clear view of the applicant. Do this so that the unaided performance reveals the raw approach with which each individual tackles the role. Don't let the prospective buyer bring a briefcase full of notes. Keep the teller's station clear of instructions, policy memos, and other cheat sheets that may typically surround the computer monitor. Furnish the call center with only a phone and one image fixed on a computer screen. After all, as Barbra Streisand demonstrated, it doesn't matter whether the props are material or not, only whether the acting genuinely fits the role. Observing the essence of how each person characterizes the role and fits into the ensemble of actors guarantees that the audition will help identify candidates well suited for particular parts.

No less an experience stager than Disney uses such a place for auditions. Disney hired Robert A. M. Stern, a renowned postmodern architect who designed many of its facilities (including Disney's Celebration living experience), to create the company's Casting Center for auditioning prospective cast members for parts. As the Project on Disney described the facility, "Stern's Casting Center tells a story about what it means to work at Disney, or, as [Stern] says, 'to clarify Disney's hiring process and give it an architectural dimension.' By channeling potential employees along a ramp between carefully spaced murals that tell a story, Stern alludes to the effects of rides at Disney World; the procession through the building's architecture is itself a kind of ride, in which one learns the story of the park's secret: that all is illusion."[26] It's also the place where Disney observes how well each actor fits into a microcosm of its larger-scale fantasies.

Regardless of the particular experience being cast, refrain from singling out any one characterization that *you* think fits the role. A vast universe of possibilities exists, and no preconceived notion of right and wrong should eliminate prospects so early in the selection process. Accept the fact that not every person has had an adequate opportunity to build a complete [characterizations = representations]; there will be time for that after casting. Rather, consider how each individual might develop into the role.

Consider for a moment the world of baseball scouts, who enjoy the great luxury of auditioning players during actual performances. Yet even in these ideal circumstances, there are dos and don'ts. The late Tony Lucadello, generally considered baseball's greatest scout, visited high school diamonds in Ohio, Indiana, and Michigan for fifty years in search of major league prospects, and in that tenure he signed more kids who eventually made it to The Show than any other scout—fifty in all, including Hall of Famer Mike Schmidt. Lucadello noted four basic approaches that various scouts used to evaluate talent, which he called "the 4 P's."[27] The "poor" scout, not a planner and never prepared, just reacts to whoever happens to be on the stage instead of rooting out potential stars. Most people evaluating talent know better or else quickly find themselves out of casting work. The next kind of scout, the "pickers," mistakenly single out a lone weakness in a player and eliminate him despite other notable strengths. "Performance-based" scouts, who account for an overwhelming majority, make their evaluations solely on the basis of the audition performance. This scouting approach has a significant flaw, which is that it places undue emphasis on the circumstances in which the player auditions, such as, perhaps, a high school star hitting or pitching against inferior talent. Finally, there is the "projector," the category in which Lucadello counted himself and all other casting directors who understand that the audition performance doesn't matter. Does the actor have the skills required to act, and act exceptionally, once cast into the role? An audition takes place to answer that question alone and to project such talent into the future of live performances.

How, then, do you select the right person to fill a role? Ironically, it's not by looking for the "ideal" person at all, at least not in terms of corresponding to some preconceived characterization. Rather, you do it by taking notice of who exhibits raw talent and acuity in making compelling choices. Do that, and you'll find someone ideal for the role—just as Michael Shurtleff found Barbra Streisand, and Tony Lucadello found Mike Schmidt.

With interviews downplayed, the onus in casting switches to asking the right questions not of the candidate *but of yourself*—questions such as the following:

- How does the actor communicate? Pay particular attention to how he listens.

- How does the actor involve and play off others? Note how he relates to fellow actors in the audition and in what circumstances he looks to seek, give, and avoid assistance.

- What does he want out of every interaction? Check for signals about what motivates the actor.

- How does the actor handle unfamiliar situations, disruptions, and interruptions? Look for demonstrations of self that emerge only when things move out of his control.

- Does his sense of rhythm and tempo make connections with the audience? Use the events in the audition to look for various sequences, progressions, and durations of activity that seem to go most smoothly.

- Does she have a sense of humor? What the actor finds funny and how he improvises his own quips indicate volumes about both his level of intelligence and willingness to learn.

- Did the actor do something unusually creative? Look for unique combinations of choices made during the audition (and not only the choices themselves).

- Were there any positive surprises? Consider how well the actor manages the audience's expectations.

Now design an audition that provides answers to questions such as these. Again, don't judge the particular choices made in the audition: auditioning remains, after all, an artificial environment. Instead, evaluate the actor's ability to make choices that create full [characterizations = representations] for his [roles = responsibilities].

You should not make final casting decisions immediately after auditioning all the prospective players. Instead, schedule callbacks for those under serious consideration, where now an interview provides valuable information. (HR departments today typically do this in reverse, interviewing all candidates while having only the one hired perform.) Probe for insights into each person's off-stage interests. Remember, individuals with the greatest reservoir of life experiences will make the most interesting choices once cast.

And finally, when making these casting decisions, consider that, as one director advises, you are "casting relationships rather than individual roles."[28] Any new actor, however well qualified for the role, is really suitable only to the extent that his addition enhances the dynamic interplay between all cast members of the [ensemble = organization].

Again, the casting director shouldn't impose his own interpretation of the part as one of the criteria for hiring. That is not his role. Rather, the casting director must assist producers and directors in finding those who also know how to fill *their* respective roles.

Recognizing the Dramatis Personae

Many people have seen the list of characters in an issue of *Playbill* or the scrolling credits at the end of a movie but may not know its name: *dramatis personae*, described by *NTC's Dictionary of Theatre and Drama Terms* as "from the Latin, meaning the characters in a play; also, the list of them. Shown at the beginning of a play script or in the printed program for a performance, the list may merely give the names of the characters and the actors who play them or may include brief descriptions of the characters. The term is also used in a joking way for the participants in any event."[29] The term deserves more serious consideration, and the practice more widespread use, in the Experience Economy.

On rare occasions, businesses acknowledge employees publicly in writing. Annual reports list senior officers. On-duty placards display the names of managers at some service establishments; ditto drivers of rental car shuttle buses. Slips of paper inform us our garment was inspected by #7, whoever that might be. Yet customers rarely see full acknowledgment of all the players involved in the production of a good or service. Why not? It's because only staged experiences merit display of a dramatis personae—and all experience stagers should display one. Of course, guests may not care to read the names of every costume designer or supporting actor who helped stage the experience (just as few stay until the end of movies to read every last credit). No matter, because the dramatis personae exists not for the customers but for the players, and not only for the stars but also for those who never set foot onstage during a performance, the business equivalents of gaffers, key grips, and Foley artists: the dramaturgs, scriptwriters, technicians, and stage crew (not to mention the casting director). The list recognizes their performances along with the onstage actors, producers, and directors who so often receive not only the credit but the fame as well. The dramatis personae sets the stage for the next production run by commemorating the preceding one.

Just as business theatre can learn from the performing arts by means of such long-standing practices, so too can the arts learn from business. *In Standing Room Only: Strategies for Marketing the Performing Arts*, Philip Kotler, marketing professor at the Kellogg Graduate School of Management at Northwestern University, and his colleague Joanne Scheff encourage those managing the arts to embrace business principles in order to keep the arts alive.[30] They recommend mixing both an "art-centered approach" that sees the arts in terms of unbridled expression and a "market-centered approach" that sees it as a hard-nosed business. What concert pianist and educator David Owen Norris shared with Kotler and Scheff regarding musical performances—"We must make the experience relevant for the audience and either satisfy or surprise audience expectations"—applies to *every* performance, no matter where or how performed, on the theatre stage or at the workplace.[31]

The output generated by those who act on farms and in factories has long been the result of theatre performances, invented worlds distinctly different from other facets of everyday living.

A two-hour performance of *King Lear* and the overnight performance of FedEx both compress time. Both—arguably one more than the other—also help us see the world differently. But which one? Today, successful businesses, like good art, must engage the audience. If you treat customers no differently than what they receive from run-of-the-mill competitors you cannot shift up the Progression of Economic Value.

The Experience Economy liberates theatre from the area behind the arched proscenium. The staged performances of government-subsidized playhouses, community theatres, movie studios, and theme parks will continue to face rising competition from unexpected sources—not only from restaurants and cafes as well as computer games and virtual worlds, but also from banks and insurance companies, airlines and hotels, and from every street corner and retooled mall. For every business is a stage.

CHAPTER 9

The Customer Is the Product

EVERY BUSINESS CAN INDEED BE a stage for offering economic experiences. Whether selling to consumers or companies, firms must recognize that goods and services are no longer enough; customers now want experiences. But to what end? Experiences can offer enjoyment, knowledge, diversion, and beauty, but more than the desire for such memorable qualities drives the Experience Economy. For not all experiences are fun, enlightening, distracting, or breathtaking.

Why, for example, do people pay good money to join fitness centers, where they expect to experience physical pain? Why do they pay $200 an hour to a psychiatrist, in whose office they may re-experience mental anguish? Why do tens of thousands of men pay admission to attend an event sponsored by the Christian organization Promise Keepers, whose goal it is to change men's behavior? And why do young managers leave well-paying jobs to spend tens of thousands of dollars on business school? There seems to be only one answer to all of these questions: to be affected by the experience.

The experiences we have affect who we are, what we can accomplish, and where we are going, and we increasingly ask companies to stage experiences that change us. Human beings have always sought out new and exciting experiences to learn and grow, develop and improve, mend and reform. But as the world progresses further into the Experience Economy, much that was previously obtained through noneconomic activity will increasingly be found in the domain of commerce. That represents a significant change. It means that to obtain what we once sought for free, we now pay a fee.

This pattern can be seen in many spheres of our culture. We see people seeking spiritual growth outside the bounds of their local, traditional place of worship. Promise Keepers is one example. Another is the rise of spiritual directors, what one writer calls "personal trainers for the soul."[1] Troubled families no longer confine their search for help to other family members and friends in their religious or social community. They often seek advice from media personalities such as Dr. Laura Schlessinger or Dr. Phil McGraw, as well as from the numerous books and tapes now available that include recipes for self-improvement. In education, businesses increasingly establish their own institutions of learning, no longer able to rely on public schools to graduate educated students. Likewise, more families pay to send their children to private school for fear that public schools won't get the job done. The changing nature of labor also drives the demand for new kinds of economic experiences. Along with the decline of the Agrarian and Industrial Economies there has been a great decline in the number of people who support themselves by doing hard, physical labor. Many of us now pay to get and stay physically fit in venues outside the workplace. It is, after all, people with desk jobs, and not meatpackers and bricklayers, who most often visit health clubs after work.

But what are people really after as they enter into all these pursuits? Experiences, yes. But there is more than that: we want to transform ourselves, to become different. While experiences are less transient than services, the individual partaking in the experience often wants something more lasting than a memory, something beyond what any good, service, or experience alone can offer. People who buy memberships in a fitness center do not pay for the pain but for ongoing exercise regimens that will increase their physical well-being, helping them go from flabby to fit. Likewise, people return to psychiatrists as long as they see improvements in their mental or emotional well-being. People head for business school because they want to affect their professional and financial well-being. Exercise routines, counseling sessions, learning courses, and religious excursions are actually means of eliciting something that is more desirable, and more valued, than the experience itself.[2]

In the healthcare industry, patients want more than pharmaceutical goods, medical services, or even a hospital experience; they want to go from sick to well. The same goes for management consulting. A struggling company wants something beyond informational goods, advisory services, or even educational experiences: it wants to grow. Companies clearly value an offering of economic growth more highly than they do the goods and services, or even isolated experiences, that still form the basis of much of the consulting industry. Even now, project methodologies (bound copies of physical goods), project team facilitators (on-site management services), and intervention programs (multidisciplinary experiences) command far lower fees than offerings such as systems outsourcing deals, which promise large-scale change.

As economic activity shifts further and further away from goods and services, those companies that stage experiences alone—without considering the effect these experiences have on the participants and without designing the experiences in such a way as to create a desired change—will eventually see their experiences become commoditized. The second time you experience something, it will be marginally less enjoyable than the first time, the third time less enjoyable than that, and so on until you finally notice the experience doesn't engage you nearly as much as it once did. Welcome to the commoditization of experiences, best exemplified by the increasingly voiced phrase "Been there, done that."[3]

The Progression of Economic Value Revisited

Experiences are not the final economic offering. Companies can escape the commoditization trap by the same route that the other offerings can take: customization. When you customize an experience to make it just right for an individual—providing exactly what he needs right now—you cannot help *changing* that individual. When you customize an experience, you automatically turn it into a *transformation*, which companies create on top of experiences (you've heard the phrase "a life-transforming experience") just as they create experiences on top of services and so forth. As shown in figure 9-1, transformations are a distinct economic offering, the fifth and final one in our Progression of Economic Value. A transformation is what the out-of-shape person, the emotionally troubled person, the young managers, the hospital patient, and the struggling company all really desire.

By staging a series of experiences, companies are better able to achieve a lasting effect on the buyer than through an isolated event. It is the revisiting of a recurring theme, experienced through distinct and yet unified events, that transforms. As multiple experiences emerge and compete for guests, companies staging these events will begin to realize that any experience can become the basis for a new offering that elicits a transformation.

Let's return to one of our favorite experiences: the birthday celebration. As more and more companies compete with the staged birthday events offered by Chuck E. Cheese's, Gameworks,

FIGURE 9-1

Completing the Progression of Economic Value

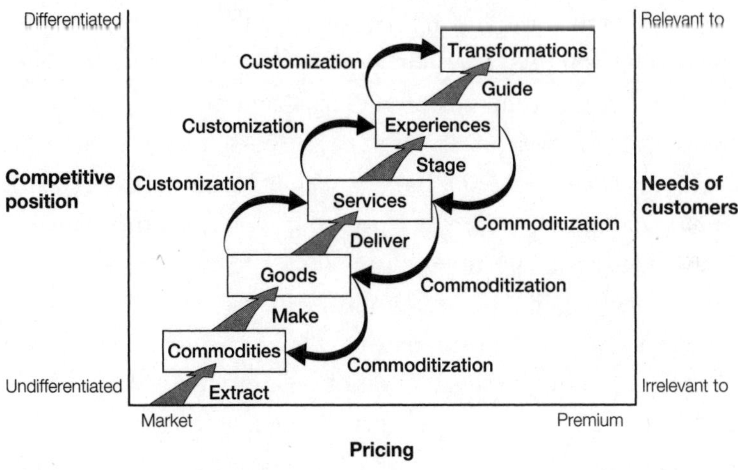

Dave & Buster's, and the like—not to mention such locally produced experiences as New Pond Farm—this genre of experience will undergo commoditization, resulting in lower prices for single birthday events. Eventually, some experience stager will realize that shifting to birthday *transformations* would increase customer value and thereby forestall commoditization. What might such a company—a transformation elicitor—do? Well, rather than focus simply on only this year's party, it might guide parents through multiple birthdays as the child grows, and it might concern itself not only with staging the party but also with selecting gifts, inviting guests, and encouraging after-party behaviors. Gifts, for example, could be aimed at a child's developmental needs. Guests might serve as professional role models, from spheres of life in which the child already shows interest—or in which the parents wish to encourage him. To help birthday children become more conscious and appreciative, the transformational birthday offering might include thank-you notes, with pre-engineered templates and stamped envelopes.[4] And most important, each year's birthday party would be treated as an incremental event in the overall management of childhood development. Such birthday guides may or may not emerge from the current birthday experience circuit, but they may just as well come from a toy manufacturer (leveraging its child development expertise), a parenting magazine (which understands child rearing as a parenting issue), a sports management firm (with a portfolio of potential role models), or a tutoring service (building on its customized curricula).

Perhaps martial arts teachers were the first experience stagers to realize the transformational power of their offerings. Many parents allow, encourage, or even force their children to join such programs as karate, kung fu, and tae kwon do. Many parents do it because they lack the skills or desire themselves to instill the proper respect and self-control in their offspring, others to complement and support what they see as their disciplinary responsibilities. Masters of martial arts promise not only to teach the skills of their ancient pursuits but to provide a set of rules by which students must live. As the business manager of one such establishment declared, when parents come for enrollment they're saying, "Fix my kid."[5] Many parents, however, want to limit the extent of this influence. In a *Forbes* story on the phenomenon, the writer reports that some parents seek out Christian or Jewish martial arts masters "to avoid schools they think may introduce their youngsters to Eastern mysticism."[6]

On a more material front, consider the food industry and the way dining experiences might progress into transformational offerings. Nutrition management may be the next shift, where grocery stores or restaurants (or more likely, start-ups from unanticipated sources) compete against Jenny Craig, Weight Watchers, and others by making healthy food interesting and exciting to eat.

Aiming all four realms of an experience at improving a guest's nutritional intake, the entertainment realm could make eating decisions fun, the educational realm might emphasize the personal effect of eating properly, the esthetic could encourage the proper pace and amount of eating, and the establishment might provide a place to escape the temptation to relapse into old behaviors. All ingredients, foods, food services, and dining experiences could be managed by a single transformation elicitor, paid not on the basis of the food itself, the service surrounding the food, nor even the experience enveloping both but for measurable improvements in cholesterol levels, fat, weight, and similar health measures. Other restaurants might guide transformations by aiming to refine people's tastes or to enhance a couple's relationship. These are all viable strategic alternatives available to those who today consider themselves to be in the business of making or serving food.

Similarly, when all bookstores add coffee and espresso bars and perhaps even reading rooms—where one pays to read in places specifically designed to maximize the reading experience—companies will surface to offer reading transformations. People would pay these establishments to guide them through intellectual pursuits by identifying books and other materials worth reading, followed by observations and perhaps even examinations—not in a traditional schoolish sense but as a new learning alternative to make sure people got the right ideas. Booksellers and publishers alike struggle to find ways to compete with online merchants such as Amazon.com (and with commoditizing e-books). Why not make this offering transformational by actually charging a premium to recommend what employees should read (via mass customized recommendations) as a means to wisely advance organization-wide intelligence?

Another industry with the potential to get into the business of guiding transformations is higher education. Consider the Harvard Business School. Its vast intellectual resources—professors, classes for undergraduate and graduate degrees, executive education programs, the *Harvard Business Review* and Harvard Business Review Press, and various and sundry newsletters, videos, blogs, various websites, and other teaching resources—make it a perfect enterprise for transforming individuals into business executives prepared to face any strategic challenge. To do so, though, it would have to extend itself beyond selling book and magazine goods, information services, and educational experiences to viewing its business as *changing* customers. And for all those colleges and universities jostling to reach the top of the various rankings now promulgated in the press, this is the route to take. One such institution of higher education that recognizes this is the London Business School. Here's what former dean John Quelch told *Fast Company* magazine:

> *We're not in the education business. We're in the transformation business. We expect everyone who participates in a program at the London Business School—whether it's for three days or for two years—to be transformed by the experience. We want people to look back on their time here as something that significantly influenced their career and possibly even their entire life. . . One nice thing about declaring that we're in the transformation business is that everyone here—from custodians to deputy deans—has become much more motivated. People are eager to take part in having an impact on the students who come here.*[7]

Such a mindset will emerge across almost every industry that today views itself as part of the service sector. Healthcare providers will shift past performing fee-for-service procedures to charging fees based on making or keeping people well. Architects will not only make the "leap from 'how it is designed' to 'how it feels,'" as Anna Klingmann describes the shift to experiences in her book *Brandscapes*, but also embrace a "changed perception of architecture, when the aspirant, rather than the artifact, is the subject of investigation."[8] Airlines and hotels will increasingly work on transforming business travelers into well-rested road warriors equipped for the next day's battles. Tourism companies will likewise get into the personal and family transformation business, for as psychologist Jeffrey A. Kottler points out, "Travel offers you more opportunities to change your life than almost any other human endeavor."[9] And, to complete only a short list of what's to come, computer service companies and system integrators will transform customers with well-running equipment into enterprises that use the equipment to run their businesses well.

And why not? Their competitors—management consultants and outsourcing firms—are already making the move to offer transformations. Many understand that customers no longer want tangible reports, intangible analyses, or memorable workshops that yield recommendations on what they should do. They're a start, but none by itself makes the customer a better company. One analyst notes that hiring a big consultant "is like going to your chiropractor. One hundred eighty-two visits later you still have to come back."[10] Rather, consulting customers aspire to become better businesses, and they want to engage consultants who yield the sustained outcomes they desire. An *InformationWeek* editorial notes, "CIOs say they're wide open to forging such deeper, 'outcome-based' partnerships, where their vendors share in the risks and rewards of major IT implementations and upgrades."[11]

Or consider the Philips Lifeline medical alert offerings, which encompass aspects of goods, services, experiences, and transformations. At the core of its offerings for the "personal response industry" lies a variety of devices (monitors, watches, and pendants); when a user presses his device, a signal goes through the telephone line to a twenty-four-hour monitoring center. There, trained monitors call back to assess the nature of the incident and, if necessary, dispatch an appropriate person—friend, relative, or public emergency personnel—to handle the situation. Fewer than 5 percent of the calls require emergency assistance, the ostensible reason for the service. Rather, most people call because they feel isolated or lonely, and talking to someone at the center makes them feel better. But in the final analysis, most customers—that is, those who are paying Philips—are relatives of the person using the device. What they are really buying is peace of mind.

What people really seek from hospitals is to be healed. Mid-Columbia Medical Center (MCMC) in The Dalles, Oregon, excels at this, drawing people from more than twenty states to its Celilo Cancer Center, where it presents a portfolio of offerings revolving around the five ways people heal: biologically, socially, intellectually, environmentally, and spiritually. Biologically, it offers state-of-the-art treatment, being the second site to offer intensity-modulated radiation therapy (IMRT). Socially, it has healing gardens for patients to enjoy with their families, as well as numerous social events. Intellectually, MCMC offers a medical library to provide patients and their families with all the information they need on their cancer situation, including information about alternative therapies. Environmentally, it places sculptured gardens on the grounds, looking out onto the Cascade Mountains. And spiritually, it added a meditation room inside and a labyrinth outside as places for people to spend time in meditation or prayer. Mid-Columbia's premise for devoting one-third of its space to such "nonfunctional" places is that it is beneficial to take patients from being stressed to relaxed, for it found that studies showed that most health issues are stress related. It therefore creates the most stress-free environment possible to accompany its treatments, including soothing harp music in the lobby, relaxation classes, massages, and steam baths. It truly considers itself to be in the transformation business.[12]

As should prisons. Corrections Corporation of America (CCA), based in Nashville, provides local, state, and federal governments with private detention and correction services. Bureaucratic wardens might simply consider it a service that keeps inmates off the street for the length of their sentences. But when asked by *Chief Executive* magazine to describe his company's "product," former CEO Doctor Crants responded that CCA produced "quality corrections," which involve not only housing people but also creating "some positive impact on the chances that those inmates will have a better life after they leave our facility than they otherwise would . . . For us, quality corrections means teaching our inmates to read and write . . . About 50 percent don't have high school diplomas, so we have GED classes and educational courses . . . For those who already have a high school diploma, we have various kinds of job training courses. We teach them a skill, such as diesel mechanics or automobile mechanics . . . And we've devised what we think is the finest drug treatment program in the world, superior to the Betty Ford Clinic. It takes seven months to get through."[13]

Crants acknowledged that CCA's methods do not work on about 20 percent of the prison population, the true psychopaths and sociopaths who cannot, at least with known methods, become productive contributors to society.[14] He further explained that the government agencies that have privatized their prisons to CCA save money, generally about 10 percent, because "what's cost effective is to give every inmate a sense of hope. He gets up in the morning and goes off to do something that, at the end of his sentence, may position him to have a chance for life outside of a prison setting."[15]

It may only be a chance, but transforming a hardened criminal or even a first-time offender into someone who won't return to prison truly is a different kind of economic offering. The same is true regarding all those who need a second chance at life, including those for whom typical schools have not worked—such as the culinary students at Bidwell Training Center in Pittsburgh. As social entrepreneur Bill Strickland says of these students, "They're human beings who are now capable of participating in the environment in an effective way . . . That's an outcome. That's a product."[16]

Discovering the Distinctions, Part 2

As with experiences, some observers will surely argue that what we are calling transformations are really only a subclass of services. But there is just too much disparity between, say, eating at a McDonald's and firming up at a fitness center, between providing information reports and partnering in business outcomes, and between cleaning a suit and cleansing a soul to classify them all as a single economic offering. As delineated in table 9-1, transformations are indeed a distinct economic offering, as distinct from experiences as experiences are from services. Identifying this new offering requires using words not normally associated with businesses and their economic output. But just as it took years for the now-familiar terms of the Service Economy—such as *intangible products, clients, delivering on demand*—to fall trippingly from the tongue, so, too, it will be a while before the new vocabulary of experiences and transformations will become second nature. But to fully discern the distinctions between all five economic offerings, consider the following:

- While commodities are fungible, goods tangible, services intangible, and experiences memorable, transformations are *effectual*. All other economic offerings have no lasting consequence beyond their consumption. Even the memories of an experience fade over time. But buyers of transformations seek to be guided toward some specific aim or

TABLE 9-1

Economic Distinctions

Economic offering	Commodities	Goods	Services	Experiences	Transformations
Economy	Agrarian	Industrial	Service	Experience	Transformation
Economic function	Extract	Make	Deliver	Stage	Guide
Nature of offering	Fungible	Tangible	Intangible	Memorable	Effectual
Key attribute	Natural	Standardized	Customized	Personal	Individual
Method of supply	Stored in bulk	Inventoried after production	Delivered on demand	Revealed over a duration	Sustained through time
Seller	Trader	Manufacturer	Provider	Stager	Elicitor
Buyer	Market	Customer	Client	Guest	Aspirant
Factors of demand	Characteristics	Features	Benefits	Sensations	Traits

purpose, and transformations must elicit that intended effect. That's why we call such buyers *aspirants*; they aspire to be someone or something different. Without a change in attitude, performance, characteristics, or some other fundamental dimension of self, no transformation occurs. And this change should be not only in degree but also in kind, not only in function but also in structure. The transformation affects the very being of the buyer.

- While companies store commodities in bulk, inventory goods after production, deliver services on demand, and reveal experiences over a duration of time, they must *sustain* transformations through time if they are to take hold, to genuinely change the aspirant. If a change—losing weight, stopping a bad habit, or becoming financially secure, say, on the consumer side, or lowering fixed expenses, stopping wasteful practices, or becoming insulated from exchange rate fluctuations on the business side—is only temporary and not sustained, then it was not really transforming but merely a momentary uptick along the same old journey. Likewise, any relapses or digressions reduce the measure or intensity of the transformation attained.

- Finally, whereas commodities are natural, goods standardized, services customized, and experiences inherently personal, transformations are *individual*. The offering does not exist outside the changed traits each aspirant desires; it is that change itself. Experiences are events to which the individual reacts and thereby creates a memory, but transformations go much further, actually changing the *being* of the buyer, whether a consumer or business. Because an experience is inherently personal, no two people can have the same one. The effect differs based on past experiences

> and current state of mind. So, too, no individual can undergo the same transformation twice; the second time it's attempted, the individual would no longer be the same person. People value transformation above all other economic offerings because it addresses the ultimate source of all other needs: why the buyer desires the commodities, goods, services, and experiences he purchases.

Indeed, with transformations, the economic offering of a business is the change in the individual person or company as a result of what the offering business does. With transformations, the *customer is the product!* The individual buyer of the transformation essentially says, "Change me." The company's economic offering is neither the materials it uses nor the physical things it makes. It's neither the processes it executes nor the encounters it orchestrates. When a company guides transformations, *the offering is the individual.*

This means that the exact form and content of any particular transformational offering have to be considered carefully. The transformation elicitor must understand customer aspirations before hoping to affect any change in the particular traits—whether they be along physical, emotional, intellectual, or spiritual dimensions. Aspirations of course relate to customer expectations; but here the expectations center not on some external function or benefit but on the customers themselves, on what they want to become.[17]

Once the Experience Economy has run its course in the decades to come, the *Transformation Economy* will take over. Then the basis of success will be in understanding the aspirations of individual consumers and businesses and guiding them to fully realize those aspirations.

Let's examine how the insurance industry, as one readily discernible example, will make the transition through successive economies. As you saw earlier, the claims adjustment process at Progressive Insurance shifted the company into the Experience Economy by providing the customers with the time and means to settle their nerves. The on-the-spot check relieves them of all worry about how to handle the situation. Traditional policy carriers merely *insure* their policyholders, meaning, as shown in figure 9-2, that clients merely secure a payment in the event of a loss. Something bad happens, they get money. That's it. The Progressive experience, on the other hand, *assures* its policyholders, meaning that guests secure confidence, encouragement, trust, or a feeling of satisfaction. When something happens, Progressive assures them that they will not only get their money but will also feel better about the whole unfortunate situation.

In the Transformation Economy, even assurance won't be enough. In addition, carriers will *ensure* policyholders, which means that aspirants will secure an actual event, situation, or outcome. For example, in 2007 Safeco Insurance of Seattle began providing "Teensurance" with the tagline "Encouraging responsibility.

FIGURE 9-2

The "insurance" industry through successive economic offerings

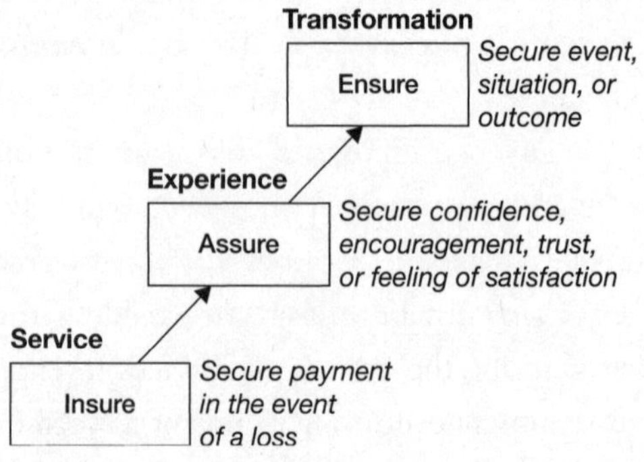

Delivering Peace of Mind." This is exactly what the company's *en*surance offering does. For teenagers, it combines an online driving assessment geared to enhance their driving skills with 24/7 roadside assistance should anything happen—not only accidents, of course, but also any car problem at all. For parents, Safeco installs a GPS monitoring device in the car that tracks not only location but also speed, distance, and time of driving. This Safety Beacon Convenience and Protection System sends an immediate alert to the parents whenever the teen exceeds preset speed limits, safe driving zone perimeters, or curfew restrictions, as well as for more mundane arrival and departure times. Online tools also enable parents and their children to discuss proper driving habits and behavior based on actual data, leading teenagers to become better drivers and thereby earn their parents' trust.

Achmea, of Zeist, The Netherlands, focuses not on automobile but health insurance, among other financial offerings. Realizing that such insurance was a low-interest product, in 2006 it sought to change itself into a health company. It created its own health centers not only to help policyholders become more fit but also to enhance their nutritional intake, posture, incident prevention, and so forth. It also created a members-only website with such features as a medical encyclopedia, diagnosis assistance, lifestyle information, and psychology consults. It rounds out its shift from mere insurance services to ensurance transformations with such additional offerings as a magazine and newsletter, wellness programs, education, travel, and health checks with its own doctors.

Now, if you're a service provider, think of your own business. What are the equivalents to *insure, assure*, and *ensure* for the industry in which your company now resides? It's unlikely you can find such simple words to describe the path from services to experiences to transformations (you may even have to invent a word or two), but thinking creatively about new economic offerings that surround the present ones will pay dividends as we move inexorably from the Experience to the Transformation Economy.

So what's a manufacturer to do? In today's Experience Economy, we already see manufacturers experientializing their goods—*inging* the thing by focusing on the experience customers have while *using* their goods. In the Transformation Economy manufacturers will of course *transformationalize* their goods—design and sell goods that help customers become something distinct. Here the focus moves from *using* to *user*: how the individual *changes* while using the good. Although offerings such as self-help books, "edutainment" software, and exercise videos and equipment begin to address this aim, they fall short of fully transformationalized offerings.[18] If exercise equipment were truly transformationalized, for instance, the manufacturers would stop thinking of their business as *selling physical* goods and start thinking of it as *developing good physiques*—and someone would show up occasionally to examine the results!

Some firms lead the way. In the greeting card business, Hallmark Card's BusinessConnections unit creates cards aimed at boosting employee morale and loyalty in the workplace (as well as customer loyalty in the marketplace). Hallmark's team of designers helps individual companies assess their needs, determines the appropriate series of messages to communicate to specific departments and individuals, and then creates customized cards for multiple occasions. Because the goal of the program is to change employee attitudes, Hallmark no longer sells the custom cards as ordinary goods but as tools for executives and HR departments to help improve employee retention and corporate culture.

Consider the automobile industry. Just as a significant factor in automobile design today is the sensation of how the doors sound when they close (something that did not matter a whit thirty years ago), in the Transformation Economy people won't buy a car unless it makes them—or their kids—better drivers. To that end, automakers have added a raft of features over the past decade or two, including collision avoidance radar, adaptive headlamps and side view mirrors, reverse backup sensors and cameras, and lane departure warning systems. Although most of these are embedded in the price of the vehicles themselves, General Motors surrounds its vehicles with the distinct transformational offering OnStar, a safety, security, and diagnostic system that ensures drivers are, well, safe and secure, with properly running vehicles.[19]

Or look at pharmaceuticals. GlaxoSmithKline (GSK) has long provided smoking cessation goods—Nicorette gum, NicoDerm CQ patches, Commit lozenges, and the like. It found, however, that the rate at which people actually achieved their aspiration of going from smoker to nonsmoker was quite small—only 24 percent.[20] So the company designed an individualized smoking cessation program called Committed Quitters. This program begins with an up-front phone conversation between the smoker and a company representative to understand the person's smoking habits, how many cigarettes he smokes a day, when he most craves one, what obstacles he faces, and so forth. GSK then sends out custom mailers—letters, brochures, tip sheets, and so on—with follow-up phone calls, e-mails, and website interactions. After the multiweek program, GSK found that people who go through Committed Quitters had a 50 percent greater likelihood of achieving their aspiration—and bought more of its manufactured goods as well.[21]

One huge arena for manufacturers to sell goods that can help transform people is fitness. A short list of products here includes Nike+, a GPS application that connects your shoes to your iPod to track miles run, and adidas' miCoach, a personal training system accessible over the Web. Another transformative product is Fitbit, a clip-on sensor from the eponymous San Francisco-based company of the same name. This device measures the number of steps you take each day, your total distance traveled, the calories burned, and even your sleep quality. DirectLife, from Philips, tracks all of your activity (except sleeping) and comes with personal fitness and nutrition coaching through its own website. And Under Armour provides apparel that compresses muscles as you work out and aids in circulation.

Further, just as many manufacturers now exploit the Experience Economy by making memorabilia for guests to buy as physical reminders of their experience, in the nascent Transformation Economy goods producers can also make the *emblems* aspirants purchase to commemorate the transformations they undergo. Rings, crosses, flags, trophies, pennants, medals, badges, medallions, insignias, diplomas, certificates, and other such emblems all tangibly signify that their bearers have transformed themselves in some way: from single to married, from team to champion, from civilian to soldier, from soldier to hero, and so forth. All of these emblems further enable people to identify those who have undergone the same transformations and thereby initiate conversations and form communities.

Guiding Transformations

Experts in grieving assert that everyone faced with a tremendous personal loss first must go through a series of experiences—such as shock, depression, confusion, guilt, anger—before recovery can occur. How much better we can handle these stages, and more quickly be transformed from grief to normal living, when someone—minister, counselor, friend—*guides* us than when we are left alone. In the same way, all transformation elicitors guide aspirants through a series of experiences.

The Progression of Economic Value forms an Economic Pyramid, viewed as successive offerings built on top of the ones below, as shown in figure 9-3. Transformation elicitors must determine exactly the right set of life-transforming experiences required to guide aspirants in achieving their goals (commemorated with goods as emblems). Experience stagers must depict what services engage the guest and then stage them in such a way as to create a memorable event (preserved with goods as memorabilia). Service providers, in turn, must devise the proper configuration of goods (such as tables and condiment dispensers in a fast-food restaurant, or hangers, plastic bags, and cleaning equipment in a dry cleaner) that enable them to deliver the set of intangible activities desired by the client. Goods manufacturers, of course, must develop sources for the appropriate commodities used as raw materials for the tangible products they make for users. And commodity traders

FIGURE 9-3

The Economic Pyramid

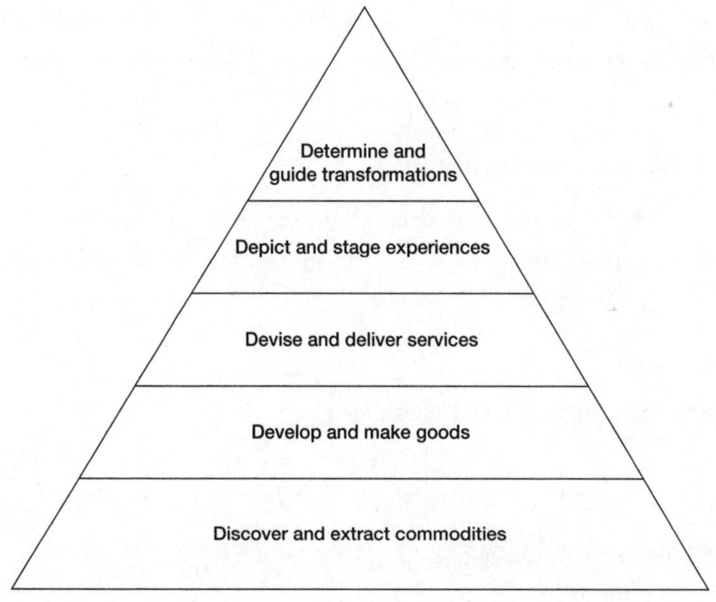

must discover where those materials lie and extract them for the markets they serve.

So transformations cannot be *extracted, made, delivered*, or even *staged*; they can only be *guided*. As the old saying goes, "You can lead a horse to water, but you can't make it drink." No one can force someone to change. All transformations occur within the very being of the customer and so, in the end, must be made by the customer. As Mark Scott, retired CEO of Mid-Columbia Medical Center, told us, "We found that some patients just did not take to stress relief well during their cancer treatments, perhaps understandably. In such cases we tried to draw in the whole family, so they could help guide the patients as well. When it worked, it worked wonderfully."

Transformation elicitors can, at best, bring about the right situation under which the proper change can occur, meaning staging the right experiences that involve the right services that . . . well, you get the idea. But that alone is not enough; there is more to guiding a transformation. As shown in figure 9-4, this economic offering requires three separate phases: diagnosing aspirations, staging transforming experience(s), and following through.

Diagnosing Aspirations

To what do customers aspire? Where are they today relative to this aspiration? Along what dimensions can this transformation be achieved? Without a proper diagnosis, customers cannot achieve

FIGURE 9-4

Phases of guiding transformations

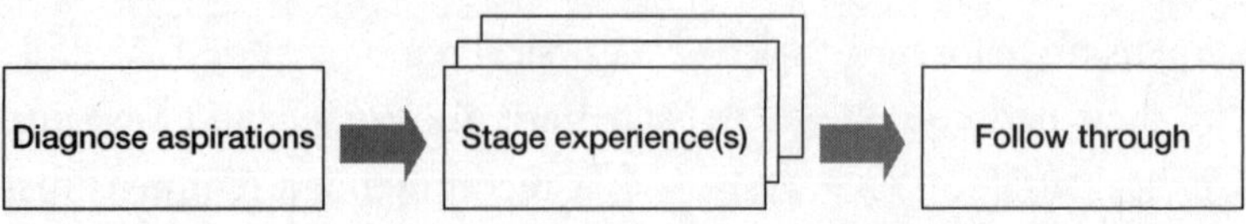

it. And—as is the case with mass customizing mere goods and services, where customers often do not know or cannot articulate what they want—aspirants often do not know or cannot articulate their hopes and dreams.[22] Or they may even have the wrong aspirations—goals and desires deleterious to their own well-being. Just as financial service firms have a fiduciary responsibility to prevent clients from making terrible investment decisions and theme park operators have a custodial responsibility to prevent guests from acting in an unsafe manner, all transformation elicitors have an ethical responsibility to prevent aspirants from attaining inappropriate or immoral traits. Of course, what those may be necessarily depends on the conscience and worldview of the particular elicitor.

Essential to every transformation, then, is understanding what customers *truly need to become* and how far away they are from fulfilling those needs within themselves, even if they do not realize it or delude themselves about the direction or magnitude of the change required. Are they really capable of achieving the aspiration? If so, how can they be guided to the proper transformation? In some cases—and this explains why triage should often precede diagnosis—individual people or companies may not be capable of becoming that to which they aspire. There's no sense even starting down the *transformation* path in these cases unless some other *preformation* activities first fortify aspirants in those areas in which they are too weak to proceed.

During the diagnosis phase, a fitness center, for example, must learn the weight, muscle strength, or body tone (or all three) desired by customers and assess their current state along each dimension before it can design a physical regimen aimed at fulfilling their particular desires. But it must also understand aspirants' medical situation to guarantee that recommended regimens first do no harm, and it must ascertain their mental and emotional dispositions to determine the possible obstacles that may arise along the way. And in the healthcare field, doctors (including psychiatrists) presume that all patients want to be physically (or mentally) well, but specific aspirations may vary greatly, from being "good as new" to returning to work with "good enough" function, from just wanting to get out of the hospital and go home as soon as possible to wanting to die in peace. Like other transformation elicitors, physicians may think some goals are set too low and may reject others for being too optimistic, but they must in any case focus on the patient's best interests when designing the proper procedures (while always leaving room for the miraculous to occur). Similarly, management consultants must understand the strategic needs of a business as well as its current capabilities, taking into account the fact that both the company and the consultant are biased observers, before designing an implementable course of action.

If you desire to offer transformations, think of diagnosis as a concrete from–to statement. Consider some of such statements we have already used here: from flabby to fit; from sick to well; from being stressed to being relaxed; from smoker to nonsmoker; from single to married; from team to champion; from grief to normal living; from just wanting to get out of the hospital and go home as soon as possible to wanting to die in peace. These statements obviously serve as generic, broad transformational directions; you must always go further, applying the from–to diagnosis down to the individual aspirant.

Staging Transforming Experience(s)

What experience or, generally, set of experiences will bring about the necessary from–to transformation? How can customers be changed from where they are today to where their aspiration lies, or should lie? Transformations, of course, build on experiences, specifically, the life-transforming experience(s) that cause customers to realize their aspirations, whether or not they can articulate what those aspirations are.

Psychiatrists, for example, hold a series of counseling sessions with patients, each one often with a different motive but all with the overarching intention of moving patients, over time, from a state of relative mental illness to one of mental health (although many psychiatrists can be accused of viewing no one as mentally well and others of "treating" the perfectly healthy). Educational institutions, including business schools, provide a series of experiences within experiences, some major, some minor, but all with the intention of educating, grooming, and molding students into graduates who will have a certain store of knowledge and abilities. Golf pros and other sports instructors combine intellectual understanding and emotional encouragement with the physical activities necessary to improve their customers' skills. As is the case with many transformations, golf pros do not limit improvement experiences to the one small act of hitting a golf ball. Rather, to turn duffers into adept players, they offer guidance on mental preparation, address, and swing; woods, irons, chipping, sand shots, and putting; rules, course management, and scoring techniques; and so forth.

Elicitors may use any one of the four realms of experience as the basis for a transformation. Entertainment experiences can alter our view of the world, while educational experiences can make us rethink how we fit into that world.[23] Escapist experiences can boost our personal capabilities and characteristics to new levels, while esthetic experiences can imbue a sense of wonder, beauty, and appreciation. But again, the most engaging life-transforming experiences center on the sweet spot composed of multiple elements from all four realms—no matter the ultimate aim of the transformation—for it is in the sweet spot that an experience best engages us and focuses our attention on its transforming nature.

Following Through

Experiences thus set the stage for transformation. But once it has occurred, how can it endure? What must be done to ensure that the change does not degenerate? It's not truly a transformation unless it is sustained through time. To make a great shot, a golfer has to have a great follow-through as well as a great swing. The same goes for great golf instruction. No one can dramatically improve his stroke after one lesson or sustain any gained improvement without continued practice and playing. Alcoholics Anonymous and other self-help groups excel in the follow-through phase of transformation, acknowledging that while it's possible to forgo one drink at one time, it's hard as all get-out to forgo that drink time after time. Similarly, marriage counselors can get a couple talking again after an adulterous affair, and perhaps even bring them to the point of forgiveness, but rebuilding the shattered trust requires a lot of long, hard work from both parties.

Transformation elicitors find follow-through the most difficult phase, and it is the one in which many fall short. Management consultants who deliver strategic analysis without guiding the client through implementation of the recommended changes remain in the service business; they are not in the transformation business. Educators who impart knowledge without ensuring that students can apply what they learn ascend only to the experience business (at best). And doctors who treat physical diseases without considering their patient's emotional needs do only half the job, a realization that is slowly dawning on the healthcare community.

Getting the Acts Together

In September 1994, the British medical journal *Lancet* created quite an angry furor in the healthcare community when it published an article applying to the work of doctors the principle that work is theatre. In "Acting in Medical Practice," Hillel Finestone and David Conter of the University of Western Ontario asserted that physicians must be trained as actors and follow the same three-phase approach outlined here to truly transform each patient. They showed how doctors, and by extension all other transformation elicitors, should employ each phase:

> *If a physician does not possess the necessary skills to assess a patient's emotional needs [diagnosis of whole person] and to display clear and effective responses to these needs [series of experiences] the job is not done. Consequently, we believe that medical training should include an acting curriculum, focused on the conveying of appropriate, beneficial responses to those emotional needs.*
>
> *In my practice . . . I frequently treat individuals who are in chronic pain. I find it essential to convey an encouraging, hopeful, often cajoling message to the patient [follow-through] to communicate concern and, more importantly, the need for the patient to work on self-improvement.*[24]

We would simply add that, since work truly is theatre, physicians should *always* act to convey the proper responsiveness and concern, and not only when it is more difficult to do so naturally.

Many physicians disagreed with, disparaged, or ridiculed the notion of doctors becoming actors. One humorous physician wrote that with drama "an official part of medical school curriculum" we would see scenes like this one: "*Problem*: Obesity. *Old way*: Doctor gives printed diet sheet. *New way*: Music swells as doctor stands in front of brilliant sunset, tears welling up, and makes the emotional, heart-rending promise, 'As God is my witness, you will always be hungry again.' "[25] But proper acting does help a patient tell more of what ails him during diagnosis, better understand treatment choices and determine the right set of experiences that will best treat him, and, finally, more readily handle the therapy and other actions required to follow through on treatment and sustain the transformation. Further, medical research backs up the contention that doctors must be actors. Numerous studies demonstrate that those doctors who deal with their patients in a more caring, empathic manner—in short, those with a better bedside manner—not only face fewer lawsuits but also have better patient treatment outcomes.[26] The personal, caring doctor of yore is not an anachronism; it's a role that must be assumed by every physician—no, make that every transformation elicitor.

The three phases of transformation—diagnosis, staged experience(s), and follow through—not only distinguish this economic offering from lesser experiences but also together represent a deeper sense of commitment to the well-being of each individual buyer than experience stagers alone may (or need to) demonstrate. Transformation elicitors must care enough to offer up-front diagnosis, to direct the staging of multiple events required for the buyer to change, and to follow through relentlessly. Noted philosopher Milton Mayeroff wrote perhaps the definitive book about this subject: *On Caring*. It should be mandatory reading for anyone truly interested in the business of offering transformations. "Caring, as helping another grow and actualize himself," writes Mayeroff, "is a process, a way of relating to someone that involves development, in the same way that friendships can only emerge in time through mutual trust and a deepening and qualitative transformation of the relationship."[27] By a "process," Mayeroff means a series of experiences that not only indicate but also *develop* caring over time. (Aren't your best friends those with whom you've had the greatest, most intense experiences?)

Further, the ongoing relationships with individual aspirants needed to sustain a transformation are possible only if executives abandon "flavor-of-the-month" imperatives in favor of enduring—yes, even timeless—operating principles. Mayeroff uses terms such as *knowing, patience, honesty, trust, humility, hope, rhythm*, and *courage* to describe caring. Why don't we find more of these terms in the mission statements of businesses? After all, transformation elicitors must also focus on the *continuation* of care. One-off experiences seldom yield a transformation, if there is no care there. Ensuring that aspirants achieve their aim usually means providing a series of experiences, each guided by a constant set of principles.

The first requirement for workers in a transformation business is that they truly care. Transformation elicitors, therefore, must first transform their own employees into caring people enriched by the work they perform before those workers can act differently to transform customers. As C. William Pollard, former chairman of The ServiceMaster Company, reminds us, "The spirits and souls of people can be enriched by what they do as they serve and work. And they can grow in the process of who they are becoming."[28] In his book *The Soul of the Firm*, Pollard relates how ServiceMaster trains and motivates employees not to deliver services but to serve. This requires a willingness among leaders to sacrifice their own needs in favor of the employees', and for employees to sacrifice their needs in order to eliminate the sacrifice of customers. Pollard relates that while Socrates said, "Know thyself" and Aristotle counseled, "Control thyself," "another great thinker changed history—and the hearts of people—with His unique approach to a meaningful life. 'Give thyself' were the words spoken by Jesus."[29]

Now, gauge your own reaction to the mere mention of Jesus' name in a business book. How does it make you feel? In the forthcoming Transformation Economy, aspirants will entrust their futures only to those with whom they share a common worldview. The transformation elicitor must embrace a context for change—the values the business enterprise seeks to promote—leading eventually to companies that practice *worldview segmentation*.

No longer can an enterprise take an agnostic attitude toward moral rightness and wrongness, hiding from such sensitive issues beneath the cloak of mere goods and services. Consciously—as with ServiceMaster—or not, all enterprises promote a worldview. Transformation issues cannot be avoided. Extracted commodities transform the earth into a subdued planet, with implications for all its inhabitants. Goods transform buyers into users of those goods, for ill or for gain. Services transform clients into recipients of those services, whether debasing or edifying. Experiences transform guests into participants in the encounter, whether the long-term effects are deleterious or therapeutic. And transformations turn aspirants into "a new you," with all the ethical, philosophical, and religious implications that phrase implies. All commerce involves moral choice.

CHAPTER 10

Finding Your Role in the World

IN THE END OF WORK, a book decrying the loss of agricultural, manufacturing, and service jobs caused by technological innovation, author and professional pessimist Jeremy Rifkin rightly points out, "We are entering a new phase in world history—one in which fewer and fewer workers will be needed to produce the goods and services for the global population."[1] Rifkin acknowledges that a "fourth" economic sector exists, which he calls the knowledge sector, but he doesn't believe it will "absorb more than a fraction of the hundreds of millions who[se jobs] will be eliminated in the next several decades."[2] Still, he confesses, "There is reason to be hopeful that a new vision based on transformation of consciousness and a new commitment to community will take hold."[3]

Indeed, there is great reason for hope: it is the natural evolution of the economy away from goods and services that brings about the need for new and more work based on experiences and transformations. As shown in figure 10-1 (an update of figure 1-3), the agricultural and manufacturing sectors actually lost jobs over the fifty-year period between 1959 and 2009. In both employment

FIGURE 10-1

Growth in employment and nominal gross domestic product (GDP) by economic offering

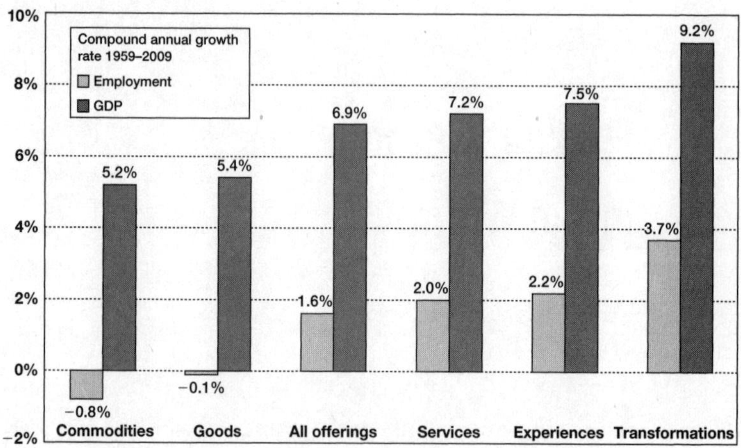

Source: U.S. Bureau of Economic Analysis; Strategic Horizons LLP; and Lee S. Kaplan, Lee3Consultants.com analysis.

and nominal GDP growth, the higher-level offerings dramatically outpaced the bottom two sectors, with transformations far exceeding even experiences in growth.[4]

Similarly, figure 10-2 updates the U.S. Consumer Price Index (CPI) statistics provided in figure 1-2, using medical care services as a transformation industry that can be cleanly separated from the "service sector" statistics gathered by the federal government. Healthcare "inflation," as it is mislabeled, not only outpaces all services, it even (as expected) increases faster than experiences.[5] But healthcare isn't alone. Management consulting fees increased tremendously in the past two decades. Today it is not uncommon for junior staff at the top consulting firms to charge more than $5,000 a day, five to eight times the per diem rates charged in the

FIGURE 10-2

Consumer Price Index (CPI) by economic offering

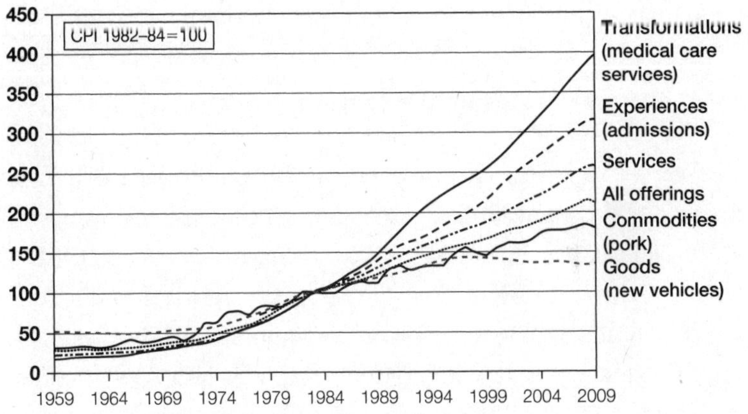

Source: U.S. Bureau of Labor Statistics; Lee S. Kaplan, Lee3Consultants.com.

1980s, on projects reaching eight or nine figures in size. And the nominal cost of total tuition, room, and board at colleges and universities quintupled from 1976–1977 to 2008–2009, greatly outpacing the rate of inflation.[6]

In short, just like the experience stagers before them, transformation elicitors are greatly increasing their share of the total economic pie. Today, the only thing better than being in the business of staging experiences is being in the business of guiding transformations. Both represent not only viable sectors of the economy but also the very engines of growth that will create more than enough jobs and output to supplant slowdowns in the lower-level sectors. This fact will take some getting used to. As former *Reason* editor Virginia Postrel accurately said, "We are, in fact, living more and more in an intangible economy, in which the greatest sources of wealth are not physical. We aren't yet used to an economy in which beauty, amusement, attention, learning, pleasure, even spiritual fulfillment are as real and economically valuable as steel or semiconductors."[7] Exactly. For the sources of wealth in these new economic sectors are not physical but intellectual.

Putting Wisdom into Work

The very idea of transforming people (or companies) demands that we think about and apply a word little used in businesses today: *wisdom*. As defined by the *Oxford English Dictionary* (OED), wisdom is "the quality of being wise, esp. in relation to conduct and the choice of means and ends; the combination of experience and knowledge with the ability to apply them judiciously; sound judgement, prudence, practical sense."[8] Elicitors require such wisdom across all phases of a transformation. In diagnosis, they need wisdom to distinguish real aspirations from false hopes, lofty goals, and self-delusions. They especially need wisdom to judge whether the individual person or company is capable of the change desired.

In the staged experiences phase, transformation elicitors need wisdom to prudently determine the right "choice of means" to fulfill the "choice of ends" decided during diagnosis. And follow-through involves the same qualified judgments, choices of action, and applications of experience and knowledge required at the beginning of the journey. Without the benefit of wisdom, people will find aspirations very difficult to achieve.

Look again at the *OED* definition of wisdom and see how it pairs experience and knowledge. As shown in figure 10-3, each level within the Progression of Economic Value corresponds with a level in what might be called the Progression of Valuable Intelligence.[9] At the bottom, commodities correspond with noise: the pure abundance of unorganized observations with little or no meaning, through which commodity extractors must wade to

FIGURE 10-3

The Progressions of Economic Value and valuable intelligence

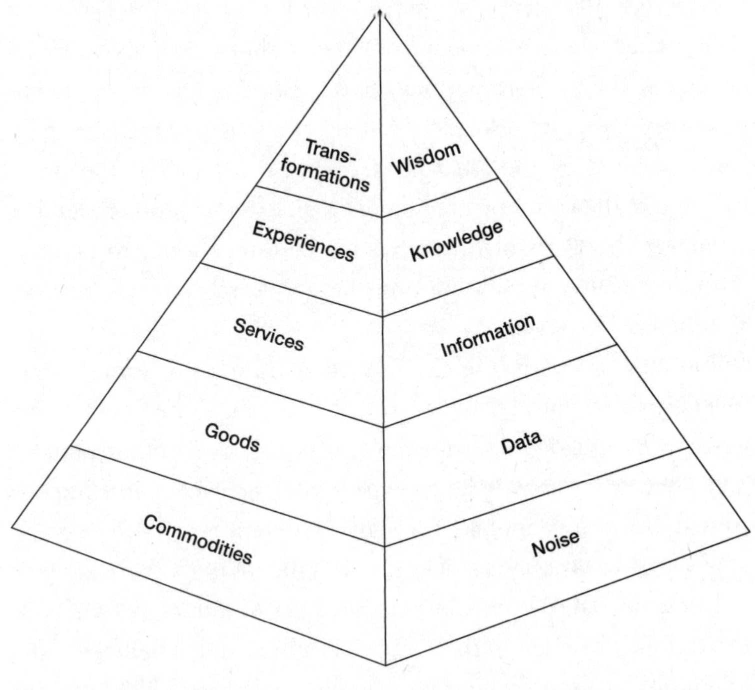

find, for example, the nuggets of gold or pockets of oil. When codified, or systematized into a code of symbols, these observations take on meaning and so become valuable data. The collection of physical and financial data is what made the Industrial Revolution possible. It was based on manufacturers' division of labor, standardized specifications, efficiency measures, and so forth. Indeed, the height of the revolution came with the creation of computers from what was once known as the data processing industry. Data became so abundant that it overwhelmed the ability of humans to process it.[10]

The term *data processing* is now an anachronism, a throwback to the 1960s and 1970s, for what we now call the *information technology* industry. This change exactly mirrors the shift from the Industrial to the Service Economy, for information is data communicated or delivered to others (a service) requiring a common context or frame of reference. Goods are manufactured in isolation and distributed to inventory; they are essentially instantiations of codified specifications. Services, on the other hand, cannot be proffered in isolation but require the common context of provider and customer together defining what particular activities the customer wants to execute. And the service of mass customizing goods, of course, substitutes information for inventory.

Now, as we shift to the Experience Economy, the term *information technology* sounds dated as well. People talk about "knowledge bases," "knowledge management," "knowledge infrastructure," and the like.[11] Knowledge is *experiential information*, intelligence gained from and applied through experiences.[12] None of the terms just mentioned relates to the embedding of intelligence within computer systems; rather, they refer to linking people with the right knowledge so that it can be immediately applied.[13] And, of course, staging experiences requires intimate knowledge of how human beings react to the cues they receive.

While we have yet to hear terms such as *wisdom technology* used, that is inevitably the next step. We do know of the first book to discuss moving beyond knowledge in companies: *Working Wisdom*, by John Dalla Costa. In it, Costa recognizes that wisdom is both *the result* of experiences—often painful ones (as with fitness centers, psychiatry, and grieving)—and *required for* transformations:

> *As a human construct with human foibles, it is inevitable that the practice of business will also include the experience of suffering. However, while other political, religious, and arts institutions see the*

> *need for suffering, valuing it as the price for the transformation to a new level of human experience, business organizations still regard suffering through that adolescent perspective of avoidance and presumed immunity.*
>
> *One reason for this institutional immaturity is that the profits of business are often based on serving a need that eliminates pain, discomfort, or unhappiness. Suffering and sorrow are words that for fifty years have been squeezed out of our consumer culture by the endless stream of products [that is, goods] and services promising relief, convenience, self-fulfillment, and instant gratification. Business in many ways provides the antidote to suffering, so it naturally tends to devalue that which it seeks to profitably eliminate.*[14]

Much greater profits will accrue to those businesses with the wisdom to shift beyond goods and services to the use of experiences, no matter how painful, to transform their customers.

Accomplishing this entails moving up the dual progressions shown in figure 10-3. While the economic offering becomes more and more intangible with each step up to the next level, the value of that offering becomes more and more *tangible*. Economists often talk about the "line of intangibility" between goods and services—to which we would add the "line of memorability" before experiences and the "line of sustainability" before transformations—but economists refer to the offering itself, and not the value it holds for the customer. As outlined in chapter 1, goods and services remain outside of the individual, while experiences actually reach inside of the individual to affect him in an inherently personal way, greatly increasing the value of the offering. But, no matter how acute an experience, one's memory of it fades over time. Transformations, on the other hand, guide the individual toward realizing some aspiration and then help to sustain that change through time. There is no earthly value more concrete, more palpable, or more worthwhile than achieving an aspiration.

Similarly, while the availability of intelligence diminishes as one ascends each level of the Progression of Valuable Intelligence (background noise is literally ubiquitous, wisdom all too scarce), the intelligence itself becomes more and more substantial. Nothing is more important, more abiding, or more wealth-creating than the wisdom required to transform customers. And nothing will command as high a price.

In his book *The Knowledge-Value Revolution*, author Taichi Sakaiya demonstrates how people in all societies "develop an empathetic impulse toward their environment that convinces them to hold off on things in short supply while making a point of using up whatever there is lots of."[15] For example, material and energy resources have always been abundant in the United States, so coal, oil, and other natural commodities have been wasted. The wealthy built enormous houses on huge plots of land and then always left the lights on simply to demonstrate their wealth. In Japan, material resources have always been scarce and therefore used sparingly. Human resources, on the other hand, existed in abundance, so to demonstrate their wealth, the affluent traditionally hired legions of people to tend their small houses, lawns, and gardens. With the economic boom of the latter half of the twentieth century, skilled labor became a scarce resource in both countries, yielding, at its zenith, disposable products that conserved labor through Mass Production techniques while simultaneously wasting materials, as they were thrown away after only one use.

In his own take on the same societal and economic shifts we identify, Sakaiya writes that more and more companies, and the people within them, are moving up the Progression of Valuable Intelligence to supply what he calls *chika* in Japanese. Translating somewhat awkwardly into *knowledge-value*, this "means both 'the price of wisdom' and 'the value created by wisdom.'"[16] Eventually, he foresees wisdom itself becoming relatively abundant:

> *It therefore follows that in the new society that is now forming, the life-style that will earn the most respect will be one in which the owner's conspicuous consumption of wisdom (in the broadest sense) is displayed, while the products that will sell best will be those that reveal their purchaser to be a person "in the know." Such products, which more than anything else manifest their owner's access to the best knowledge, information, and accumulated wisdom to be had, possess what I will hereafter refer to as "knowledge-value." It is my contention that we are entering a new phase of civilization in which the value attached to knowledge is the driving force.*[17]

And it is our contention that the "products" that best display knowledge-value—the economic offerings that result from accumulated wisdom—are those that transform the customer. The offering is not, however, the wisdom itself; that is only a means. The offering is the changed individual. The customer is the product.

You Are What You Charge For: Once More with Caring

Very few of the enterprises that work to change people or companies are truly in the transformation business. Far too many view their offerings as mere services, and, as a result, they far too often fail to elicit the transformation or to capture the full economic value delivered when it is elicited. More important, few charge for the transformation itself. Being in the transformation business means charging for the demonstrated outcome the aspirant achieves—the transformation itself—and not for the particular activities the company performs.

If a fitness center were truly in the transformation business, for example, it wouldn't charge (solely) via membership fees or by the amount of time members spend on machines. Rather, it would charge for meeting the health and well-being aspirations of its members. If the aspirations were not met within a fixed period of time, the fitness center would not be paid—or it would be paid less, on some sliding scale commensurate with the progress achieved. In other words, it would charge not for the pain but for the gain.

Think about what such a business would do differently were it truly a transformation elicitor. First, it would spend much more time up front, before it agreed to accept an individual as a member—on understanding the individual's true aspirations and, more important, his or her current capabilities, both physical and mental. Many people do not have the temperament to stick to a physical regimen and cannot sustain progress toward a defined goal. Indeed, we suspect that many fitness centers derive much of their revenue from people who pay their money but rarely encounter pain on the machines. Signing up such people may be profitable for one period, but surely it leads to the costly churn of constantly replacing expiring memberships. Meanwhile, fitness centers lose much greater profits by not charging for the full value gained by those who do have the mindset to follow through on their aspirations and by not first attempting to change the temperament of those initially incapable of follow-through. (And these diagnostic activities should themselves be treated and explicitly charged for as an experience and, for some, a transformation—yielding profits right up front before someone even becomes a member!)

Once a fitness center determines that an individual can both physically and mentally achieve a specific aspiration, then and only then would it lay out the charge for a specific achievement, including reaching interim goals along the way. And the amount would be two or three or perhaps even ten times what such places charge today for mere machine usage. Who wouldn't pay more for a guarantee that he would lose those thirty pounds, gain those five extra inches of pure muscle around the chest, bench press 250 pounds, or (more subjectively) develop washboard abs or perfectly tight buns? And once it made such a commitment, the fitness center would be sure to design exactly the right set of experiences to make sure the aspirant achieved his goals—and therefore be paid in full. Personal trainers earn so much more than fitness center instructors precisely because they ensure their patrons follow the proper regimen.

Workers need personal trainers, too, such as those supplied by Priority Management of Vancouver, Canada. Using the slogan "A Better Way to Work," Priority Management changes people's behavior—generally yielding at least a 20 percent improvement in business and personal productivity, among other clear benefits—while they work through a productivity challenge that diagnoses current levels of productivity, stages training workshops, and then gives personal follow-through by a certified trainer. Key to success: a guarantee that if the person does not meet his aspirations, he doesn't have to pay. As retired franchise owner Roger Wangen of Burnsville, Minnesota, told us, "With our training methods, most clients readily achieve their productivity goals. But if someone's in danger of falling behind the goals we've mapped out together or isn't taking to the new way of managing his priorities I've shown him, I redouble my efforts to make sure he gets the results he desires." It's no wonder that more than 95 percent of Priority Management's customers continue with the program. Even if it doesn't call its customers aspirants, this company truly is in the transformation business.

Consider also the business-to-business example of management consulting, another industry that typically charges for the service activities workers perform, rather than for the actual transformation of clients. If consultants truly viewed themselves as being in the business of transformation, they would, like fitness centers, spend much more time in the up-front diagnosis phase, identifying clients' strategic needs as well as their capacity for change. They would stop writing analytical documents (the tangible goods of the present-day, PowerPoint-driven consulting industry) and start staging memorable events that would enable the client first to experience what it would be like to live and work in a world where the strategy has been achieved and then to actually create that future world (while, of course, providing appropriate memorabilia for each experience that would be very different from today's sterile binders). Most important, they would follow through to ensure that each client actually achieved its stated strategy, or else risk losing some or all of its fee.[18] Wholly successful engagements, perhaps commemorated with appropriate emblems, would result in even greater revenue than that received today for mere services.

We already see many consulting engagements paid in whole or in part through stock options or a percentage of the business results achieved. London-based Celerant Consulting, for example, considers itself to be in the transformation business, with its website home page declaring, "We believe the benefits of consultancy shouldn't disappear when the consultant does. Our approach is designed to produce positive change in your business that lasts."[19] So naturally the company, whose tagline is "Changing business for good," often puts a significant portion of its fees at risk, tied to performance benchmarks. As Executive Vice President Gary Traylor says, "Clients want some certainty. When they hire a consultant, they're taking a big risk. This shows them a commitment on our part."[20] And Starizon Studio of Keystone, Colorado—founded by Gary Adamson explicitly to transform manufacturers and service providers into premier experience stagers—puts 25 percent of its fees at risk through its "transformational guarantee." Clients may pay all of this portion, none of it, or anywhere in between, depending solely on their view of whether they achieved the transformation they sought.

You really are what you charge for. So let's be very clear about this as it applies to each level of customer value:

- If you charge for *stuff*, then you are in the *commodities* business.
- If you charge for *tangible things*, then you are in the *goods* business.
- If you charge for the *activities you execute*, then you are in the *services* business.
- If you charge for the *time customers spend with you*, then you are in the *experiences* business.
- If you charge for *the demonstrated outcome* the customer achieves, then and only then are you in the *transformations* business.

It's not easy being in the business of transforming customers. Extracting commodities out of the ground may be the most physically demanding practice, but eliciting transformations out of customers is the most intellectually demanding, and it sometimes involves great physical (for example, fitness centers) and emotional (hospitals) demands as well.

Work *Is* Theatre: Act 2, Scene 1

Transformation elicitors still must stage experiences, extending them by orchestrating themes, impressions, cues, and even memorabilia in such a way as to move the buyer toward his aspiration and not only to present the experience itself. Work is therefore still theatre, but an important shift in roles occurs between buyer and seller with this new offering. With an experience, the employees of the staging company are actors performing parts, creating roles, and building characters to engage guests in entertaining, educational, escapist, and/or esthetic ways. With a transformation, all these experiential realms merely set the stage for helping *the customer* learn to act. Erving Goffman, the sociologist who first proclaimed theatre to be a model for work, points to boot camp as a means of personal transformation from cynical to sincere performance for a "raw recruit who initially follows army etiquette in order to avoid physical punishment and eventually comes to follow the rules so that his organization will not be shamed and his officers and fellow soldiers will respect him."[21]

Consider again a birthday transformation offering. The selection of gifts, the invitation of guests, the after-party thank-you notes, and other aspects should all aim to help children learn to act; at first, acting "as if" they are thankful, for example, and later drawing on their emotional reservoir of thankful deeds past to make their own personal statements of appreciation whenever appropriate. Such an offering supplements the parent's most fundamental role, that of developing children into independent adults acting on their own. The entire ensemble of a transformation elicitor assumes a singular role itself, that of directing the aspiring actor to perform new parts. (And remember the metadrama involved: directing is still work, and work is still theatre!)

Director Harold Clurman says that theatre techniques "must be ultimately judged by their contribution to our human needs, our aspirations, moral concerns and philosophies. These questions lead to the role played by the audience in the theatre … The audience is the theatre's wellspring, its leading actor. This is not a metaphor, it is a historical fact."[22] And the audience's role is to become part of the play itself, its members thereby becoming something different from what they were before the performance began. Unless customers act differently, there is no transformation. Transformation elicitors cannot change for the customer; they can only direct the change. And customers must be willing to put themselves in the hands of a guiding director. How does a company gain the confidence of customers to earn such responsibility?

For starters, *customize*. No individual will entrust himself—or any part of himself—to an enterprise that has not established a one-to-one relationship with him. Mass produced, mass marketed, and mass distributed offerings send one clear message to potential buyers: we don't care enough to know you individually. Buyers inevitably respond, You cannot help change me if you do not even care enough to know me. Getting your act together by mass customizing your offerings establishes connections with customers that signal you care.

Second, *stage truly engaging experiences*. Make it the goal of each individual relationship to hear customers say that when the two of you work together, they discover things about themselves they did not know before. Then go further: make it your aspiration to hear them say that only when they interact with you do they gain the deepest understanding of some part of themselves. Make your customers' most memorable experiences their moments with you. These set the stage for creating a bond between you and your customers, a bond that fosters communication of their ultimate aspirations.

Third, *furnish places for actors to rehearse new behaviors*. Use knowledge of each customer's individuality to orchestrate the appropriate set of experiences to guide the desired transformation. Bring together buyers with similar aspirations into a community, eager to learn not only from you and the overall experience but also from one another. Create *ensembles* of like-minded customers, not to lump them into detached and anonymous market segments but to form a close-knit cast of characters able to strengthen and confirm the rightness of the aspirations each seeks.

Take a cue from the late Robert Lucid, emeritus professor of English at the University of Pennsylvania, who, in his role as faculty master of Penn's Hill House dormitory, understood the aspirations of matriculating students. As Lucid explained, "When people come to a university, they're interested in it almost exclusively for certain utilitarian reasons—they're looking for a job or whatever it is—but they're also interested in it as a theater, in which they're going to act out a certain part. They've been thinking about it for quite a while, and they're ready to act it out now if only the other actors are there. And it's that almost desperate search for the other players—they've got the script pretty clear in mind; it's just that they want to be sure that they're in the right place."[23] Iron sharpens iron, and most performances—especially transformational ones—demand that the stage be shared with other people, so that each character is framed by the characters of others performing the same theatre. The interchange between actors is often the vital factor that drives transformational outcomes.

Finally, *direct the actors*. If aspirants could do it all themselves, they wouldn't purchase a transformational offering or entrust their aspirations to an outside party. They know that they need some guidance, but they don't wish to be told what to do. Handling this delicate balance between assistance and interference is the director's responsibility. Guiding is directing! And again, a skilled director embodies two seemingly contradictory roles: collaborator and commander. Directing certainly takes on the flavor of collaboration, with shared control of outputs and dialog with actors about how best to portray their roles. But there are moments within the transformation when the director must force decisions and dictate a particular course of action, helping the actors realize their aspirations. The director guides the moment-to-moment orchestration of themes, impressions, and cues.

Everything else is only a prop supporting this guiding activity. Any good (and the commodities it comprises) must be used only to help a customer learn to act, just as acting instructors use masks and other objects to facilitate the learning of new skills. Any service must be used only to accelerate this learning. Likewise, any experience must be staged only to promote the actor's progression of personal value.

The lower-order offerings that will retain the greatest value in the forthcoming Transformation Economy will be those filled with intention, those existing *in order to* help individual customers become all they seek to be. The issue of how one's economic offerings affect buyers will be unavoidable and inherent to any purchasing decision. In this world, businesses succeeding in the Experience Economy must confront the reality—always present, but previously veiled in economies dominated by commodities, goods, and services—that everything they do affects the character of those for whom the work is done. The intentions of every business will be scrutinized as never before, and the outcome of the assessment will determine which enterprises prosper and which become impoverished.

Ample Waves of Gain

To enrich an enterprise with greater intention, focus on the four universal elements that together constitute how businesses ultimately create value:

- *Origination*: Work that generates value from something new
- *Execution*: Work that generates value from something done

- *Correction*: Work that generates value from something improved
- *Application*: Work that generates value from something used[24]

Everything eventually offered for commerce must originate from somewhere and something. Commodities, preexisting to commercial enterprise, are extracted from animal, mineral, or vegetable substances. Since the beginning of economic activity these materials have been the wellspring from which a stream of new goods and services—and now experiences and transformations—flows.

All forms of economic output, however, require that the supplier execute some key activity to create the offering. And any activity, no matter how well it is done, remains prone to error (we are, after all, only human). The company must then correct any flaws or failures that affect the offering. As Henry Petroski points out, "It is not that form follows function but, rather, that the form of one thing follows from the failure of another thing to function as we would like it."[25] The offering is improved—by adding, subtracting, or modifying aspects of the offering—until it is *applied* to a specific person or enterprise. At that point, the offering is exchanged for monetary payment, and the act of putting an offering to use connects with the original request to fulfill an individual want or need.

Every business needs a strategy to manage these four dimensions of value generation (which reflect the four forms of theatre as illustrated in figure 7-1, which in turn mirror the four business models described in figure N-1 in endnote 24 of chapter 7). As figure 10-4 then illustrates, companies must define their economic offerings (commodities, goods, services, experiences, and transformations) in terms of the type of work performed (originating, executing, correcting, and applying) for specific kinds of buyers (markets, users, clients, guests, or aspirants). Systematically examining this new competitive landscape and filling it with company-unique intention, each business must define its own offerings, core activities, corrective triggers, and buyer relationships to first explore and then exploit for persistent advantage.

FIGURE 10-4

The new competitive landscape

	Commodities The material is the offering	→ Goods The product is the offering	→ Services The operation is the offering	→ Experiences The event is the offering	→ Transformations The individual is the offering
Origination	New substances are discovered	New inventions are developed	New procedures are devised	New scripts are depicted	New aims are determined
Execution	Extracting is the core activity of the trader	Making is the core activity of the manufacturer	Delivering is the core activity of the provider	Staging is the core activity of the stager	Guiding is the core activity of the elicitor
Correction	A poor site triggers further exploration	A problem triggers fixing of a mistake	A reaction triggers a response	Forgetting triggers preservation of memory	A relapse triggers stronger resolve
Application	A trade connects in markets	A transaction connects with users	An interaction connects with clients	An encounter connects with guests	Persevering connects with aspirants

The performance of commodity suppliers like Archer Daniels Midland and Cargill demonstrates that companies can compete successfully at the lowest level and that sometimes focusing on the supply of commodities represents the right strategy for a business. Drawing from the four universal elements of work just discussed, any company doing so must excel at the primary value-generating work required of commodity-based companies:

- Discovering new substances
- Extracting materials efficiently
- Exploring alternative sites
- Trading in markets

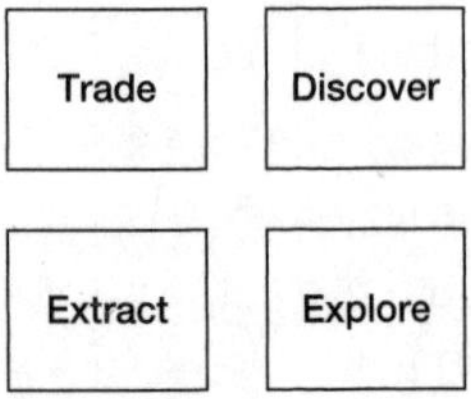

Trade Discover
Extract Explore

Only a remnant of agricultural and mining companies has survived the competitive attrition of previous eras. Most materials have traded for ages through firmly established markets, but whenever someone discovers a new substance, the processes of extracting, exploring, and trading form new markets. Access to these true marketplaces remains critical to success, and poor selection of sourcing and destination market sites can spell disaster for these commodity extractors.

Location theory and practice, however, no longer play as vital a role as they once did in the success of goods-based businesses. Companies still make efforts to optimize plant, warehouse, and distribution sites, but these facilities do not provide the primary source of sustained strategic advantage. Instead, value must be generated from the following:

- Developing new inventions
- Making products efficiently
- Fixing mistakes
- Transacting with users

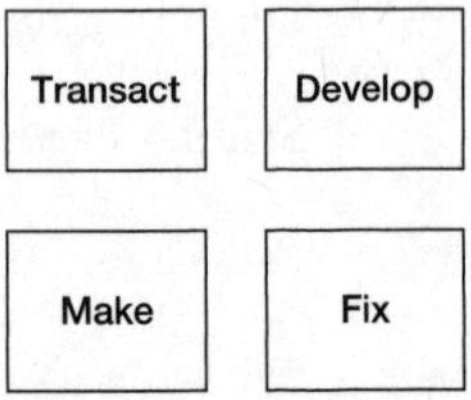

Transact Develop
Make Fix

These elements of success differ significantly from the activities of commodity businesses. Research and development efforts must constantly invent new solutions to old problems as product life cycles continue to decrease. Efficiency—and quality—in manufacturing, whether based on craft production or more modern techniques, is critical to success. And transactions with customers must satisfactorily meet the needs of customers.

The increased importance of high-quality processes to create these goods has led to wholly new economic enterprises supporting manufacturers and, eventually, to entirely new service industries. These service providers found ways to perform highly valued activities that manufacturers otherwise left for the customer to do. Their tasks involve the following:

- Devising new procedures
- Delivering operations efficiently
- Providing responses
- Interacting with clients

Interact	Devise
Deliver	Provide

Innovation in services does not come via the isolation of the R&D lab but in face-to-face interactions with individual clients. Two-way communication—genuine dialog—becomes critical to ensure the routine delivery of outstanding service operations.

Similarly, mere service operations do not suffice in the staging of experiences. Work needs to be orchestrated, converting routine interactions into memorable performances by means of the following:

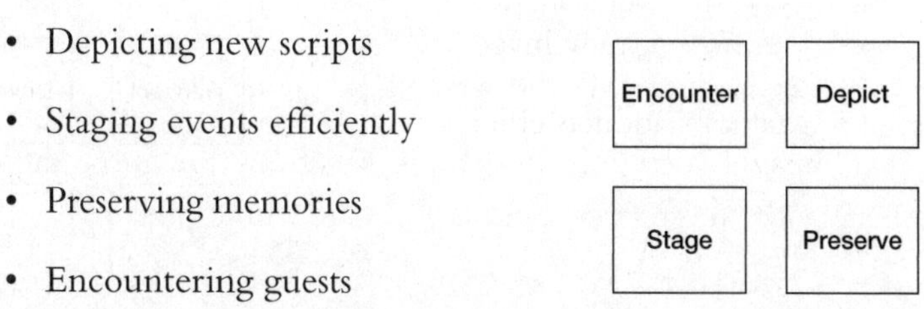

Any business, from repair firm to parking lot, can advance from delivering services to staging experiences if it declares experiences to be the business in which it competes, exploits the inherent sacrifice gaps of traditional service offerings in its industry, and designs an event enriching enough to charge admission.

Recognizing experiences as a distinct economic offering provides the key to future economic growth. Jeremy Rifkin was right to suggest that fewer workers will be needed to deliver services in the future, just as past innovations have greatly reduced the need for factory workers to produce goods and, before that, for farm workers to harvest agricultural commodities. But Rifkin, neo-Luddite Kirkpatrick Sale, political pundit Pat Buchanan, anchor Lou Dobbs, and others like them who bemoan the automation and offshoring of jobs are wrong in stating that the overall demand for labor will decrease. The future waves of economic growth will present ample opportunities to generate more wealth and create new jobs. Indeed, the masses will be employed by those businesses that recognize and create experiential output as a distinct economic offering—and learn to do it well.

Even higher-paying jobs will accompany experiences that richly understand, articulate, and ensure transformations (beginning perhaps with experts in transforming enterprises into experience stagers!). The processes required for transforming an aspirant prove more exacting and elusive than those needed for the buyer of any other economic offering. They involve the following:

- Determining new aims
- Guiding individuals efficiently
- Strengthening resolve
- Persevering with the aspirant

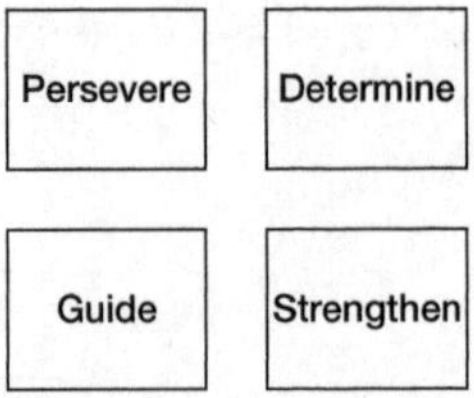

Persevere	Determine
Guide	Strengthen

Companies certainly find transformations the most difficult offering to supply, for elicitors must be intentional about their own processes while also helping their customers learn to act with intention. Customers, however, value these offerings most highly, for they address the ultimate source of all other needs: the reason the buyer wants what he wants.

So What Do You Intend to Do?

The capabilities required to transform a customer are not unlike those needed to transform an entire industry: one must first aspire to bring about a desired change. Not change for the sake of change, which too often results in aimless wandering and constant doubting of one's direction, but something more. One must apply the principle of intention to strategy.

Premier strategists Gary Hamel and the late C.K. Prahalad popularized the notion of *strategic intent*, observing that "too many mission statements fail entirely to impart any sense of mission. For this reason we prefer goals that are focused on making a real difference in the lives of customers." Exactly. Hamel and Prahalad encourage organizations to embrace passion and pathos, and they point out that strategic intent is "as much about the creation of meaning for employees as it is about the establishment of direction." They even commend Jesus Christ's imperative, "Go into all the world and preach the gospel" as "[p]erhaps one of the most ambitious, and emotionally compelling strategic intents ever articulated."[26]

We believe that Hamel and Prahalad assert something profound: strategic intent is the foundation of any organization's energy and ambitions. It supplies purpose and meaning to otherwise humdrum activities. Recognizing the importance of strategic intent alone, however, is not sufficient to set the direction or establish the meaning of an enterprise. There remains the question of what one means by *intention*.

The intention of any company's mission statements, strategic plans, and action steps must be grounded in it's uniqueness, and not in a fixation on the activity of competitors. This does not mean that the company is striving to be differentiated but rather that it is seeking to discover the unexamined dimensions of self, with competitive differentiation resulting as a natural by-product. This corporate self-examination provides the wellspring of renewal (just as examining the uniqueness of customers opens the wellspring of unarticulated needs often pointed out by Hamel and Prahalad). The strategy of a business confers meaning only if those called on to execute it understand—ideally, viscerally—how the company plans to alter the very structure of the world through its industry. Every activity of the company must be performed *in order to* advance external change. The firm can then fulfill its specific strategic intention not by competing for the future but by actively attaining that future.[27] And that can only be accomplished through rigorous thinking about what business the company truly is in.

We do not wish to see executives use the frameworks presented here just to argue over whether they today deliver services, stage experiences, or guide transformations. That is not our intent. Any such debate should serve only as a means to discover new ways of generating value. The Progression of Economic Value simply articulates a new competitive reality for the strategic options facing any enterprise today. The opportunities are vast, but so are the challenges. As the Experience Economy continues to unfold, manufacturers and service providers will increasingly see their offerings commoditized as more and more businesses charge explicitly for the memorable encounters they stage. And as the Experience Economy naturally progresses into the Transformation Economy, even experience stagers will find their offerings commoditized as more and more businesses charge explicitly for the demonstrated outcomes they elicit.

You must find your own role in the world. What business are you really in? Five economic offerings—commodities, goods, services, experiences, and transformations—yield five very distinct possibilities, with tremendous ramifications for your business, your employees, and your customers.

★ ENCORE ★

Exit, Stage Right

CUSTOMERS AND COLLEAGUES OFTEN ASK US, "What's next after transformations?" The question comes up particularly when people begin wondering whether transformations, like the other economic offerings before them, will be commoditized. The healthcare industry, after all, continues to undergo, as it has for the past two decades, tremendous pressure to cut costs via uniform coverage, resulting in fewer procedures and routine treatment. That same pressure is beginning to be applied on tuition costs, just as Internet-based learning programs increase access to and slash the costs of college education. Management consulting firms find themselves competing against business schools that hire out their MBAs at remarkably reduced billing rates.[1] At the same time, they also face new competition from India and increased Web-based delivery of advice to small- and medium-sized enterprises—at a fraction of traditional consultancy costs. Are these signs of commoditized transformations? Perhaps.

Remember, in the nascent Transformation Economy, the customer is the product and the transformation is an aid in changing the traits of the individual who buys it. Transformations that effect this kind of change automatically ward off commoditization, because there can be no greater differentiation than a transformed person or company; every individual is unique. Certainly, competitors can duplicate specific diagnoses, experiences, and follow-through devices. But no one can commoditize the most important aspect of a transformation: the unique relationship formed between the guided and the guide. It is the tie that binds.

An offering of a higher order can supersede lower-level relationships. But the only offering that can displace a transformation is yet another transformation—one aimed at another dimension of self, or at the same dimension but from a different worldview. By worldview, we mean a particular way—often religious or philosophical—of interpreting one's own existence. We already see companies and their customers acknowledge rival worldviews—ideologies, if you will—as the legitimate domain of business and as differentiators of competing offerings. The question, "What's next?" therefore becomes highly personal. To answer it truthfully requires us sharing our worldview with you. Consider the fundamental nature of each offering:

- Commodities are only raw materials for the goods they make.
- Goods are only physical embodiments of the services they deliver.
- Services are only intangible operations for the experiences they stage.
- Experiences are only memorable events for the transformations they guide.[2]

Then reflect on our personal belief that

- Transformations are only temporal states for the eternalities they glorify.

All economic offerings do more than effect an exchange of value in the present; they also, implicitly or explicitly, promote a certain worldview. In the full-fledged Transformation Economy, we believe buyers will purchase transformations according to the set of eternal principles the seller seeks to embrace—what together they believe will last.[3]

Like every other economic offering, transformations will be scrutinized, lionized, and criticized—but not commoditized. Still, they must be customized to remain differentiated. Imagine the most highly customized transformation possible. What would be so right for a particular person that it would transform that person into someone who needs no additional change? What would the ultimate customer-as-product be? The utmost would be *perfection*, the perfect human being. According to our own worldview, there can be no sixth economic offering because perfecting people falls not in the domain of human business but under the province of God, the Author and Perfecter of our faith. As the Apostle Paul said, "For by grace you have been saved through faith. And this is not your own doing; it is the gift of God, not a result of works, so that no one may boast. For we are his workmanship."[4] We believe that no one can be in the business of extending this offer; it is a *free* gift. It cannot be fulfilled as an economic offering supplied by mankind, but only as an atoning act of God. And so, we contend, transformations are the fifth and final offering.

When transformations finally constitute the preponderance of economic commerce, many businesses and individuals will claim to provide the ultimate offering and charge for revealing its secrets. In doing so, they will glorify whatever they view as ultimate. Since all commerce is moral choice, every business is a stage for glorifying something. Who or what does your business glorify? Your answer may or may not help you accept what is next, but it will certainly help guide what you do today.

Notes

Chapter 1

1. For a backstage tour of the technology of Walt Disney World, see Scott Kirsner, "Hack the Magic: The Exclusive Underground Tour of Disney World," *Wired*, March 1998, 162–168, 186–189.

2. So pervasive had theme restaurants become that on April 15, 1998, online satirical magazine *The Onion* (www.theonion.com) posted a story with the title "Nation's Last Themeless Restaurant Closes," ostensibly about Pat's Place in Dubuque, Iowa, being replaced by the town's seventh "Paddy O'Touchdown's Irish Sports Bar & Good-Tyme Internet Grill."

3. Steven E. Prokesch, "Competing on Customer Service: An Interview with British Airways' Sir Colin Marshall," *Harvard Business Review* 73, no. 6 (November–December 1995): 103. For a response to this interview that incorporated the first publishing of the concept of experiences as a distinct economic offering, see B. Joseph Pine II, "Customer Service on British Airways," letter to the editor, *Harvard Business Review* 74, no. 1 (January–February 1996): 162–164.

4. Howard Riell, "Upscale Grocer Chain Grows," *Stores*, March 1995, 26.

5. Russell Vernon, "Fighting Back—A Small Retailer Takes on the EEOC," *Retailing Issues Letter* 8, no. 2, Center for Retailing Studies, Texas A&M University (November 1996): 2. See also Leonard L. Berry, *On Great Service: A Framework for Action* (New York: Free Press, 1995), 90–92 in particular.

6. See, for example, Louise Palmer, "There's No Meetings Like Business Meetings," *Fast Company*, April–May 1996, 36, 40.

7. Tibor Scitovsky, *The Joyless Economy: The Psychology of Human Satisfaction*, revised edition (New York: Oxford University Press, 1992), 67.

8. "Household Data Annual Averages 2009," *Bureau of Labor Statistics*, http://bls.gov/cps/cpsaat18.pdf. See also Julian L. Simon, *The Ultimate Resource 2* (Princeton, NJ: Princeton University Press, 1996), 416 and 109. This book is a tremendous (and very possibly the ultimate) resource of data on how humans have fared with all the commodities discovered on earth.

9. For a summary background on the American System of Manufactures and the system of Mass Production, see B. Joseph Pine II, *Mass Customization: The New Frontier in Business Competition* (Boston: Harvard Business School Press, 1993), chapters 1 and 2.

10. Deuteronomy 28:11 (King James Version): "The lord shall make thee plenteous in goods, in the fruit of thy body, and in the fruit of thy cattle, and in the fruit of thy ground, in the land which the lord sware unto thy fathers to give thee." Work (the

fruit of thy body) here is clearly seen as extracting from animal (thy cattle), vegetable (thy ground), and mineral (the land) to make goods.

11. W. W. Rostow, *The World Economy: History and Prospect* (Austin: University of Texas Press, 1978), 52–53, cited in Alfred D. Chandler, *Scale and Scope: The Dynamics of Industrial Capitalism* (Cambridge, MA: Belknap Press of Harvard University Press, 1990), 4.

12. David A. Hounshell, *From the American System to Mass Production, 1800–1932: The Development of Manufacturing Technology in the United States* (Baltimore: Johns Hopkins University Press, 1984), 228.

13. "Household Data Annual Averages 2009," Bureau of Labor Statistics, http://bls.gov/cps/cpsaat18.pdf.

14. Demian McClean, "Farming Ousted by Service Sector as Top Employer," *Cleveland Plain Dealer*, October 21, 2007, citing the report "Key Indicators of the Labor Market," issued by the United Nations International Labour Organization.

15. A great set of principles and frameworks for manufacturers to use in wrapping services around their goods can be found in Christopher Lovelock, *Product Plus: How Product + Service = Competitive Advantage* (New York: McGraw-Hill, 1994).

16. See, for example, "Big Mac Currencies," *Economist*, April 12, 1997, 71.

17. Suzanne Woolley, "Do I Hear Two Bits a Trade?" *Business Week*, December 8, 1997, 112. Patrick McGeehan and Anita Raghavan, in "On-Line Trading Battte Is Heating Up as Giant Firms Plan to Enter Arena," *Wall Street Journal*, May 22, 1998, said that the slashing of online commissions "threatened to lapse into absurdity" when Ricketts said this.

18. Stan Davis and Christopher Meyer, *Blur: The Speed of Change in the Connected Economy* (Reading, MA: Addison-Wesley, 1998), demonstrate that the markets for goods and services increasingly act like financial markets; that is, they're commoditizing. The authors then provide compelling strategies for living in such a "blurred" world. See especially 96–110.

19. The dual forces of service commoditization and manufacturers wrapping services around their goods have led to a blurring of the lines between the two, as in Davis and Meyer, *Blur*, and Michael Schrage, "Provices and Serducts," *Fast Company*, August–September 1996, 48–49.

20. Adam Smith, *An Inquiry into the Nature and Causes of the Wealth of Nations*, Modern Library edition (New York: Random House, 1994), 361.

21. This is why the best entertainers make astronomical amounts of money. See Robert La Franco and Ben Pappas, "The Top 40," *Forbes*, September 21, 1998, 220–246.

22. Travis J. Carter and Thomas Gilovich, "The Relative Relativity of Material and Experiential Purchases," *Journal of Personality and Social Psychology* 98, no. 1 (2010): 146–159. This builds on the earlier work of Leaf Van Boven and Thomas Gilovich, "To Do or to Have? That Is the Question," *Journal of Personality and Social Psychology* 85, no. 6 (2003): 1193–1202.

23. "Economics Discovers Its Feelings," *Economist*, December 23, 2006, 34.

24. "Relative Importance of Components in the Consumer Price Index, 2009," Bureau of Labor Statistics, www.bls.gov/cpi/cpiri2009.pdf.

25. Prices for the higher-level offerings tend to increase not only because customers desire them more highly but also because those companies offering them may have lower relative productivity gains over time and create their offerings less efficiently. This is to be expected, because efficiency and productivity are tightly

bound with the forces of commoditization. Until competition becomes more intense, there is little incentive for experience stagers to lower their costs.

26. Recall also the late economist Julian Simon's famous bet with Malthusian Paul Ehrlich to demonstrate whether or not the earth was running out of raw materials, retold by Simon in *The Ultimate Resource 2*, 35–36. Ehrlich and two colleagues chose five commodities and bet that the sum of their prices would be higher in 1990 than in 1980. They lost hands down to Simon. As Simon makes clear, the prices of commodities always decrease relative to those of goods and services over the long term, as do the prices of commoditized goods and services relative to their noncommoditized brethren and of course to experiences.

27. Nominal GDP was used because it uses actual prices and does not take inflation into account. As noted earlier, the inflation deflator does not accurately reflect the shift from goods to services (much less the shift to experiences). Therefore, real GDP does not accurately show the growth in services and experiences. Furthermore, the increased prices of higher-level offerings, as noted earlier, reflect, at least in part, higher demand and not only higher costs of inputs.

28. The employment and the GDP of experiential industries were calculated as follows to reflect an educated guess of which portions of certain services were experiences: retail trade (NAICS code 44-45; 20% of annual value); information (51; 50%); professional, scientific, and technical services (54; 20%); management of companies and enterprises (55; 33.3%); arts, entertainment, and recreation (71; 100%); accommodation and food services (72; 30%); and other services except public administration (81; 20%). For more, albeit dated, statistics on the rise of experiences, see the amazingly prescient report by James A. Ogilvy (now with the Global Business Network), "The Experience Industry: A Leading Edge Report from the Values and Lifestyle Program," *Business Intelligence Program Report*, no. 724 (Fall 1985).

29. Economist Stanley Lebergott, in *Pursuing Happiness: American Consumers in the Twentieth Century* (Princeton, NJ: Princeton University Press, 1993), makes the point: "Consumers buy bazaars full of goods, but only to create the diversified experience they ultimately seek" (p. 3) and goes on to show with a wealth of data that these goods (and services, for that matter) that enable consumer experiences have seen tremendous growth in the twentieth century. See also Virginia I. Postrel, "It's All in the Head," *Forbes ASAP*, February 26, 1996, 118.

30. Peter Guttman, *Adventures to Imagine: Thrilling Escapes in North America* (New York: Fodor's Travel Publications, 1997), describes these adventures, each of which Guttman personally experienced and photographed. The book also includes a detailed directory of outfitters to contact for each adventure.

31. Quoted in Tim Stevens, "From Reliable to 'Wow,'" *Industry Week*, June 22, 1998, 24, emphasis added. Other sources for wowing customers include Paul Levesque, *The Wow Factory: Creating a Customer Focus Revolution in Your Business* (Chicago: Irwin Professional Publishing, 1995); Tom Peters, *The Pursuit of Wow! Every Person's Guide to Topsy-Turvy Times* (New York: Vintage Books, 1994); and, in a slightly different but exemplary vein, Ken Blanchard and Sheldon Bowles, *Raving Fans: A Revolutionary Approach to Customer Service* (New York: William Morrow and Company, 1993).

32. Bernd Schmitt and Alex Simonson, *Marketing Aesthetics: The Strategic Management of Brands, Identity, and Image* (New York: Free Press, 1997), provide a great resource for marketing an experiential brand.

33. *Experientialize* and *sensorialize* are not the most euphonious of words, but as Stan Davis and Bill Davidson point out in reference to the word *informationalize*, "We use it because it is more self-explanatory and complete, even though cumbersome. We suspect that 'industrialize' sounded equally unnatural when it first appeared." See *2020 Vision* (New York: Simon & Schuster, 1991), 207, n. 1.

34. Christian Mikunda explores how manufacturers in particular create experience places in *Brand Lands, Hot Spots & Cool Spaces: Welcome to the Third Place and the Total Marketing Experience* (London: Kogan Page, 2004).

35. So far removed are suburban and urban kids from the Agrarian Economy that just being on a farm is an experience! Indeed, staging farm experiences is the next big wave in agrimarketing. See Julie V. Iovine, "A New Cash Crop: The Farm as Theme Park," *New York Times*, November 2, 1997, and Rick Mooney, "Let Us Entertain You," *Farm Journal*, March 1998, H-8, H-9.

36. The initial term *progression of value* and its depiction were suggested to us by the late Rohan Champion when he was vice president of new services strategy at AT&T.

37. Of course, each economic offering has its own set of fixed costs to which margins contribute, such as a farm for commodities, a factory for goods, an office or outlet for services, and back to a farm for this particular experience.

38. See Eben Shapiro, "Discovery Zone Slides into Bankruptcy Court," *Wall Street Journal*, March 26, 1996.

Chapter 2

1. See, for example, Colin Berry, "The Bleeding Edge: If You're Looking for What's Next in Online Technology and Commerce, Just Follow the Gamers," *Wired*, October 1997, 90–97.

2. See also Amy Jo Kim, "Killers Have More Fun," *Wired*, May 1998, 140–144, 197–198, 209.

3. *The New Shorter Oxford English Dictionary*, vol. 1, A–M, s.v. "entertainment."

4. Stan Davis and Jim Botkin, *The Monster Under the Bed: How Business Is Mastering the Opportunity of Knowledge for Profit* (New York: Simon & Schuster, 1994), 125.

5. Judith Rodin, "A Summons to the 21st Century," *Pennsylvania Gazette*, December 1994.

6. Although he didn't use the term *edutainment*, Philip Kotler, professor of marketing at the Kellogg Graduate School of Management, Northwestern University, made the first foray into making education entertaining that we're aware of in "Educational Packagers: A Modest Proposal," *Futurist*, August 1978, 239–242. There he introduced "the metaphor of classroom as *theater*" and encouraged "educational packagers" (as opposed to publishers) to be "like a Hollywood film producer" in providing a "multimedia experience" where "students are both instructed and entertained."

7. Psychologist Mihaly Csikszentmihalyi refers to optimal experiences of this kind as "the process of total involvement with life I call *flow*," in *Flow: The Psychology of Optimal Experience* (New York: HarperPerennial, 1990), xi. We here equate it with the escapist realm, but arguably it corresponds more broadly to hitting the sweet spot across all four realms.

8. Michael Krantz dubs those producing motion-based attractions and the like the "experience industry" in "Dollar a Minute: Realies, the Rise of the Experience Industry, and the Birth of the Urban Theme Park," *Wired*, May 1994, 104–109, 140–142.

9. This is a slightly changed formulation from William Irwin Thompson, *The American Replacement of Nature: The Everyday Acts and Outrageous Evolution of Economic Life* (New York: Doubleday Currency, 1991), 35. It should be noted that Thompson is very much a critic of staged experiences, believing that they are replacing natural ones.

10. Kotler was prescient in this regard, discussing escapist experiences in "'Dream' Vacations: The Booming Market for Designed Experiences," *Futurist*, October 1984, 7–13. Tibor Scitovsky, *The Joyless Economy: The Psychology of Human Satisfaction*, revised edition (New York: Oxford University Press, 1992), makes the point that many affluent people pay for increasingly comfortable lifestyles, something that decreases the pleasure they receive from everyday experience. Those growing up in such an environment then "are prone to take up dangerous sports and become involved in reckless adventures. Could it be that, deprived of the simple pleasures by too much comfort, they seek compensation in pleasures which accompany excitement and threat? Perhaps the increasing violence of our increasingly affluent society can be similarly explained" (p. 74).

11. John Ed Bradley, "SWM, tall, handsome, 29, professional football player, seeks beautiful, intelligent young woman to help design dream house and create family equivalent of America's Team. Must like quiet evenings at home, either cruising America Online or admiring tropical fish tank. Must spend Sundays in crowded stadiums rooting for Dallas Cowboys. Dislike of 49ers and Redskins a plus, but not required," *Sports Illustrated*, January 15, 1996, 80–90.

12. Steve Hamm, with Amy Cortese and Cathy Yang, "Microsoft Refines Its Net Game," *Business Week*, September 8, 1997, 128.

13. MIT professor Sherry Turkle, *Life on the Screen: Identity in the Age of the Internet* (New York: Simon & Schuster, 1995), discusses the tendency of computer-mediated reality to encourage people to take on multiple online personas. Some people do so to the degree that RL (real life) "can be 'just one more window'" (p. 14).

14. Frank Rose, "Keyword: AOL," *Wired*, December 1996, 299.

15. See William Powers, *Hamlet's Blackberry: A Practical Philosophy for Building a Good Life in the Digital Age* (New York: HarperCollins, 2010), as one example of those now articulating ways to escape the distractions of digital life.

16. Ray Oldenburg, *The Great Good Place: Cafés, Coffee Shops, Community Centers, Beauty Parlors, General Stores, Bars, Hangouts and How They Get You Through the Day* (New York: Marlowe & Company, 1997).

17. In *The Theming of America: Dreams, Visions, and Commercial Spaces* (Boulder, CO: Westview Press, 1997), 115, Mark Gottdiener points out that many themed environments fulfill "the desire for community and pedestrian communion in public spaces, along with what is often a much-needed holiday from the normal routines of everyday life. People seem to crave this street-level intimacy—a need created by the destruction of public space in contemporary society through suburbanization and the terror of urban crime."

18. The concept of flow experiences is applied to those of the esthetic kind in Mihaly Csikszentmihalyi and Rick E. Robinson, *The Art of Seeing: An Interpretation of the Aesthetic Encounter* (Malibu, CA: J. Paul Getty Museum and the Getty Center for Education in the Arts, 1990).

19. The live butterflies placed in the first prototype store had the unfortunate habit of dropping onto customer's plates.

20. Quoted in Chris Niskanen, "Big Big Business," *St. Paul Pioneer Press*, March 29, 1998.

21. Michael Benedikt, *For an Architecture of Reality* (New York: Lumen Books, 1987), 4.

22. Ibid., 48. We argue, however, that architectural masterpieces are similarly "non-real" in that they are only constructions of our own making. If Benedikt's own definition were taken literally, the only truly esthetic experiences would occur when one is immersed solely in God's creation.

23. Ada Louise Huxtable, *The Unreal America: Architecture and Illusions* (New York: New Press, 1997), 75.

24. For more on the Experience Economy and authenticity, see James H. Gilmore and B. Joseph Pine II, *Authenticity: What Consumers* Really *Want* (Boston: Harvard Business Press, 2007), chapter 6 in particular.

25. Huxtable, *The Unreal America*, 58.

26. Tom Carson, "To Disneyland," *Los Angeles Weekly*, March 27, April 2, 1992. Carson also quotes Charles Moore, from the book *The City Observed*, in a chapter on Disneyland, saying, "People often use Disneyland as a synonym for the facile, shallow and fake. It just doesn't wash: this incredibly energetic collection of environmental experiences offers enough lessons for a whole architectural education in all the things that matter—community and reality, private memory and inhabitation, as well as some technical lessons in propinquity and choreography."

27. Charles Goldsmith, "British Airways's New CEO Envisions a Marriage of Travel and Amusement," *Wall Street Journal*, November 6, 1995.

28. Other Unique Experiences periodically offered by American Express include a customized Napa Valley Wine Country tour, a New York culinary experience at the French Culinary Institute, a country music extravaganza, and a Champagne harvest at Veuve Clicquot in France. Treating these offerings as economic experiences, American Express requires a huge number of reward points be redeemed, sometimes as high as half a million, meaning $500,000 would ordinarily have been charged to the card member's American Express card!

29. Anthony Rooley, in *Performance: Revealing the Orpheus Within* (Longmead, UK: Element Books, 1990), 108–109, delineates seven stages of any performance that seem to spiral around the sweet spot: "The arts must delight in order to attract our further attention, and lead us subtly to a more profound contemplation. This happens in seven stages during a performance as it:

(a) delights the senses
(b) invites curiosity
(c) involves the mind
(d) encourages deeper study
(e) encourages regular practice
(f) expands love
(g) opens up knowledge"

30. Witold Rybczynski, *Home: A Short History of an Idea* (New York: Penguin Books USA, 1986), 66.

31. Ibid., 62.

32. See James H. Gilmore and B. Joseph Pine II, foreword to *The Power of the 2×2 Matrix: Using 2×2 Thinking to Solve Business Problems and Make Better Decisions*, by Alex Lowry and Phil Hood (San Francisco: Jossey-Bass, 2004), xv.

Chapter 3

1. A look at the origin of the English word *theme* explains this relationship between *theme* and *place*. John Ayto, *Dictionary of Word Origins* (New York: Arcade Publishing, 1990), 527, tells us that the "Greek théma denoted etymologically 'something placed,' hence a 'proposition' (it was formed from the base **the-*, source of *tithénai* 'place, put' and distant relative of English *do*). English acquired the word via Latin thêma and Old French **teme* as *teme*, but soon reverted to the Latin spelling." Experiences occur in places, and the best of those places are themed.

2. James Champy, *Reengineering Management* (New York: Harper Business, 1995), 56–57. See also I. Jeanne Dugan, "The Baron of Books," *Business Week*, June 29, 1998, 108–115.

3. Quoted in Bob Thomas, *Walt Disney: An American Original* (New York: Hyperion, 1994), 11.

4. Ibid., 13.

5. Ibid., 247.

6. Ibid., 246.

7. For a comprehensive look at the Geek Squad's theming, see Gosia Glinska, James H. Gilmore, and Marian Chapman Moore, *The Geek Squad Guide to World Domination: A Case for the Experience Economy* DVD-ROM (Charlottesville, VA: Darden Business Publishing, 2009).

8. For a great article on the art of storytelling applied to new media such as CD-ROMs and the World Wide Web—but generally applicable beyond that—see Brent Hurtig, "The Plot Thickens," *New Media*, January 13, 1998, 36–44.

9. Randy White, "Beyond Leisure World: The Process for Creating Storyline-Based Theming," *FEC Magazine*, November–December 1998.

10. Mark Gottdiener, *The Theming of America: Dreams, Visions, and Commercial Spaces* (Boulder, CO: Westview Press, 1997), 144–151. In *Marketing Aesthetics: The Strategic Management of Brands, Identity, and Image* (New York: Free Press, 1997), 137–139, Bernd H. Schmitt and Alex Simonson recommend that corporations use as a source of themes the five cultural domains of the physical world; philosophical/psychological concepts; religion, politics, and history; the arts; and fashion and popular culture. They also suggest (pp. 129–135) that companies relate themes—which the authors define as "the content, the meaning, the projected image of an identity" (p. 124)—to their mission, vision, objectives, and strategies; core capabilities; legacy; corporate or brand personality; and values. For existing corporations, we think it's especially important to honor the legacy of the business.

11. Schmitt and Simonson, *Marketing Aesthetics*, 128–129.

12. For more on Mike Vance's "Kitchen of the Mind," see Mike Vance and Diane Deacon, *Think Out of the Box* (Franklin Lakes, NJ: Career Press, 1995), especially 96–97 and 103–109.

13. Henry M. Morris with Henry M. Morris III, *Many Infallible Proofs: Evidences for the Christian Faith* (Green Forest, AR: Master Books, 1996), 118. Morris further

points out that each of the three entities of the tri-universe is itself a trinity: space has three dimensions; matter can be energy, motion, or phenomena; and time has past, present, and future.

14. So good is Lori's faithful re-creation of the 1950s diner that about the only thing that intrudes on the illusion are the drinks offered on the menu and the earrings on the waiters and the tattoos on the waitresses. The restaurants are, after all, located in San Francisco.

15. Schmitt and Simonson, *Marketing Aesthetics*, 172–185.

16. *Roget's International Thesaurus*, 4th ed., rev. Robert L. Chapman (New York: Harper & Row, 1977), xvii–xxiv. Never purchase a thesaurus in dictionary form; the categorized version is the only way to go.

17. CEO Betts and his team orchestrated such an engaging experience that in February 1997 The Walt Disney Company itself honored East Jefferson with its "Mouscar" Award—a takeoff on the Oscar that had never before been bestowed outside Disney. Betts quipped, "It no longer bothers me when people refer to the hospital as 'a Mickey Mouse operation.'"

18. Regarding mechanics, there is a significant discussion in the literature on the marketing of services on "servicescapes," a term coined by Arizona State University professor Mary Jo Bitner to describe the physical surroundings of (what are generally thought of as) service providers. It is very similar to what Carbone calls "mechanics clues." See, for example, Mary Jo Bitner, "Consumer Responses to the Physical Environment in Service Settings," in *Creativity in Services Marketing*, eds. M. Venkatesan, Diane M. Schmalensee, and Claudia Marshall (Chicago: American Marketing Association, 1986), 89–93; Mary Jo Bitner, "Servicescapes: The Impact of Physical Surroundings on Customers and Employees," *Journal of Marketing* 56, no. 2 (Spring 1992): 57–71; Kirk L. Wakefield and Jeffrey G. Blodgett, "The Importance of Servicescapes in Leisure Service Settings," *Journal of Services Marketing* 8, no. 3 (1994): 66–76; and, for an entire book dedicated to the subject with numerous excellent articles, John F. Sherry Jr., ed., *ServiceScapes: The Concept of Place in Contemporary Markets* (Lincolnwood, IL: NTC Business Books, 1998). Perhaps the first article in this vein was Philip Kotler, "Atmospherics as a Marketing Tool," *Journal of Retailing* 49, no. 4 (Winter 1973): 48–64.

19. Donald A. Norman, *Turn Signals Are the Facial Expressions of Automobiles* (Reading, MA: Addison-Wesley, 1992), 19.

20. Tom Huth, "Homes on the Road," *Fortune*, September 29, 1997, 307, emphasis added.

21. As Alvin Toffler predicted long ago in *Future Shock* (New York: Bantam Books, 1970), 226, consumers would one day "begin to collect experiences as consciously and passionately as they once collected things."

22. Leonard L. Berry, *On Great Service: A Framework for Action* (New York: Free Press, 1995), 10.

23. Ibid., 91.

24. Anthony Rooley, in *Performance: Revealing the Orpheus Within* (Longmead, UK: Element Books, 1990), 103–104, points out, "The five senses form two distinct levels: smell, taste, and feeling belong to the body and are the lower senses, providing essential information for good functioning; sight and hearing feed the mind."

25. One could say that British Airways and other airlines do charge customers just for entering their "place," but here the "just" is important. Even though they control

the entire immersive environment of an airplane, they don't charge *just* for getting on it but for the service of transporting people from one city to another. Interestingly, Israeli airline El Al had an offering it called the Flight to Nowhere, in which it charged large groups the equivalent of about $85 to fly on a plane, eat dinner and dessert, sing songs, and watch movies. According to El Al spokesman Nachman Kleiman, "You don't necessarily have to go to London or Paris to have a good time." Associated Press, "Israeli Airline Offers 'Flight to Nowhere,'" *Daily Tribune* (Hibbing, MN), December 29, 1997. In contrast, one of the reasons that Planet Hollywood and other theme restaurants have trouble is that they do not charge admission. Because the entire experience is paid for by consumers through the price of their meals, they impute a higher value to the food, which does not (indeed, cannot) live up to their expectations. A cheeseburger must be awfully good to justify an $8.95 price tag; with a $5 admission fee, however, a $3.95 burger doesn't have to be nearly as good—as long, of course, as the experience itself is worth $5.

26. Ozlem Sandikci and Douglas B. Holt discuss this phenomenon in "Malling Society: Mall Consumption Practices and the Future of Public Space," in Sherry, *ServiceScapes*, 305–336, calling it "product foreplay." They even suggest (333–334) that the next step in the "evolution of the mall" will be for mall operators "to sell this space to consumers" because "mall development is driven by the need to commodify [i.e., sell as something of value] social experience."

27. "Niketown Comes to Chicago," press release, Niketown Chicago, July 2, 1992, cited in Sherry, "The Soul of the Company Store: Niketown Chicago and the Emplaced Brandscape," in his *ServiceScapes*, 109–146.

28. In nearly every mall in the United States, developers failed to capture revenue for the experience occuring before store doors open every morning, namely, senior citizens valuing the space as a place to walk. The owners should charge admission for the escapist value created for guests.

Chapter 4

1. "Fiscal Year 2010 Financial Charts," Dell, http://content.dell.com/pr/en/corp/d/corp-comm/fy10-financial-charts.aspx.

2. "Michael Dell Email to Employees," *The HR Capitalist*, http://www.networkworld.com/news/2007/013107-dell-ceo.html.

3. For more on Mass Customization, see Stanley M. Davis (who coined the term), *Future Perfect* (Reading, MA: Addison-Wesley, 1987), also available in a tenth anniversary edition from the same publisher; B. Joseph Pine II, *Mass Customization: The New Frontier in Business Competition* (Boston: Harvard Business School Press, 1993); B. Joseph Pine II, Bart Victor, and Andrew C. Boynton, "Making Mass Customization Work," *Harvard Business Review* 71, no. 5 (September–October 1993): 108–119; for manufacturers only, see David M. Anderson, *Agile Product Development for Mass Customization* (Chicago: Irwin Professional Publishing, 1997); and Bart Victor and Andrew C. Boynton, *Invented Here: Maximizing Your Organization's Internal Growth and Profitability* (Boston: Harvard Business School Press, 1998).

4. There are at least six types of modularity (as well as myriad ways of implementing each type, depending on a company's particular circumstances); see Pine, *Mass Customization*, 196–212. Other good resources on this topic include Karl

T. Ulrich and Steven D. Eppinger, *Product Design and Development* (New York: McGraw-Hill, 1995); G. D. Galsworth, *Smart, Simple Design: Using Variety Effectiveness to Reduce Total Cost and Maximize Customer Selection* (Essex Junction, VT: Omneo, 1994); Toshio Suzue and Akira Kohdate, *Variety Reduction Program: A Production Strategy for Product Diversification* (Cambridge, MA: Productivity Press, 1990); Ron Sanchez and Joseph T. Mahoney, "Modularity, Flexibility, and Knowledge Management in Product and Organization Design," *Strategic Management* 17 (December 1996): 63–76; Marc H. Meyer and Alvin P. Lehnerd, *The Power of Product Platforms: Building Value and Cost Leadership* (New York: Free Press, 1997); and Carliss Y. Baldwin and Kim B. Clark, "Managing in an Age of Modularity," *Harvard Business Review* 75, no. 5 (September–October 1997): 84–93. The six types of modularity discussed in *Mass Customization* are based on earlier work by Ulrich and one of his students.

5. This is something one of the authors of this book got wrong in his earlier *Mass Customization*.

6. Quoted in Clayton Collins, "Five Minutes with J. D. Power III," *Profiles*, October 1996, 23.

7. Add up all the sacrifice existing across all these dimensions—each designed for the average—and one begins to understand why airline travel generally provides such an unpleasant experience. The biggest sacrifice customers encounter, of course, is arriving at an airport terminal when where they want to be is at home, a hotel, or some other specific destination—a sacrifice impossible to eliminate, short of a *Star Trek*–like transporter. Virgin Airways at least reduced it through its program of picking up and dropping off upper-class passengers in limousines—a much better experience than the antics required to get in and out of the typical airport. Airlines could further reduce this sacrifice by allowing passengers to act as *if* they were already at their destinations—by providing onboard check-in with rental cars and hotels, along with transferring bags directly to the final destination.

Chapter 5

1. Daniel Roth, "Netflix Inside," *Wired*, October 2009, 124.

2. Dorothy Leonard and Jeffrey F. Rayport, "Spark Innovation Through Empathic Design," *Harvard Business Review* 75, no. 6 (November–December 1997): 104.

3. For more on Ross Controls, see Steven W. Demster and Henry F. Duignan, "Subjective Value Manufacturing at Ross Controls," *Agility and Global Competition* 2, no. 2 (Spring 1998): 58–65.

4. For more information on learning relationships, see B. Joseph Pine II, Don Peppers, and Martha Rogers, "Do You Want to Keep Your Customers Forever?" *Harvard Business Review* 73, no. 2 (March–April 1995): 103–114. Robust details on one-to-one marketing can be found in Peppers and Rogers's fine books, *The One to One Future: Building Relationships One Customer at a Time* (New York: Currency Doubleday, 1993), and *Enterprise One-to-One: Tools for Competing in the Interactive Age* (New York: Currency Doubleday, 1997). All marketers and anyone else concerned with how their companies should adapt to a world filled with interactive technologies should read these books.

5. Of course, as with the old learning curve, the path followed is never as smooth as that pictured.

6. For more information on these four approaches, see the original article on which this section is based: James H. Gilmore and B. Joseph Pine II, "The Four Faces of Mass Customization," *Harvard Business Review* 75, no. 1 (January–February 1997): 91–101.

7. For more on Lutron, which practices collaborative and cosmetic as well as adaptive customization, see Joel S. Spira and B. Joseph Pine II, "Mass Customization," *Chief Executive* 83 (March 1993): 26–29, and Michael W. Pessina and James R. Renner, "Mass Customization at Lutron Electronics—A Total Company Process," *Agility and Global Competition* 2, no. 2 (Spring 1998): 50–57.

8. For a discussion of the benefits of adaptive over collaborative customization, see Eric von Hippel, "Economics of Product Development by Users: The Impact of 'Sticky' Local Information," *Management Science* 44, no. 5 (May 1998): 629–644.

Intermission

1. Quoted in Steven E. Prokesch, "Competing on Customer Service: An Interview with British Airways' Sir Colin Marshall," *Harvard Business Review* 73, no. 6 (November–December 1995): 106.

2. T. Scott Gross, *Positively Outrageous Service: New and Easy Ways to Win Customers for Life* (New York: MasterMedia Limited, 1991), 5–6. Gross defines positively outrageous service as "unexpected service delivered at random . . . It is a memorable event and is so unusual that the customer is compelled to tell others." See also Gross, *Positively Outrageous Service and Showmanship: Industrial Strength Fun Makes Sales Sizzle!!!* (New York: MasterMedia, 1993), which discusses "signature showmanship" and "retail theater." Because Macaroni's has since been expanded into the restaurant chain Romano's Macaroni Grill, apparently it lost its wonderful customer surprise in the process of becoming a chain.

3. Perhaps Continental did practice customer surprise for its top-mileage customers without publicizing it to the rest of the world (something that would only have set expectations for frequent fliers who fly frequently enough to rate this level of customer surprise!), as Delta has done. See Nancy Keates, "The Nine-Million-Mile Man," *Wall Street Journal*, July 24, 1998.

Chapter 6

1. Michael Shurtleff, *Audition: Everything an Actor Needs to Know to Get the Part* (New York: Walker and Company, 1978), 162–164.

2. Selling shares to the public in 1998, the Cleveland Indians Baseball Co. stock prospectus (p. 4) explains: "Fans at Jacobs Field are offered a customer-focused experience in an attractive, comfortable environment featuring a variety of amenities, concessions and merchandise options and a courteous, well-trained staff."

3. George F. Will, *Men at Work* (New York: Macmillan Publishing Co., 1990), 6.

4. Others go even further by taking Shakespeare's proclamation, "All the world's a stage" to heart. For example, musician and sculptor Anthony Rooley, in *Performance: Revealing the Orpheus Within* (Longmead, UK: Element Books, 1990), 2–3, expresses "a philosophical view which understands that from birth to death, our entire 70-year span (or whatever is our allotted length) is nothing, but nothing, other than a play, a

performance. Each of us plays a part, or a series of parts, more or less willingly, more or less consciously, more or less capably. Every action, interplay of relationships, pursuits of all kinds can be seen as 'performance.'"

5. Preston H. Epps, trans., *The Poetics of Aristotle* (1942; reprint, Chapel Hill, NC: University of North Carolina Press, 1970), 13–29.

6. Books could be written interpreting Aristotle's *Poetics*—and scores have been. We take this brief exposition primarily from Richard Hornby, *Script to Performance: A Structuralist Approach* (New York: Applause Books, 1995), 79–91.

7. Peter Brook, *The Empty Space* (New York: Touchstone, 1968), 9.

8. Brenda Laurel, *Computers as Theatre* (Reading, MA: Addison-Wesley, 1993), xviii.

9. Ibid., 32–33.

10. Ibid., 86–87.

11. For an excellent treatment of the importance and role of "being watched" in human performance, see Paul Woodruff, *The Necessity of Theatre: The Art of Watching and Being Watched* (New York: Oxford University Press, 2008).

12. Erving Goffman, *The Presentation of Self in Everyday Life* (New York: Anchor Books, 1959), 18.

13. Ibid., 73–74. Goffman's ideas were used to analyze the noncustomer work situation in labor negotiations in Raymond A. Friedman, *Front Stage, Backstage: The Dramatic Structure of Labor Negotiations* (Cambridge, MA: MIT Press, 1994).

14. A number of articles in the services literature use the "dramaturgical perspective" to analyze service work. Although theatre is used more as a metaphor than a model, this line of inquiry provides a great wealth of information along these lines. See in particular Stephen J. Grove, Raymond P. Fisk, and Mary Jo Bitner, "Dramatizing the Service Experience: A Managerial Approach," *Advances in Services Marketing and Management* 1 (1992): 91–121; S. Grove and R. Fisk, "Impression Management in Services Marketing: A Dramaturgical Perspective," in *Impression Management in the Organization*, eds. R. Giacalone and P. Rosenfeld (Hillsdale, NJ: Lawrence Erlbaum Associates, 1989), 427–438; J. Czepiel, M. Solomon, and C. Curprenant, eds., *The Service Encounter: Managing Employee/Customer Interaction in Service Businesses* (Lexington, MA: Lexington Books, 1985); Christopher Lovelock, *Product Plus: How Product + Service = Competitive Advantage* (New York: McGraw-Hill, 1994), 86–96; Ron Zemke, "Service Quality Circa 1995: A Play with Many Acts," in *The Quality Yearbook 1995*, eds. James W. Cortada and John A. Woods (New York: McGraw-Hill, 1995), 119–126; Carl Sewell and Paul B. Brown, *Customers for Life: How to Turn That One-Time Buyer into a Lifetime Customer* (New York: Pocket Books, 1990), 113–117; T. Scott Gross, *Positively Outrageous Service and Showmanship* (New York: MasterMedia Limited, 1993), 89–106; and Sam Geist, *Why Should Someone Do Business with You . . . Rather Than Someone Else?* (Toronto: Addington & Wentworth, 1997), 86–116.

15. Richard Schechner, *Performance Theory* (New York: Routledge, 1988), 30, n. 10. While limiting his analysis to theatre and to a lesser degree the related activities of ritual, play, games, sports, dance, and music (the seven "public performance activities of humans," p. 10), in this endnote Schechner cites Goffman and acknowledges that "performance is a 'quality' that can occur in any situation rather than a fenced-off genre . . . Or, as John Cage has argued, simply framing an activity 'as' performance—viewing it as such—makes it into a performance." We wholeheartedly agree.

16. Ibid., 72.

17. Ibid., 72, 70.

18. Ibid., 72.

19. Thus the importance of understanding both the *product* and the *representation*, which together constitute any offering and yield the four approaches to customization discussed in chapter 5.

20. Schechner, *Performance Theory*, 72.

21. Ibid., 71.

22. *Fish! Catch the Energy. Release the Potential* (Burnsville, MN: ChartHouse International Learning Corporation, 1998). See also the book based on the video: Stephen C. Lundin, Harry Paul, and John Christensen, *Fish! A Remarkable Way to Boost Morale and Improve Results* (New York: Hyperion, 2000).

23. Michael Chekhov, *On the Technique of Acting* (New York: HarperPerennial, 1991), 71.

24. Eric Morris, *Acting from the Ultimate Consciousness: A Dynamic Exploration of the Actor's Inner Resources* (Los Angeles: Ermor Enterprises, 1988), 152.

25. Ibid., 153.

26. Julius Fast, *Subtext: Making Body Language Work in the Workplace* (New York: Viking, 1991), 3–4, provides a fuller delineation: "The subtext in any exchange is a mixture of many different elements. In part, it is composed of each person's body language, posture, hand movements, eye contact, how he or she handles space, and the ability to use subtle touch at the right moment. The way we use our voices also influences how our words are interpreted."

27. Karen Klugman, Jane Kuenz, Shelton Waldrep, and Susan Willis, *Inside the Mouse* (Durham, NC: Duke University Press, 1995), 110–111, emphasis added. Despite, or because of, this book's strikingly critical examination of Disney offerings from a leftist political perspective, the authors provide a wealth of insights about the inner workings of Disney.

28. For an outline of the "Elements of an Action," including the "Magic If," see Sonia Moore, *The Stanislavski System* (New York: Penguin Books, 1984), 25–45.

29. Michael Kearns, *Acting = Life: An Actor's Life Lessons* (Portsmouth, NH: Heinemann, 1996), 75.

30. Moore, *The Stanislavski System*, 30.

31. Ibid., 83.

32. Kearns, *Acting = Life*, 42.

33. Ibid., 45. Although the acting literature abounds with admonishments to infuse performances with intention, we particularly like Kearns's formulation and his straightforward description of its application.

34. Laura Johannes, "Where a Woman Lives Influences Her Choice for Cancer Treatment," *Wall Street Journal*, February 24, 1997.

35. Note that the key for doctors here is to get patients to properly consider the alternatives, and not to get them to choose a particular alternative. As Michael Kearns says in *Acting = Life*, 43, "Many actors confuse result with intention. When I ask for an intention, I'm invariably given a result word: happy, sad, tragic, overjoyed, jealous, angry. Those are emotions that result from playing an intention; they are not intentions . . . An actor who attempts to play resentful, hurt, or ecstatic is acting a result and it's bad acting, usually accentuated by mugging (there's a lot of this on sitcoms).

An actor who plays an intention, allowing the emotions to emerge naturally, is on the road to good acting."

36. Quoted in Edward Felsenthal, "Lawyers Learn How to Walk the Walk, Talk the Talk," *Wall Street Journal*, January 3, 1996.

37. Richard B. Schmitt, "Judges Try Curbing Lawyers' Body-Language Antics," *Wall Street Journal*, September 11, 1997.

38. Barb Myers retired in 1997. She was replaced not by a machine but by her former understudy, Joyce Lewis, who made memories for a yet another generation of Penn students.

Chapter 7

1. While not always explicitly pointed out in the text, this description of an actor at work exemplifies the following elements of theatre:

- As if
- Charting
- Costuming
- Cut 95 percent
- Dragging out
- Exiting all the way off
- Intention
- Making an entrance
- Props
- Roles and characterization
- Subtext: body language, props, costumes

Note that some techniques (such as the use of props) appear multiple times. If you're reading this note prior to reading the vignette, we encourage you to look for exactly where Linda uses each one.

2. Anthony Rooley, in *Performance: Revealing the Orpheus Within* (Longmead, UK: Element Books, 1990), 50, urges performers to use this technique before beginning any performance:

> *Another procedure is to use the eyes. Extend your sightlines to the far corner of the room, right to the dimly-lit recesses and encircle the audience with your vision. Moving further in, towards oneself, the eyes might meet those of another individual, perhaps someone who is ready to smile in recognition of this moment's importance, or someone who needs a little reassurance that it is all right to relax. Then the eyes of the front row, who are there because they choose to be there—sitting on the front row is a very conscious choice. These people deserve careful attention and a smile perhaps (certainly better, in most instances, than a stern encounter).*

3. John Rudin, *Commedia dell'Arte: An Actor's Handbook* (London: Routledge, 1994), 51. See also *Scenarios of the Commedia dell'Arte: Flaminio Scala's Il Teatro delle favole rappresentative*, trans. Henry F. Salerno (New York: Limelight Editions, 1996).

4. See in particular Edward de Bono, *Serious Creativity: Using the Power of Lateral Thinking to Create New Ideas* (New York: HarperBusiness, 1992).

5. A good guide to improvisational techniques is Brie Jones, *Improve with Improv: A Guide to Improvisation and Character Development* (Colorado Springs, CO: Meriwether Publishing, 1993).

6. Commedia dell'Arte was also performed on a raised (outdoor) platform, but without the formality of a proscenium, much less a written-out script.

7. One of the best platform theatre books is by playwright and director David Mamet, *True and False: Heresy and Common Sense for the Actor* (New York: Pantheon Books, 1997).

8. "Prepping the Chief for the Annual Meeting or Other Event Can Mean Practice," *Wall Street Journal*, March 20, 1997. See also Quentin Hardy, "Meet Jerry Weisman, Acting Coach to CEOs," *Wall Street Journal*, April 21, 1998.

9. William Grimes, "Audio Books Open Up a New World for Actors," *Cleveland Plain Dealer*, January 9, 1996. See also Rodney Ho, "King of Audio-Book Narrators Makes 'Readers' Swoon," *Wall Street Journal*, April 10, 1998.

10. "California Dream$," *Forbes*, December 16, 1996, 114. Note that while most broadcast television relies on matching theatre, live productions are pure platform.

11. The term *jump cut* has become a somewhat pejorative term in the entertainment industry, because many directors overuse the technique to hide flaws in the script or in actor performances.

12. Richard Dyer MacCann, ed., *Film: A Montage of Theories* (New York: E. Dutton & Co., 1966), 23.

13. Quoted in Jeffrey M. Laderman, "Remaking Schwab," *Business Week*, May 25, 1998, 128.

14. Thomas W. Babson, *The Actor's Choice: The Transition from Stage to Screen* (Portsmouth, NH: Heinemann, 1996).

15. Sally Harrison-Pepper, *Drawing a Circle in the Square: Street Performing in New York's Washington Square Park* (Jackson: University Press of Mississippi, 1990), 140.

16. Bim Mason, in *Street Theatre and Other Outdoor Performances* (London: Routledge, 1992), writes, "One of the aims of this book is to show how much craft and expertise there is involved in this area of work" (p. 4). He also points out (p. 5) how much street theatre there is in real life: "There is plenty of drama outdoors and an element of performances starts to occur if the participants become conscious of spectators and 'play up' to them. For example, the demolition of houses in Barcelona . . . was watched by a large group of locals, so the bulldozer drivers began to show off their skill with exaggerated nonchalance." Work is, indeed, theatre.

17. For a terrific guide to selling that introduces many routines, see Don Peppers, *Life's a Pitch: Then You Buy* (New York: Currency Doubleday, 1995).

18. Rudin, *Commedia dell'Arte*, 23.

19. Mel Gordon, *Lazzi: The Comic Routines of the Commedia Dell'Arte* (New York: Performing Arts Journal Publications, 1983), 29, 43, 18, 23, and 18, respectively. Interestingly, such well-rehearsed routines are now labeled "comic stage business" (p. 4).

20. Tony Vera, quoted in Harrison-Pepper, *Drawing a Circle*, xiii.

21. Carl Asche, quoted in Harrison-Pepper, *Drawing a Circle*, 114.

22. For more on The Hartford's PLIC call center, see B. Joseph Pine II and Hugh Martin, "Winning Strategies for New Realities," *Executive Excellence* 10, no. 6 (June 1993): 20.

23. For how an environmental "sense and respond" capability relates to Mass Customization, see Stephan H. Haeckel and Richard L. Nolan, "Managing by Wire," *Harvard Business Review* 71, no. 5 (September–October 1993): 122–132. See also

Stephen P. Bradley and Richard L. Nolan, eds., *Sense and Respond: Capturing Value in the Network Era* (Boston: Harvard Business School Press, 1998).

24. The Four Forms of Theatre model derives from prior work on a Mass Customization model known as the Product-Process Matrix" in which the axes are Product [= performance] Change and Process [= script] Change. Then, the four quadrants become the four generic business models that any company can have:

> [Invention = improv theatre]
> [Mass Production = platform theatre]
> [Continuous Improvement = matching theatre]
> [Mass Customization = street theatre]

Just as performers of work must cycle between each successive form of theatre to reach street theatre, companies must cycle from Invention to Mass Production—through the activities of *development*—then to Continuous Improvement—through the activities of *linking*—before reaching Mass Customization—through the activities of *modularization*. When mass customizers are faced with "capability failures"—customers requiring capabilities the company does not possess—they must return to Invention—through the activities of *renewal*—to create a new capability, just as street performers renew their capabilities through on-the-spot improvising. While Mass Customization provides the highest levels of customer value, it is not appropriate everywhere, just as street performance is not the appropriate form of theatre for every situation.

The Product-Process Matrix (figure N-1) was originally developed by Bart Victor and Andy Boynton, two University of North Carolina professors (now dean of the Carroll School of Management at Boston College and the Cal Turner Professor of Moral Leadership at Vanderbilt University, respectively) and extended in collaboration with Joe Pine, and now enhanced and applied to theatre primarily through the efforts of Jim Gilmore. It has evolved considerably over time to become a very robust way of looking at the world of business competition. To trace that evolution, see Andrew C. Boynton and Bart Victor, "Beyond Flexibility: Building and Managing the Dynamically Stable Organization," *California Management Review* 34, no. 1 (Fall 1991): 53–66; B. Joseph Pine II, *Mass Customization: The New Frontier in Business Competition* (Boston: Harvard Business School Press, 1993), 215–221; Andrew C. Boynton, Bart Victor, and B. Joseph Pine II, "New Competitive Strategies: Challenges to Organizations and Information Technology," *IBM Systems Journal* 32, no. 1 (1993): 40–64; B. Joseph Pine II, Bart Victor, and Andrew C. Boynton, "Making Mass Customization Work," *Harvard Business Review* 71, no. 5 (September–October 1993): 108–119; B. Joseph Pine II, Bart Victor, and Andrew C. Boynton, "Aligning IT with New Competitive Strategies," in *Competing in the Information Age: Strategic Alignment in Practice*, ed. Jerry N. Luftman (New York: Oxford University Press, 1996) 73–96; James H. Gilmore and B. Joseph Pine II, "Beyond Goods and Services: Staging Experiences and Guiding Transformations," *Strategy and Leadership* (May/June 1997): 10–18; B. Joseph Pine II, "You're Only as Agile as Your Customers Think," *Agility and Global Competition* 2, no. 2 (Spring 1998): 24–35; and, finally, Bart Victor and Andrew C. Boynton, *Invented Here: Maximizing Your Organization's Internal Growth and Profitability* (Boston: Harvard Business School Press, 1998). Victor and Boynton's book, while curiously eliminating the axes of the framework, provides a masterful look at how an organization must learn and leverage knowledge to make the transition to each successive business model.

FIGURE N-1

The Product-Process Matrix

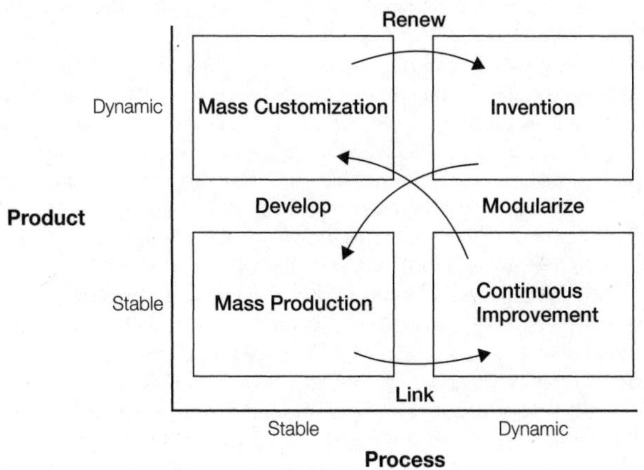

Source: Bart Victor, Andrew C. Boynton, and B. Joseph Pine II.

25. In *Drawing a Circle*, Harrison-Pepper relates that street performers create new acts through "a process of revision, refining, and personalizing" (p. 80)—that is, flowing from improv to platform (revision), then to matching (refining), and finally to street (personalizing).

26. Harrison-Pepper, *Drawing a Circle*, 117.

Chapter 8

1. We agree with our friends Stan Davis and Bill Davidson in *2020 Vision* (New York: Simon & Schuster, 1991), 113, when they say, "*The best place to look for the basis of organization change is in the future business, and the worst place to look is in the current organization*. The present organization, however, may be a good predictor of what will *prevent* you from developing the kind of organization you will need."

2. As James A. Ogilvy writes, "The Experience Industry: A Leading Edge Report from the Values and Lifestyles Program," report 724, SRI International Business Intelligence Program, Meno Park, CA, Fall 1985, 22, "The bad news is that marginal utility is not the only concept that won't carry over from industrial economics to the economics of the experience industry. Other familiar categories may be equally misleading . . . [S]uch basic terms as *inventory* or even *capital* become problematic. As they say in Hollywood, 'You're only as good as your last movie.' If this saying is an accurate indication of the way value can or cannot be accrued in the experience industry, then the very concept of fixed assets calls for radical revision."

3. Edward Felsenthal, "Lawyers Learn How to Walk the Walk, Talk the Talk," *Wall Street Journal*, January 3, 1996.

4. Jonnie Patricia Mobley, *NTC's Dictionary of Theatre and Drama Terms* (Lincolnwood, IL: National Textbook Co., 1992), 49. This book is an excellent resource for understanding the various terms of theatre.

5. This is not altogether different from the way the mechanization of Industrial Age jobs led to the rise in the human-to-human activity of delivering services.

6. According to Charles Marowitz, *Directing the Action: Acting and Directing in the Contemporary Theatre* (New York: Applause Theatre Books, 1991), the role of director did not exist in the performing arts until the late nineteenth century. Initially, the position involved coordinating fellow actors, simply directing on- and offstage activities as an equal among peers. Gradually, directing began to include coaching actors in how to portray their respective roles. What we today know as the modern director, people "who leave their mark on material as much as they do on actors" (p. 2), did not fully emerge within the arts until the 1920s and 1930s in France and Russia. Interestingly, the rise of directing as a profession in the performing arts of these two countries coincides with the rise of professional management in the industrialized world of Britain, Germany, and the United States, as demonstrated in Alfred D. Chandler Jr., *Scale and Scope: The Dynamics of Industrial Capitalism* (Cambridge, MA: Belknap Press of Harvard University Press, 1990). Directors here and there entered the world of theatre; the two sets of countries simply chose different stages. Today's Experience Economy, however, demands that the performing arts and business merge.

7. As Marowitz points out in *Directing the Action*, 6, "Too infrequently do we recognize that the central function of the man is to rethink and recreate the materials with which he works. The director who does not engage the animate and inanimate materials at his disposal and transmute them into an image of himself, is merely going through the motions. Some other title must be found for him. Call him a coordinator, a controller, a foreman, or a traffic cop, but do not confuse him with an artist of the theatre."

8. Elizabeth Weil, "Report from the Future: Every Leader Tells a Story," *Fast Company*, June–July 1998, 38. Another article from the same issue by author and publisher Harriet Rubin, "The Hitchhiker's Guide to the New Economy," profiling Douglas Adams, makes the point that "the art of the storyteller is the art of the new economy" (p. 178).

9. David Kahn and Donna Breed, *Scriptwork: A Director's Approach to New Play Development* (Carbondale: Southern Illinois University Press, 1995), 20.

10. Gordon Shaw, Robert Brown, and Philip Bromiley, "Strategic Stories: How 3M Is Rewriting Business Planning," *Harvard Business Review* 76, no. 3 (May–June 1998), 44; 47. See also Thomas A. Stewart, "The Cunning Plots of Leadership," *Fortune*, September 7, 1998, 165–166, and Rob Wilkens, "Strategic Storytelling," *Lifework* 1, no. 5 (October 1998): 23–25.

11. A couple of good resources on scriptwriting are J. Michael Straczynski, *The Complete Book of Scriptwriting* (Cincinnati: Writer's Digest Books, 1996), and Syd Field, *Screenplay: The Foundations of Screenwriting* (New York: MJF Books, 1994). For a wonderful book on how to read scripts as literature and then turn them into engaging performances, see Richard Hornby, *Script to Performance: A Structuralist Approach* (New York: Applause Books, 1995). Interestingly, Hornby dislikes the performance theory approach of Richard Schechner because "structure cannot be separated from substance without degenerating into triviality" (p. xv). Hornby further calls Schechner's work "sometimes insightful and sometimes Rube Goldberg fabrication." Let us assure you that we adapted from the insightful parts.

12. Michael Hammer, "Reengineering Work: Don't Automate, Obliterate," *Harvard Business Review* 68, no. 4 (July–August 1990): 104–112.

13. See also James H. Gilmore, "Reengineering for Mass Customization," *Journal of Cost Management* 7, no. 3 (Fall 1993): 22–29, and Gilmore, "How to Make Reengineering Truly Effective," *Planning Review* 23, no. 3 (May/June 1995): 39, as well as B. Joseph Pine II, "Serve Each Customer Efficiently and Uniquely," *Network Transformation: Individualizing Your Customer Approach*, supplement to *Business Communications Review* 68, no. 4 (January 1996): 2–5.

14. Gary Hamel and C. K. Prahalad, *Competing for the Future: Breakthrough Strategies for Seizing Control of Your Industry and Creating the Markets of Tomorrow* (Boston: Harvard Business School Press, 1994).

15. For how Gallatin Steel mass customizes steel—a near, but not quite, commodity—see David H. Freeman, "Steel Edge," *Forbes ASAP*, October 6, 1997, 46–53. For more on how Pilkington Brothers took a laborious five-step glass-making process down to one-step float glass, see James M. Utterback, *Mastering the Dynamics of Innovation: How Companies Can Seize Opportunities in the Face of Technological Change* (Boston: Harvard Business School Press, 1994), 104–120. All process and product developers should read this book.

16. Bob Thomas, *Walt Disney: An American Original* (New York: Hyperion, 1994), 264.

17. Francis Reid, *Designing for the Theatre* (New York: Theatre Art Books/ Routledge, 1996), 19.

18. Felsenthal, "Lawyers Learn How to Walk the Walk."

19. Angie Michael, *Best Impressions in Hospitality: Your Professional Image for Excellence* (Manassas Park, VA: Impact Publications, 1995), provides a good resource in this area.

20. Michael Holt's classic manual on costuming, *Costume and Make-Up* (New York: Schirmer Books Theatre Manuals, 1988), 7, lays out the importance of these cues: "Costume is part of the actors' apparatus. It helps them to create their characters. Every item of clothing sends signals of one kind or another to the audience. As soon as the actors appear, even before they speak, the audience will have gleaned a great deal of information. They can see by the shape and colour of the costume whether a character is to be welcomed or feared. The whole image is composed of signs that they will react to both consciously and unconsciously."

21. Quoted in Erik Hedegaard, "Fools' Paradise," *Worth*, June 1998, 76.

22. Pauline Menear and Terry Hawkins, *Stage Management and Theatre Administration* (New York: Schirmer Books Theatre Manuals, 1988), 7.

23. Julian Fast, *Subtext: Making Body Language Work in the Workplace* (New York: Viking, 1991), 13.

24. Leonard A. Schlesinger and James L. Heskett, "Breaking the Cycle of Failure in Services," *Sloan Management Review* 32, no. 3 (Spring 1991): 26.

25. Given that this section is written from the perspective of the auditors, we refer aspiring actors who wish to perform well at auditions to Michael Shurtleff, *Audition: Everything an Actor Needs to Know to Get the Part* (New York: Bantam Books, 1978).

26. The Project on Disney, *Inside the Mouse* (Durham, NC: Duke University Press, 1995), 214–215.

27. Mark Winegardner, *Prophet of the Sandlots: Journeys with a Major League Scout* (New York: Prentice Hall Press, 1990), 97.

28. Robert L. Benedetti, *The Director at Work* (Englewood Cliffs, NJ: Prentice-Hall, 1985), 87.

29. Mobley, *NTC's Dictionary of Theatre and Drama Terms*, 4.

30. Philip Kotler and Joanne Scheff, *Standing Room Only: Strategies for Marketing the Performing Arts* (Boston: Harvard Business School Press, 1997).

31. Ibid., 13.

Chapter 9

1. As Lisa Miller reports on the phenomenon of spiritual directors in the *Wall Street Journal*, "Americans have long hired people to care for their children, their bodies and their finances. Now, they're hiring personal trainers for their souls." In "After Their Checkup for the Body, Some Get One for the Soul," July 20, 1998.

2. For a study on the vast possibilities and sheer magnitude of change individuals seek, see Grant McCracken, *Transformations: Identity Construction in Contemporary Culture* (Bloomington: Indiana University Press, 2008).

3. Interestingly, boot camps, flight simulators, business games, and virtual reality training tools all purposefully commoditize experience in order to change people. By having them go through simulations of real-world experiences over and over and over again, these experiences help their reactions become second nature, greatly increasing their ability to react to fast-changing, often life-threatening, situations quickly. As training executive Tom Orton told *Industry Week*, users of his company's semiconductor plant simulator "feel as though they've already been there and done that" ("25 Winning Technologies," December 15, 1997, 52).

4. We anticipate the day when the proliferation of FedEx packages, faxes, and e-mail will restore the receipt of good old U.S. mail as a memorable experience, much as a trip to a farm has become.

5. David Bacon, quoted in Susan Warren, "Parents Are on a Kick for Tae Kwon Do as a Disciplinary Art," *Wall Street Journal*, October 3, 1997.

6. Tim W. Ferguson, "Let's Talk to the Master," *Forbes*, October 23, 1995, 142.

7. Quoted in Lucy MacCauley, "Measure What Matters," *Fast Company*, May 1999, 111.

8. Anna Klingmann, *Brandscapes: Architecture in the Experience Economy* (Cambridge, MA: MIT Press, 2007), 313 and 323, respectively.

9. Jeffrey A. Kottler, *Travel That Can Change Your Life: How to Create a Transformative Experience* (San Francisco: Jossey-Bass Publishers, 1997), xi.

10. Mark Wolfenberger, quoted in Nikhil Hutheesing, "Reducing Sticker Shock," *Forbes*, November 3, 1997, 151.

11. Rob Preston, "Down to Business: Outsourcing's Next Big Thing," *InformationWeek*, August 31, 2009, 48.

12. For more on Mid-Columbia Medical Center, see Mark Scott and Leland Kaiser, with Richard Baltus, *Courage to Be First: Becoming the First Planetree Hospital in America* (Bozeman, MT: Second River Healthcare Press, 2009).

13. Quoted in J. P. Donlon, "The P&G of Prisons," *Chief Executive*, May 1998, 28–29.

14. Kairos Prison Ministry International, a nonprofit Christian ministries organization based in Orlando, Florida, specifically targets this recalcitrant prison

population through a series of annual events that aim to change prisoners' hearts, beginning with the most hardened leaders. Understanding exactly how tough this is, Kairos employs platform theatre, wherein its workers script and rehearse every word spoken over a three-day period.

15. Donlon, "The P&G of Prisons," 29.

16. Quoted in Sara Terry, "Genius at Work," *Fast Company*, September 1998, 176.

17. Each of the four *S*'s in the 3-S Model still applies. First, customer satisfaction relative to expectations: how well did the transformation elicitor achieve my aspirations? Then, customer sacrifice: what gaps exist between what the customer should truly aspire to and what the customer was able to achieve? Third, customer surprise: transcending customer aspirations by eliciting change along a dimension the customer never expected. And finally, customer suspense: heightening the anticipation the customer has for what dimension the elicitor will help change next.

18. As pointed out in chapter 6 of this book, Brenda Laurel makes the point in *Computers as Theatre* (Reading, MA: Addison-Wesley, 1993), xviii, that human–computer interfaces should be "designed experiences." In "Interface Design: Diversity in Your Audience," *Interactivity*, February 1997, 69, Eric Justin Gould, principal of MONKEY media, an interface design and production studio, goes even further by encouraging interface designers to think of the transformative power of technology: "When you bring new technology into someone's life (be it cutting-edge hardware or just a new way of interacting), you can't help but have an effect on them. To respect a culture is to consider, during the design process, what influence your product might have on the people who interact with it." Exactly.

19. In a syndicated *Chicago Tribune* column by Jim Mateja, titled "OnStar Diagnostic System Brings Aid with a Call" in the *St. Paul Pioneer Press*, October 25, 1997, OnStar's chief engineer, Walt Dorfstatter, says, "We look at remote diagnostics as giving motorists instant peace of mind."

20. Britton Manasco, "SmithKline Beecham's Smoking Cessation Program," *Inside 1to1*, August 6, 1998.

21. Ibid.; see also Joyce A. Sackey, "Behavioral Approach to Smoking Cessation," Real Doctors (Life Makers), May 8, 2006, www.real-doctors.com/forums/index.php?PHPSESSID=d7d058b1ee1131ada4d9f0cbc6b5ee80&action=printpage;topic=654.0, and "These Are the Champions," *PROMO Magazine*, November 1, 1999, promomagazine.com/mag/marketing_champions/.

22. Rolf Jensen, *The Dream Society* (New York: McGraw-Hill, 1999).

23. In *The Experience Economy: New Perspectives* (Amsterdam: Pearson Education Benelux, 2007), 19–29 and throughout, Albert Boswijk, Thomas Thijssen, and Ed Peelen argue that companies should emphasize more meaningful experiences—denoted by the Dutch word *erfahrung*—as opposed to the more emotional, staged experiences denoted by *erlebnis*. These take off on the educational elements of an experience whenever "a person dwells on the question of what a particular experience . . . means for him" (p. 24). Such meaningful experiences are at least a half-step to becoming transformational. For a good model on meaningful experiences, the Experience Triangle (with levels of motivation, physical, rational, emotional, and mental), see Sanna Tarssanen and Mika Kylänen, "What Is an Experience?" in *Handbook for Experience Tourism Agents*, third edition, ed. Sanna Tarssanen (Rovaniemi, Finland: University of Lapland Press, 2006), 6–21.

24. Hillel M. Finestone and David B. Conter, "Acting in Medical Practice," *Lancet* 344, no. 8925 (September 17, 1994): 801.

25. Mark DePaolis, "Doctors Can Act as If All the World's a Stage," *Minneapolis Star-Tribune*, January 27, 1995.

26. See, for example, Gregory W. Lester and Susan G. Smith, "Listening and Talking to Patients: A Remedy for Malpractice Suits?" *Western Journal of Medicine*, March 1993; Jerry E. Bishop, "Studies Conclude Doctors' Manner, Not Ability, Results in More Lawsuits," *Wall Street Journal*, November 23, 1994; Daniel Goleman, "All Too Often, The Doctor Isn't Listening, Studies Show," *New York Times*, November 13, 1991; Dennis H. Novack, Anthony L. Suchman, William Clark, Ronald M. Epstein, Eva Najberg, and Craig Kaplan, "Calibrating the Physician: Personal Awareness and Effective Patient Care," *Journal of the American Medical Association*, 278, no. 6 (August 13, 1997): 502–509; Eric B. Larson and Xin Yao, "Clinical Empathy as Emotional Labor in the Patient-Physician Relationship," *Journal of the American Medical Association*, 293, no. 9 (March 2, 2005): 1100–1106.

27. Milton Mayeroff, *On Caring* (New York: HarperPerennial, 1971), 1–2.

28. C. William Pollard, "The Leader Who Serves," *Strategy & Leadership* 25, no. 5 (September/October 1997): 50.

29. C. William Pollard, *The Soul of the Firm* (New York: HarperBusiness and Grand Rapids, MI: Zondervan Publishing House, 1996), 130. The last of Pollard's twenty-one principles of leadership (p. 166) demonstrates the power of a serving attitude: "We have all been created in God's image, and the results of our leadership will be measured beyond the workplace. The story will be told in the changed lives of people." Make no mistake: such serving yields no mere service but rather a caring transformation.

Chapter 10

1. Jeremy Rifkin, *The End of Work: The Decline of the Global Labor Force and the Dawn of the Post-Market Era* (New York: G. Putnam's Sons, 1995), xvi.

2. Ibid., xvii. Part of Rifkin's "solution" is to put a value-added tax "on the entertainment and recreation industries, which are among the fastest-growing sectors of the economy." The reason: "Few of the nation's poor can afford home computers, cellular phones, and expensive trips to theme parks, resorts, and casinos" (p. 271). It's axiomatic that the economy gets less of whatever gets taxed, so this would seem to be the economic equivalent of cutting off one's nose to spite one's face—taxing experiences when that's where the new jobs will be created. It's also not surprising that someone who doesn't trust market mechanisms would look to target the fastest-growing economic sector for sources of revenue for more government programs and regulations.

3. Ibid., 247. See also Rifken, *Age of Access: The New Culture of Hypercapitalism Where All of Life Is a Paid-for Experience* (New York: Penguin Putnam, 2000), where he more explicitly discusses the Experience Economy. Our summary of this somewhat contradictory book: this shift to an economy wherein all of life becomes a paid-for experience is a terrible thing, and the worst part about it is that the poor do not have access to the same (terrible) opportunities.

4. To create the transformations category, we used employment and GDP government statistics in these five sectors: professional, scientific, and technical services (NAICS code 54; 60% of annual value); management of companies and enterprises (55; 33.4%); educational services (61; 100%); healthcare and social assistance (62;

100%); and other services except public administration (81; 20%). As with experiences, there are certainly transformation businesses left in the service statistics, as they could not be broken out separately. We believe that a true breakout into these newly identified economic offerings of what today are classified as services would show an even more pronounced shift in these statistics to the higher-order offerings.

5. Indeed, prior to a brief reprieve forced by political pressure in 1994, healthcare spending grew consistently in double digits over the previous decade, far outpacing almost any other industry.

6. *Digest of Education Statistics: 2009*, National Center for Education Statistics, nces.ed.gov/programs/digest/d09/tables/dt09_334.asp, Table 334. As with recent reductions in the rate of price increases in healthcare, the education statistics are affected by politics. In particular, the increasing amount of student aid available from the government in various forms makes it easier for colleges and universities to increase their tuition commensurately.

7. Virginia I. Postrel, "It's All in the Head," *Forbes ASAP*, February 26, 1996, 118. To give her full credit, Postrel further states, "Increasingly, people aren't just buying goods and services. They're buying experiences."

8. *The New Shorter Oxford English Dictionary*, vol. 2, N–Z, ed., s.v. "wisdom."

9. There are other versions of this sort of intelligence progression, such as Haeckel's Hierarchy, named after Stephan H. Haeckel of the IBM Advanced Business Institute, which includes intelligence itself as a level between information and knowledge. See Vincent P. Barabba and Gerald Zaltman, *Hearing the Voice of the Market: Competitive Advantage Through Creative Use of Market Information* (Boston: Harvard Business School Press, 1990), 37–58.

10. The word *computer* originally referred to the people who made calculations for weapons delivery during World War II.

11. For example, a special issue on "Knowledge and the Firm" was published by *California Management Review* 40, no. 3 (Spring 1998).

12. Diane Senese, in "The Information Experience," *Information Outlook*, October 1997, 29–33, discusses how "information professionals" can "enjoy a unique role in preparing [their] corporations for the experience economy" when they "re-imagine [their] roles" as helping corporate customers in "experiencing knowledge."

13. Michael Schrage writes of the need to view technology from the standpoint of its effect on relationships, as opposed to information, in *No More Teams! Mastering the Dynamics of Creative Collaboration* (New York: Currency Doubleday, 1995).

14. John Dalla Costa, *Working Wisdom: The Ultimate Value in the New Economy* (Toronto: Stoddart Publishing Co., 1995), 24.

15. Taichi Sakaiya, *The Knowledge-Value Revolution, or a History of the Future* (Tokyo: Kodansha International, 1991), 20–21.

16. Ibid., 235.

17. Ibid., 57–58.

18. As consultant and author Robert H. Schaffer says, "For a consulting assignment to be considered successful, delivering a report with the 'right solutions' or installing a new system is not sufficient. The project must actually yield measurable bottom-line results for the client and, equally important, the client must develop the ability to sustain those benefits." From Ian White-Thomson and Robert H. Schaffer, "Getting Your Money's Worth," *Chief Executive*, November 1997, 41. See also Robert H. Schaffer, *High-Impact Consulting: How Clients and Consultants Can Leverage Rapid*

Results into Long-Term Gains (San Francisco: Jossey-Bass Publishers, 1997).

19. Celerant Consulting, www.celerantconsulting.com/index.aspx.

20. Quoted in Daniel Lyons, "Skin in the Game," *Forbes*, February 16, 2004, 78.

21. Erving Goffman, *The Presentation of Self in Everyday Life* (New York: Anchor Books, 1959), 20.

22. Harold Clurman, *On Directing* (New York: Collier Books, 1972), 154–155.

23. Quoted in Samuel Hughes, "Lucid Observations," *Pennsylvania Gazette*, October 1996, 28. One of the places within a place Lucid furnished for student-actors to rehearse was the Hill House Pit Stop, a student-run convenience store that competed with the likes of WaWa Food Markets, located within Hill House and managed by one of the authors in his junior year.

24. This section is based on James H. Gilmore and B. Joseph Pine II, "Beyond Goods and Services: Staging Experiences and Guiding Transformations," *Strategy & Leadership* 25, no. 3 (May/June 1997): 18. These four universal elements—origination, execution, correction, and application—derive from the same framework behind figure 7-1, Four Forms of Theatre, known as the Product-Process Matrix (see chapter 7, n. 24). The figure-eight pattern in this framework is a fractal, a pattern detectable at any level of analysis, where the level of analysis used here is the most general.

25. Henry Petroski, *The Evolution of Useful Things* (New York: Vintage Books, 1992), 86.

26. Gary Hamel and C. K. Prahalad, *Competing for the Future* (Boston: Harvard Business School Press, 1994), 133–134. Note that the words of Jesus they quote are not found in the Acts 1:8 passage they cite but in Mark 16:15.

27. We provide a model for doing so, Here-and-Now Space, in chapter 9 of *Authenticity: What Consumers* Really *Want* (Boston: Harvard Business Press, 2007), 179–218.

Encore: Exit, Stage Right

1. Peter Haynes and Dolly Setton, "McKinsey 101," *Forbes*, May 4, 1998, 130–135.

2. This articulation of the Progression of Economic Value was inspired by James Brian Quinn in *Intelligent Enterprise: A Knowledge and Service Based Paradigm for Industry* (New York: Free Press, 1992), who on p. 7 used the exact formulation given here for goods, except in choosing the word *product* instead.

3. Issues have arisen already from the demand some individuals place on perpetuating biological life. See Andrew Kimbrell, *The Human Body Shop: The Engineering and Marketing of Life* (New York: HarperCollins, 1993), and Margaret Jane Radin, *Contested Commodities: The Trouble with Trade in Sex, Children, Body Parts, and Other Things* (Cambridge, MA: Harvard University Press, 1996), for thoughtful preludes to what lies ahead. Let us point out that these issues concern what *should* be permissible to buy and sell, and not what *can* be. While statecraft and other nonmarket forces may strive to restrict the supply of such economic commerce, only individual soul searching and changed human hearts will eradicate the demand.

4. Ephesians 2:8–10a (English Standard Version).

Index

Credits

Every business a stage, and all our thoughts and words merely play to bring this reality to light. Many men and women have exited and entered our working lives, each playing a part in this particular written production. Like many speeches on Oscar night, the following credits are sure to leave out someone who deserves proper thanks. Still, we do want to acknowledge those who have lent their hands, heads, and hearts to this endeavor.

First, the infancy of the ideas in this book emerged about a year after Joe left IBM, while Jim was still working at CSC Consulting & Systems Integration. While speaking on the subject of Mass Customization at the IBM Advanced Business Institute, Joe shared the often-mentioned point that mass customizing a good automatically turns it into a service. An astute audience member raised his hand and asked, "You say companies can mass customize services as well. Into what does customization turn a service?" To which Joe intuitively replied, "Mass Customization automatically turns a service into an *experience*." Instantly, Joe recognized the significance of his response, and later that evening he called Jim. "Guess what I said today! . . . Now let's go figure out what it means." After many months of thinking, reading, and discussing, we concluded that experiences were indeed distinct economic offerings, just like goods and services. So to that unknown IBMer we owe a very large debt for asking the question that demanded not only an immediate answer but ultimately this entire book.

We are also indebted to CSC and the IBM Advanced Business Institute, particularly Dave DeRoulet, Gary Cross, and Roger Kallock when they were at the former, and Al Barnes when at the latter, for supporting (both intellectually and financially) our research into first Mass Customization and then the Experience Economy. Many partners we worked with at Pricewaterhouse-Coopers's Diamond Advisory Services, where we were once Diamond Fellows, also provided great support, particularly Mel Bergstein, Jim Spira, Barry Uphoff, Chap Kistler, and Chunka Mui. Diamond's Rachel Parker scoured the depths of government statistics and helped us interpret just how the shift through successive economies played out in the numbers. In this, the updated edition, Lee Kaplan of LEE3 Consultants ably performed this task. Lee really dug into the most recent government data and showed us what was going on. Thank you, Rachel and Lee for going to school on the data when we were unwilling!

People at a number of companies loved these ideas while they were still being formulated, invited us to work with their organizations, and applied them in their relationships with their own customers. Although many of these people are no longer at the companies that embraced the Experience Economy, we still would like to thank in particular ARAMARK (especially Lynn McKee), Scudder Kemper Investments (especially Mark Casady and Lin Coughlin), Hillenbrand Industries (especially Fred Rockwood, Chris Ruberg, Brad Reedstrom, Brian Leitten, and Rob Washburn, among others), enable (Mort Aaronson), Lutron Electronics Co., Inc. (Joel Spira and Mike Pessina), CompuCom (Ed Anderson), ChemStation (George Homan and Russ Gilmore), UCLA Executive Education (Jim Aggen, Grace Siao, and again Al Barnes), Penn State Exec Ed (Al Vicere, Gini Tucker, Maria Taylor, and Bob Prescott, among others), and the U.S. Chamber of Commerce's Institutes for Organization Management (Maggie Elgin and

Nancy Turnbull). Companies that through our work with them helped us further understand experience staging after the first edition was published include LEGO Systems A/S (Mark Hansen), The Walt Disney Company (Scott Hudgins), Risto Nieminen (Veikkaus Oy), the Carlson Companies (Marilyn Carlson Nelson and Curtis Nelson), MGM Resorts (Felix Rappaport), Microsoft (Nadine Kano), Chick-fil-A (Dan Cathy and Jon Bridges), Duke Corporate Education (Cheryl Stokes), Exhibitor Magazine Group and Exhibitor Learning Events (Lee Knight and Dee Silfies, respectively), Gallery Furniture (Jim McIngvale), HelmsBriscoe (David Peckinpaugh), Marriott (Mike Jannini and Steve Weisz), and Whirlpool (Josh Gitlin). The late Rohan Champion deserves special mention for pushing his former employer, AT&T, to shift beyond its commoditized services, and it was Rohan himself who first thought of expressing experiences and transformations in the form of a progression of value.

A number of individuals soldiered the discoveries we made along the way and influenced how we extended our thinking, including Jim Utterback of the MIT Sloan School of Management; Shlomo Maital of MIT and Technion University; Marvin Zonis of the University of Chicago; David Reed of SAP Labs; Mark Dehner of Land as Art; Jim Rogers of Advance Management Group; Lou Carbone of Experience Engineering; Stephan Haeckel of Adaptive Business Designs; Randy White of White Hutchinson Leisure & Learning Group; Larry Keeley of the Doblin Group; Dave Wright of Maxwell Technologies; David Anderson and Stephen Fraser, then of GATX Corporation; Hugh Martin, then of The Hartford; Alan Hald, a founder of MicroAge; John Sviokla of PricewaterhouseCoopers's Diamond Advisory Services; Jeffrey Rayport, formerly of the Harvard Business School; Tim Gallwey, author of the *Inner Game* books; and Mark Hatch of TechShop. Individuals who have helped extend our thinking since the first edition include Robert Stephens (the Geek Squad), Chip Conley (Joie de Vivre Hospitality), Waynn Pearson (Cerritos Public Library, retired), Don Taranto (TST, Inc.) and Ed Goodman (Spiral Experiences, LLC), Maxine Clark (Build-A-Bear Workshop), Gary Adamson (Starizon Studio), Sonia Rhodes (Sharp HealthCare), Jeff Kallay (TargetX), Steve Dragoo (Service Solutions Consulting), Doug Johnson (General Growth Properties), Amy Sanders (American National Bank of Texas), Mark Greiner (Steelcase), Albert Boswijk (European Centre for the Experience Economy), Pat Esgate (Esgate & Associates), Dave Norton (Stone Mantel), Rick Worner (Oppenheimer & Company), Conny Dorrestijn (Shiraz Partners), Sanna Tarssanen (Lapland Experience Organization), Ann Marie Fiore (Iowa State University), Toon Abcouwer and Rik Maes (University of Amsterdam), Jon Jerde (The Jerde Partnership), Bob Rogers (BRC Imagination Arts), Doug Wilson (Hillenbrand Industries), Chris Voss (London Business School), John Sherry (University of Notre Dame), Rolf Jensen (Dream Company), and Gosia Glinska, Jeanne Liedtke, Marian Moore, Phil Pfeifer, and Elliott Weiss (all at the Darden School at the University of Virginia). Our respective fathers, Haydn Gilmore and Bud Pine, both reviewed drafts of the initial manuscript and provided valuable encouragement and feedback, and Julie Pine helped formulate the first description of how each economic offering differed from the others.

We must also do justice to a number of thinkers and authors who were amazingly prescient in identifying some of the trends we discovered, some long before us and all unbeknownst to us until we started researching the Experience Economy. Back in 1970, futurist Alvin Toffler included a chapter in *Future Shock* titled "The Experience Makers." Even before that, in 1959, sociologist Erving Goffman, in *The Presentation of Self in Everyday Life*, applied the principles of theatre to work and social situations. In the 1970s marketing professor Phil Kotler of Northwestern University foresaw how education and travel would become more and more experiential. In 1995 Gerhard Schulze wrote of the "experience society" in *Die Erlebnisgesellschaft: Kultursoziologie der Gegenwart* (which we still hope someone someday translates into English). More recently, professors Mary Jo Bitner of the Arizona State University, Raymond Fisk of Texas State University–San Marcos, and Stephen Grove of Clemson University have done the most in researching and promoting within academia the notion of experiential environments (which Bitner calls "servicescapes") and taking a dramaturgical perspective on service offerings. In many ways, the best writers on services point to the shift to experiences, most notably Chris Hart, Christopher Lovelock, Leonard Berry, Earl Sasser, James Heskett, and Leonard Schlesinger. Brenda Laurel of the California College of the Arts applied drama to computer interactions in her wonderful book *Computers as Theatre*. Jay Ogilvy, cofounder of the Global Business Network, wrote *The Experience Industry*, a 1985 report for SRI International, demonstrating that demand for "vivid experiences" already drove marginal growth in the U.S. economy. There are surely others whom we should be mentioning, and we hope that they receive due recognition for their parts in predicting and describing the rise of the Experience Economy.

A number of people, while they did not necessarily write or discuss with us views directly related to the subject of this book, significantly influenced our thinking about a range of issues that could not help manifesting themselves as we wrote. Those full of wise saws include Stan Davis, Edward de Bono, Joel Barker, Don Peppers and Martha Rogers, Michael Schrage, the late Peter Drucker, George Gilder, James Brian Quinn, Taichi Sakaiya, Virginia Postrel, Larry Downes and Chunka Mui (again—again), Donald

Norman, David Gelernter, Joel Kotkin, Grant McCracken, R. C. Sproul, and the late masters Henry Morris and James Boice. And we learned most of what we know about theatre and how to apply its principles to work from the writings of such performing arts authors as David Mamet, Peter Brook, Richard Schechner, Richard Hornby, Michael Kearns, Michael Shurtleff, Eric Morris, Thomas Babson, Anthony Rooley, Charles Marowitz, David Kahn and Donna Breed, Harold Clurman, Richard Olivier, and especially Sally Harrison-Pepper, through whose work we gained a greater understanding of street performance—that form of theatre that Jim has venerated since his more youthful days of watching a Pantaloon named Robert Armstrong perform on the streets of San Francisco as Butterfly Man.

Of course, the idea of this book would have quickly faced mere oblivion without a number of people contributing across a wide range of disciplines. Our agent, Rafe Sagalyn, helped find us exactly the right publisher and provided guidance at many important junctures in the writing. Many at Harvard Business School Press enthusiastically supported us from the beginning. Nick Phillipson first rallied enthusiasm for the project. Our wonderful editor, Kirsten Sandberg, pointed out the many deficiencies in early drafts and pushed and cajoled us to make each draft better. Also, Sarah Merrigan and Morgan Moss greatly improved the final manuscript through their meticulous editing. And Carol Franco was an unswerving champion of our ideas ever since her involvement in publishing *Mass Customization* many years ago. So much of what we've thought has been published first in the *Harvard Business Review* that we want to thank our longtime editor, Steve Prokesch, as well as Tom Richman, Cathy Olofson, Regina Fazio Maruca, and Nan Stone. Personal editing assistance with the manuscript and industry analysis were provided by, respectively, freelancers Robin Schoen and Chris Roy, while

Word Plus Project Support of Cleveland created the original graphics for many of the figures; our thanks to Petra Haut, Tim McCluskey, and the late Ruthanne Fait. We do greatly appreciate the encouragement and support of Courtney Schinke Cashman in producing this updated edition.

Of course, we would have been sans figures, sans manuscript, sans business, sans everything were it not for our managing partner Doug Parker, who handles many of the day-to-day aspects of running our business and took on even more thankless tasks in order to provide the time, energy, and focus we needed to write. He also marshals all of the marketing activities that keep us in business. We owe Doug a great debt of gratitude. Scott Lash, also a partner in Strategic Horizons LLP, performed many tasks essential to completing this work, including researching a number of the companies we highlight, and does so much that we appreciate in the company.

And thank you to our families—Julie, Becca, and Lizzie Pine; Beth, Evan, and Anna Gilmore—for living through our fixation on all things experiential and giving us the time to write, and to our parents—Bud Pine and the late Marilou Burnett Pine and Norman Burnett; and Haydn and Marlene Gilmore and the late Jean Gilmore—for their loving support and guidance throughout our lives. Finally, we acknowledge the providential work of a triune God, who placed all these people in our footpaths and gave us the curiosity and capabilities to discover what He first made clear.

About the Authors

B. JOSEPH PINE II and **JAMES H. GILMORE** are cofounders of Strategic Horizons LLP, an Aurora, Ohio-based thinking studio dedicated to helping enterprises conceive and design innovative ways of adding value to their economic offerings via mass customizing, staging experiences, rendering authenticity, and guiding transformations. They are coauthors of *Authenticity: What Consumers* Really *Want* (Harvard Business School Press, 2007) and coeditors of *Markets of One: Creating Customer-Unique Value through Mass Customization* (Harvard Business School Press, 2000). Mr. Pine, who also wrote *Mass Customization: The New Frontier in Business Competition* (Harvard Business School Press, 1993) and *Infinite Possibility: Creating Customer Value on the Digital Frontier* (Berrett-Koehler, 2011), is a Visiting Scholar with the MIT Design Lab as well as a Senior Fellow with both the Design Futures Council and the European Centre for the Experience Economy, which he cofounded. Mr. Gilmore is a Batten Fellow and Adjunct Lecturer at the Darden School of Business at the University of Virginia as well as a Visiting Lecturer in Apologetics at Westminster Seminary California.